THE
PROOF IS
in the
DOUGH

THE PROOF IS *in the* DOUGH

RURAL SOUTHERN WOMEN, EXTENSION, AND MAKING MONEY

KATHRYN L. BEASLEY

The University of Georgia Press | Athens

Parts of chapters 3 and 5 previously appeared in the *Alabama Review*. Parts of chapters 4 and 6 appeared in "Feeding the Bank Account: Florida Women, Home Demonstration Programming and Using Florida for Disposable Income, 1914–1925," *Florida Historical Quarterly* 100, no. 2 (Fall 2021): 189–213. Copyright © 2021 Florida Historical Society and the Florida Historical Quarterly.

© 2025 by the University of Georgia Press
Athens, Georgia 30602
www.ugapress.org
All rights reserved
Designed by Melissa Bugbee Buchanan
Set in Adobe Garamond Pro

Most University of Georgia Press titles are available from popular e-book vendors.

Printed digitally

Library of Congress Cataloging-in-Publication Data
Names: Beasley, Kathryn L., 1987– author.
Title: The proof is in the dough : rural southern women, extension, and making money / Kathryn L. Beasley.
Description: Athens, Georgia : The University of Georgia Press, [2025] | Includes bibliographical references and index.
Identifiers: LCCN 2024031459 | ISBN 9780820367927 (hardback) | ISBN 9780820367910 (paperback) | ISBN 9780820367934 (epub) | ISBN 9780820367941 (pdf)
Subjects: LCSH: Rural women—091734. | Income—History.
Classification: LCC HQ1240 .B42 2025 | DDC 305.409173/4—dc23/eng/20240820
LC record available at https://lccn.loc.gov/2024031459

This book is dedicated to H. R. F. and L. R. F.—what can I say except I love and miss you both.

This book is also in memory of Dr. Laurie Wood, who was part of this research from the beginning, with encouragement and suggestions, as well as one of my favorite oral defense comments: "Reading this made me hungry."

CONTENTS

Acknowledgments   ix

INTRODUCTION
Women and Developing Rural Reform
in the Twentieth-Century South   3

CHAPTER ONE
Sowing a Progressive Bucolic Haven   11

CHAPTER TWO
Rural Alabama Women and Cultivating
Commerce   28

CHAPTER THREE
Growing Disposable Income through Florida's
Home Demonstration Programs   49

CHAPTER FOUR
Curb Markets, Finding Customers, and
Ripening Bank Accounts   68

CHAPTER FIVE
Harvesting Tropical Fruits and Milk and
Using Florida Grown   89

CONCLUSION
Reaping the Profits from Gardens to
Grapefruit   106

Selected Recipes   111

Notes   127

Index to Recipes   183

Index   185

ACKNOWLEDGMENTS

This book is the result of research, not just for its original iteration as my doctoral dissertation, but because I wanted to introduce these rural women and focus on their determination, creativity, and capabilities when they sought to financially help themselves and their families. Bringing their voices from the past was an essential part of the research journey.

I want to start at the beginning of that journey, at Florida State University. A paper I wrote in 2014 for a seminar on the Gilded Age and the Progressive Era, which was later published as an article, was on a different topic: the Cooperative Extension Service. However, as someone who grew up with the Cooperative Extension Service, land-grant universities, and agriculture as a core foundation, I found it was an easy decision to focus on the intersection of agricultural, rural, southern, and women's history.

Jennifer Koslow, my dissertation adviser, was one of the first to help shape my research during the writing and revising process, with advice and support. I was also fortunate to have a fantastic committee—Andrew Frank, Katherine Mooney, Laurie Wood, and Meegan Kennedy—all of whom offered feedback I used when I began the dissertation-to-book process.

The time I spent at the archives, on the phone, and through email all came together to help fashion this book. At Auburn University's Special Collections and Archives, Jennifer Wiggins, John Varner, Elizabeth Bates, and Tommy Brown were especially generous with their time and efforts. I would like to thank Tommy Brown for his help in obtaining photos. Veronica Henderson of the University Archives and Special Collections at Alabama A&M University's J. F. Drake Memorial Learning Resources Center, along with Kristan Ford and the staff at the Archives Research Center at the Atlanta University Center's Robert W. Woodruff Library, who offered emailed and digital scans of archival material when travel was not an option for me. Jaimie Kicklighter, Meredith McDonough, and Amelia Chase at the Alabama Department of Archives and History were another source of help, for which I am grateful.

I especially want to thank the Special and Area Studies Collection at the George A. Smathers Libraries at the University of Florida. The travel grant I received as a doctoral student was pivotal in my chapters about Florida, and I received great help from the staff and archivists there: Florence Turcotte, Peggy McBride, Steven Hersh, and Michelle Wilbanks. I particularly want to thank Caleb del Rio for his time and help in finding the photos for this book. The

State Archives of Florida (known online as Florida Memory) was also extremely helpful in allowing the use of their images. The archives at Florida A&M University and Vanderbilt University also helped with crucial information, for which I am very thankful.

Parts of this book's chapters appeared as articles in the *Alabama Review* and the *Florida Historical Quarterly*. I would like to extend my gratitude toward Matthew Downs and Connie Lester, the respective editors, for their gracious permission in allowing me to reprint those portions of the articles that appear in the chapters.

Finding a home for this book at the University of Georgia Press has been a joy for my first experience in publishing a manuscript. Nathaniel Holly has been a fantastic editor, with patience, good humor, helpful advice, and the ability to help me navigate these uncharted waters. Jon Davies and Anne Coulling have been incredibly helpful in guiding my book to the finish line. The rest of the editorial and marketing team at UGA Press have also been enjoyable to work with, from start to finish.

Most importantly, I want to thank my family and friends. First, my parents, who were my steadfast research assistants, draft and proof readers, and sounding board. My extended family, who were all supportive every step of the way. Patrick for always being there. My friends who let me keep them updated over the progress of this book: Phillip, Miriam, Nick, Taka, Steph, Tom A., Sheryl, and Catherine O., to name a few. Last, I want to dedicate this book to my grandparents, H. R. and Lynnell—my biggest supporters and cheerleaders, who would have been so excited that this book is out in the world. I am proud every day that I am your granddaughter. I also want to dedicate this book to my former professor and committee member, Dr. Laurie Wood, who offered incredibly helpful advice and suggestions during my time at FSU. I was looking forward to talking to her about the book. The profession has lost an incredible historian.

I would like to note I conducted research at the Special and Area Studies Collections at the George A. Smathers Libraries at the University of Florida in 2018, based on the archive's finding aid at the time, which had been created in October 2012. The archives reorganized the home demonstration and Cooperative Extension Service records, creating a new finding aid in August 2022. These records were merged and revised under the University of Florida Institute for Food and Agricultural Sciences (IFAS) Extension Records, series 093, with four subseries of archival material, which includes the home demonstration records. This change is reflected in my citations.

THE PROOF IS *in the* DOUGH

INTRODUCTION

WOMEN AND DEVELOPING RURAL REFORM IN THE TWENTIETH-CENTURY SOUTH

In 1927, Mary Bailey, the home demonstration agent (HDA) for Lee County, Alabama, included a letter from Florence Ellington Robertson in her annual report of home demonstration work. Robertson, a local farmer's wife, praised the creation of Opelika's curb market for the financial opportunities it provided to her family: "[We] paid all the running expenses of home . . . kept two children in school . . . furnished one room complete in antique furniture . . . yard improvement[s]. . . . See from the total of sales how much the Curb Market has meant to a family of four. My sales from last Nov. 1st to this Nov. 1st has amounted to $1134.35."[1] Robertson sold two days a week at the Opelika curb market and made almost 25 percent of the average income earned in Alabama in 1927.[2]

Robertson's story is illustrative of the multiple ways rural white and African American women in Alabama and Florida transformed home demonstration programs between 1914 and 1929 to enhance their own financial situations and fiscal opportunities, as well as to improve their socioeconomic circumstances. At the same time, for African American women, racism and discrimination created layers of adversity that became part of their experiences with home demonstration programming. Examining the role of home demonstration programming in Alabama and Florida illuminates how rural women's uses of statewide programming, while similar, were also distinct from one another. By capitalizing on the skills learned during demonstrations and information about new approaches to food, clothing, homes, and more, women formed ways of easing their economic needs.

In the late nineteenth century, southern political leaders attempted to transform the region into the "New South" by advocating for industrial development and other modernization projects.[3] But change came more dramatically to some regions than to others. For example, Birmingham, Alabama, became a thriving industrial center, known for its iron and steel, yet the state's population remained primarily rural: 83 percent in 1910, 78 percent in 1920, and 72 percent in 1930. During the same period in Florida, tourism and real estate booms drew in new people; however, much of the population remained in rural areas: 71

percent in 1910, 63 percent in 1920, and 48 percent in 1930. However, not all those who lived in rural areas were farmers, while farmers did live in rural areas.[4]

Meanwhile, as the nation became increasingly urban, reformers (also referred to as progressives) advocated for governmental regulations to mitigate the negative effects of industrialization and urbanization. They focused on cities, as the population shifted toward more residents living in urban areas than rural ones. Yet, even before the desperate economic conditions of the 1930s, the South struggled with its own compounding issues and cycles of poverty. The rise of a new South, which exalted business and urban centers, provided a somewhat glossy veneer that masked the reality of rural southern life, where tenancy, sharecropping, mill towns, and economic disparities prevailed. Long stretches of farmers' fields, pine trees, and small to moderate-sized towns hid persistent poverty. Racism, disenfranchisement, and racial violence were prevalent in urban and rural areas alike. The South's demographics were also changing, as many African Americans sought a better life by moving out of the region in what became known as the "Great Migration."[5] The statistical tables on the following pages, drawn from U.S. Census information, provide a look at the population and demographics in both Florida and Alabama for the years 1910, 1920, and 1930.[6]

Overall, the statistics from this period emphasize that the majority of the population in the two states lived in rural areas (although more people lived on farms in Alabama than in Florida, and by 1930, Florida's urban population narrowly exceeded its rural share). In both states, white women outnumbered African American women, especially in rural areas, and indeed, while the percentage of white women on farms in both states remained steady, the number of African American women in rural or farm settings decreased. Still, the number of both white and African American farmers remained high well into the 1920s. In 1929, the *Modern Farmer*, a publication of the National Federation of Colored Farmers, cited census statistics showing that Alabama's Dallas County had 6,606 farms, with 638 white farmers and a far greater number—5,968—of African American farmers. In a separate news item, the *Modern Farmer* highlighted Conecuh County, also in Alabama, where the 1,779 white farmers outnumbered the 1,335 African American ones. (Nonetheless, the paper noted, "if these 1,335 colored farmers are in an organization they can wield more power and get better loans. If the white farmers organize and the colored do not, it will be a very easy matter to tell what will happen.")[7]

For most rural residents, nineteenth-century middle-class ideals about creating separate gendered spaces and a "domestic sphere" versus a "work" or "public

TABLE 1 | ALABAMA OVERALL POPULATION

Census year	Total population of Alabama	# of white individuals	% of total population	# of African American individuals	% of total population
1910	2,138,093	1,228,832	57%	908,282	42%
1920	2,348,174	1,447,032	62%	900,652	38%
1930	2,646,248	1,700,775	64%	944,834	36%

TABLE 2 | ALABAMA OVERALL POPULATION BY RACE & GENDER

Census year	Total female population in Alabama	# of white women	Female % of overall white population	% of overall female population in Alabama (white)	# of African American women	Female % of overall African American population	% of overall female population in Alabama (African American)
1910	1,063,884	602,941	49%	57%	460,488	51%	43%
1920	1,175,069	713,993	49%	61%	460,873	51%	39%
1930	1,331,239	843,253	50%	63%	487,690	52%	37%

TABLE 3 | ALABAMA URBAN POPULATION BY RACE & GENDER

Census year	Urban population of Alabama	% of overall population	White population	# of white women	% of total urban population	African American population	# of African American women	% of total urban population
1910	370,431	17%	213,756	106,069	29%	156,603	83,024	22%
1920	509,317	22%	312,410	156,848	31%	196,833	103,861	20%
1930	744,273	28%	475,660	242,778	33%	268,450	145,323	20%

TABLE 4 | ALABAMA RURAL POPULATION BY RACE & GENDER

Census year	Rural population of Alabama	% of overall population	White population	# of white women	% of total rural population	African American population	# of African American women	% of total rural population
1910	1,767,662	83%	1,015,076	496,872	28%	751,679	377,464	21%
1920	1,838,857	78%	1,134,622	557,145	30%	703,819	357,012	19%
1930	1,901,975	72%	1,225,115	600,475	32%	676,384	342,367	18%

TABLE 5 | ALABAMA RURAL FARM POPULATION BY RACE & GENDER

Census year	Rural population on farms of Alabama	% of overall rural population	White population	# of white women	% of white women on farms	African American population	# of African American women	% of African American women on farms
1920	1,334,513	72%	819,162	400,458	30%	515,082	263,816	20%
1930	1,336,409	70%	839,530	407,777	31%	496,542	251,846	19%

TABLE 6 | ALABAMA RURAL NONFARM POPULATION BY RACE & GENDER

Census year	Rural population on nonfarms of Alabama	% of overall rural population	White population	# of white women	% of white women on nonfarms	African American population	# of African American women	% of African American women on nonfarms
1920	504,344	27%	315,460	156,687	31%	188,737	93,196	18%
1930	565,566	30%	385,585	192,698	34%	179,842	90,521	16%

TABLE 7 | FLORIDA OVERALL POPULATION

Census year	Total population of Florida	# of White individuals	% of total population	# of African American individuals	% of total population
1910	752,619	443,634	59%	308,669	41%
1920	968,470	638,153	66%	329,487	34%
1930	1,468,211	1,035,205	71%	431,828	29%

TABLE 8 | FLORIDA OVERALL POPULATION BY RACE & GENDER

Census year	Total female population in Florida	# of white women	Female % of overall white population	% of overall female population in Florida (white)	# of African American women	% of overall African American population	% of overall female population in Florida (African American)
1910	358,453	211,089	48%	59%	147,307	48%	41%
1920	473,150	310,509	47%	66%	162,331	49%	34%
1930	730,536	513,389	50%	70%	216,680	50%	30%

TABLE 9 | FLORIDA URBAN POPULATION BY RACE & GENDER

Census year	Urban population of Florida	% of overall population	White population	# of white women	% of total urban population	African American population	# of African American women	% of total population
1910	219,080	29%	130,302	63,328	29%	88,586	44,675	20%
1920	355,825	37%	235,026	117,218	33%	120,598	62,290	18%
1930	759,778	52%	549,025	279,114	37%	210,292	111,708	15%

TABLE 10 | FLORIDA RURAL POPULATION BY RACE & GENDER

Census year	Rural population of Florida	% of overall population	White population	# of white women	% of total rural population	African American population	# of African American women	% of total rural population
1910	533,539	71%	313,332	147,761	28%	220,083	102,632	19%
1920	612,645	63%	403,127	193,291	32%	208,891	100,041	16%
1930	708,433	48%	486,180	234,275	33%	221,536	104,972	15%

TABLE 11 | FLORIDA RURAL FARM POPULATION BY RACE & GENDER

Census year	Rural population on farms of Florida	% of overall rural population	White population	# of white women	% of white women on farms	African American population	# of African American women	% of African American women on farms
1920	279,370	46%	191,678	91,795	33%	87,602	43,537	16%
1930	274,949	39%	199,360	94,968	35%	75,469	36,858	13%

TABLE 12 | FLORIDA RURAL NONFARM POPULATION BY RACE & GENDER

Census year	Rural population on nonfarms of Florida	% of overall rural population	White population	# of white women	% of white women on nonfarms	African American population	# of African American women	% of African American women on nonfarms
1920	333,275	54%	211,449	101,496	30%	121,289	56,504	17%
1930	433,484	61%	286,820	139,307	32%	146,067	68,114	16%

sphere" did not make sense or even exist.[8] Perceptions and beliefs about "women's work" endured, but rural farm women were often coproducers, blurring the assumed lines between separate spheres. The workspaces of rural men and women were complex and were not easily distinguished. Women labored in the fields during planting and harvesting to help ensure the success of a particular farming operation. For such a farm woman, as Kathleen Babbitt has written of their counterparts in New York and of home economists, "Income of her own was important to the farm woman's self-esteem and identity as a worker."[9] However, the work of the Cooperative Extension Service was not intended to transform traditional expectations about proper gender roles or aspects of performative femininity.

The lives of twentieth-century southern rural women have recently been a research area for historians, especially with regard to the nuances of the relationship of rural women to local economic networks. The overall historical conversation has recentered how such women's lives and labor provide a greater context in which to understand their evolving, often overlapping, roles as producers and consumers. As Lu Ann Jones has stated concerning North Carolina women's rural commerce, it was "a continuous and relatively stable source of income that enabled farms to endure."[10] The income rural women made allowed them to "mitigate their economic dependence upon men," while "women's trade evolved as the regional economy developed and in response to the needs of their families and to their own personal goals."[11]

For example, home demonstration agents taught rural women the art of canning tomatoes so that they would have a ready and yearly food supply. With the help of early female demonstration agents, young girls, and sometimes their mothers, learned how to properly cook, measure, and weigh what was to be canned and how to adequately sanitize the cans. Agents viewed this as a scientific process, but training in such matters also educated students about finance. If there was excess, agents wanted the women to be able to determine values and to market their goods for a profit. Minoa D. Uffelman asserts, "The extra money earned by farm wives and girls could be used in any number of ways to improve the lives of their families."[12] Participating in tomato-canning clubs signaled a chance to change fiscal circumstances. Similarly, Elizabeth S. D. Engelhardt writes of these clubs, "Putting money in the hands of people generally disempowered by society and trusting them to make decisions about spending it gave the girls a powerful sense of agency and freedom."[13]

Tomato-canning clubs are one example of an early, but important, approach to creating a sense of economic and personal accomplishment for such women—successfully using an agent's predetermined program or plan. Rural women could take an idea and use it to bring about a financially beneficial outcome. They figured out how to take new technological ideas regarding food, clothing, animal husbandry, and crafts and use them at their personal discretion, turning these programs into personal antipoverty opportunities. Other historians of rural women, such as Melissa Walker and Rebecca Sharpless, recognize farm women as producers as well as contributors to their respective local and regional economies.[14] Some rural women actively embraced elements of modernization, while others did not. That dichotomy was the push and pull between maintaining a historical tradition and modernizing or completely restructuring a life based on changing economic or other conditions. Women elected to participate in some Extension-based programs and avoided others because of issues involving racial discrimination, which, in turn, shaped the programs themselves.[15]

Home demonstration programs and home demonstration agents have also drawn scholarly attention, with discussions of these programs and people through lenses of region, race, and gender. Historians have probed the Cooperative Extension programs by analyzing the collision of reform, scientific farming, domestic science, gender, and race. Scholarship after 1990, particularly, has discussed advantages gained from home demonstration programs, with rural women serving as examples of the success of HDAs.[16] From its start, the Cooperative Extension Service was nationwide and not exclusive to southern states.[17] Home demonstration agents originated as a key component in the initial federal legislation launching the Extension Service, the Smith-Lever Act of 1914, establishing their role in delivering unbiased, research-based, scientific information via one-on-one contact. Historians have since created rich narratives about the regional differences and parallel difficulties faced by HDAs and the rural women they sought to reach in these early years of the service.[18]

In her research regarding Virginia women's engagement with urban markets for their personal gain, historian Ann E. McCleary notes, "[They] hoped to regain some measure of economic control over their lives . . . to shift the marketing of their home-produced goods back into their own hands, and to gain a cash income over which they could have greater control."[19] She writes that farm women "carved out new public spaces" and "articulated a modern vision of the rural woman as farm producer, business person, and entrepreneur."[20] Curb markets, in particular, provided a means, motive, and opportunity for rural women to become consumers and producers.[21] Curb markets are similar to today's farmers' markets, with regard to idea and use, and they became a solution for rural women looking for new methods to help themselves economically. "Many women," notes Lu Ann Jones, writing about rural southerners, "believed they made more money at the curb market than anywhere else."[22] In Alabama and Florida, curb markets became major ways for women to build their bank accounts. Such markets, discussed in chapter 4, were often initiated or run by women or by a specially appointed local HDA. Their creation encouraged the standardization of products, quality control, pricing, salability of items, supply and demand, holding a buyer's interest, and consumer contact.[23]

Since the 1980s, historians have sought to broaden the study of home demonstration programs to include the experiences of African American HDAs, who usually worked under the umbrella of white agents and in a culture of segregation and disenfranchisement. Racial discrimination, socioeconomic conditions of rural African American and white families, and the sheer physical distance between homes and towns meant that HDAs had to work harder at cultivating relationships to persuade individuals to attend their meetings. Although one narrative tendency is to regard the HDAs as the sole alleviators of problems in rural life, such a focus oversimplifies the complex relationship and reality of rural women's interactions with the Cooperative Extension Service and HDAs.

In writing about African American HDAs in Florida, Barbara Cotton notes that male and female agents alike faced "severe obstacles."[24] These included not only lower pay and resources than white agents received, but also the difficulty of proving themselves professionally.[25] In both states, female African American HDAs worked within a two-tier system of bias not faced by their white HDA counterparts, who encountered discrimination based only on gender. However, these African American agents achieved a remarkable degree of success, even in ways that were unanticipated. In the words of Carmen V. Harris, "Although whites expected that extension work among blacks would produce a mollified peasantry, black extension work turned out to be a subversive force that undermined white supremacy and contributed to the demise of the Jim Crow South."[26]

Jim Crow laws meant that African American HDAs had to construct their own State Council of Home Demonstration Clubs. Female-led groups and clubs like these helped create "safe, women-centered spaces" for their members.[27] Indeed, the "Negro Division" became a vector for economic and social change as both male and female African American agents sought to stabilize and bring economic opportunities to their communities.[28]

By using newly learned foodways and clothing techniques, inculcating better health and nutritional habits, or creating a more aesthetically pleasing home, rural women demonstrated the influence of home demonstration agents in their everyday lives. Moreover, by taking advantage of their newfound knowledge to create moneymaking paths, rural white and African American women in Alabama and Florida gained more control over the present and future economic circumstances for themselves and their families. Whether these enterprises were enhanced by the privilege of skin color or were hindered by racial discrimination, the way women used these ventures had common threads.[29] Alabamian and Floridian women revealed why and how they used the money, which shows how home demonstration programming allowed rural women to take a more active role in guiding their own personal economic agendas during this fifteen-year period.

This is ultimately a story of how extra eggs came to mean more than adding to a morning breakfast for one's children; they also provided income to pay taxes or school tuition. Vegetables grown in the garden appeared not just on the dinner table, but in the marketplace, where the price they fetched bought new clothes, other household goods, or even a car.

Having a new source of disposable income brought intangible benefits as well as material ones. As Lu Ann Jones writes, "Earnings might also shift the balance of power within families, giving women more influence over farm decisions and enhancing their sense of dignity and personal worth."[30] While the HDAs instituted the initial programming, rural white and African American women in Alabama and Florida took it further, utilizing their new skills and knowledge for the betterment of their family's lives and their own.

CHAPTER ONE

SOWING A PROGRESSIVE BUCOLIC HAVEN

Home demonstration agents and the Cooperative Extension Service have their roots in three pieces of federal legislation—the Morrill Land-Grant Act of 1862, the Hatch Act of 1887, and the Second Morrill Act of 1890. Another catalyst was the Country Life Movement, which helped to idealize bucolic living and sought to motivate people to remain in rural areas rather than moving to cities. The creation of the land-grant system and other federal and state-based agricultural programs coalesced with an increased emphasis on scientific farming techniques. All of these infrastructural forces converged in the passage of the Smith-Lever Act of 1914, which formally established the Cooperative Extension Service.

A BRIEF HISTORY OF LAND-GRANT UNIVERSITIES

Michigan started the symbolic ball rolling with its 1850 state constitution, which specified, "The legislature shall encourage the promotion of intellectual, scientific and agricultural improvement; and shall, as soon as practicable, provide for the establishment of an agricultural school . . . for instruction in agriculture and the natural sciences connected therewith."[1] In 1855, the Agricultural College of the State of Michigan (now known as Michigan State University) became an early "prototype for the entire land-grant system."[2] New York's state senate passed a resolution in March 1852 to seek funding for land on which to create agricultural-focused institutions, and Massachusetts followed a month later with similar language. In 1853, Illinois became the first state to pass a resolution petitioning Congress for federal lands to help establish one institution in each state to provide for "the more liberal and practical education of our industrial classes and their teachers."[3] Among those pushing for the resolution was Jonathan Baldwin Turner, an abolitionist, working-class industrial education advocate, botanist, and Illinois College professor, who advocated for agricultural education.[4]

Lyman Trumbull, an Illinois senator, wrote to representative—and future senator—Justin Smith Morrill of Vermont, calling him a "warm friend of agriculture" who could more easily advance the land-grant idea. The tactic worked, and between 1857 and 1862, Morrill was the chief advocate and promoter of a land-grant bill.⁵ The bill was passed by Congress, only to be vetoed by President James Buchanan, but it was later taken up again, advocated by Morrill and Benjamin F. Wade of Ohio on the Senate side, and finally, on July 2, 1862, President Abraham Lincoln signed the Morrill Land-Grant Act into law. The legislation bore the name of the Vermont congressman, and it was not until the mid-1910s that, at the behest of Turner's daughter and others, Jonathan Turner received credit for originating the land-grant university idea.⁶

The Morrill Act was rooted in ideas about opening higher education to those of a lower economic status or class—including farmers and other "average" Americans—who could not afford traditional colleges and universities such as Yale, Harvard, and Princeton. It also changed concepts "broadly defining . . . what 'educated' means . . . adding practical things into that education," and these new universities and colleges indicated how "the state will give . . . opportunities to rise," which, in turn, would help the country succeed.⁷

While the first Morrill Act helped create new agricultural and mechanical education–based colleges, it was later expanded to include existing universities that achieved land-grant status by offering the same academic programs. The land-grant system meant each state received "30,000 acres of federal land . . . indigenous land for the most part" for each member of Congress—the land could be sold, with the proceeds used to establish a land-grant institution. Ultimately, the land "grew to an allocation of 100 million acres."⁸ Universities created with or subsequently given land-grant status are present in every state and territory and include Kansas State (1863), Pennsylvania State (1863), Iowa State (1864), Cornell (1865), Purdue (1869), Virginia Tech (1872), Louisiana State (1874), Mississippi State (1878), North Carolina State (1887), Clemson (1889), New Mexico State (1889), Oklahoma State (1890), and University of Hawai'i at Mānoa (1907).⁹ Established universities such as the University of Georgia, the University of Tennessee, and Rutgers had their status applied retroactively. The majority of land-grant institutions in the South were established after 1865, because the 1862 act specifically stated, "No State while in a condition of rebellion or insurrection against the government of the United States shall be entitled to the benefit of this act."¹⁰

While the Morrill Act opened the academic doors to many new students, one group continued to be systematically excluded, particularly in the South—African Americans. "White leaders were openly questioning the need for higher education for Blacks," notes Frederick S. Humphries, "and where the Supreme Court decisions, such as the Civil Rights cases of 1883 and *U.S. v. Cruikshank* in 1876, were eroding most civil rights gains, a new initiative was needed by Congress to assure land-grant education for black people."[11] After the first Morrill Act passed, Justin Smith Morrill called for a similar land-grant university system for African Americans, stating "they are members of the American family, and their advancement concerns us all."[12] However, publicly funded African American agricultural-based or land-grant colleges did not become a reality until the Second Morrill Act, or the Agricultural College Act of 1890. Enacted on August 30, 1890, the legislation was primarily directed at southern states and instituted a specific requirement if they wished to receive extra funding for land-grant universities: "No money shall be paid out under this act . . . for the support and maintenance of a college where a distinction of race or color is made in the admission of students, but the establishment and maintenance of such colleges separately for white and colored students shall be held to be a compliance with the provisions of this act if the funds received . . . be equitably divided as hereinafter set forth."[13]

The African American universities created as land-grant universities or receiving that status retroactively included Alcorn State, Fort Valley State, Lincoln, Kentucky State, Central State, Langston, and North Carolina A&T. Colloquially, these institutions are known as "1890s schools." While the Morrill Act of 1890 was said to replicate the 1862 law, in reality its application was rife with inequality, lacked adequate and consistent funding, and, sometimes, ignored the agricultural component altogether. The 1890 legislation also began encouraging a "separate but equal" concept even before the Supreme Court declared it constitutional in 1896's *Plessy v. Ferguson*. In the words of historian Thomas Aiello, the newer public "HBCUs" (historically Black colleges and universities) were founded by "white state governments, largely on an industrial training model. They are distinguished in that type of nomenclature from private 'HBCUs' that were engaged in a more liberal arts–centered curriculum."[14]

Meanwhile, the mission of land-grant institutions increasingly became linked with scientific research, which was considered critical for advancing agriculture and technology. These institutions looked to create research-specific locations that helped their overall mission. The solution was in Connecticut, and the pioneering idea was an agricultural research center.

As early as the 1840s, John Pitkin Norton, a Yale University professor of agricultural chemistry, articulated the "concept of a nationwide system of agricultural experiment stations."[15] Norton's ideas influenced one of his students, Samuel William Johnson, who became a leader in scientific agricultural education and an advocate for agricultural experiment stations, like those he saw during an extended academic period in Germany. In 1875, the first Connecticut

Experiment Station was founded at Wesleyan University. Johnson was named its director in 1877 and held the position for two decades. The station moved to New Haven and became part of Yale in 1879.[16] Similar experiment stations were established in California, North Carolina, New York, and New Jersey from 1875 to 1880, with others taking root in states from Alabama to Wisconsin to Vermont. Early "farmer institutes," a precursor to experiment stations, sporadically appeared, especially in the Midwest. At the federal level, William Hatch of Missouri and Mississippi's James Z. George introduced bills calling on Congress to allocate federal funds to land-grant colleges to create agricultural experimental research stations. In 1887, the Hatch Act passed.[17]

A key aspect of the Hatch Act was to set up a mechanism for disseminating information. The legislation provided "that bulletins or reports of progress shall be published at said stations at least once in three months . . . and to such individuals actually engaged in farming as may request the same."[18] No postage was required for these reports and bulletins, which made scientific and agricultural discoveries more widely available to the public. Obstacles remained, however. For one example, some rural residents were illiterate, while discrimination meant African American universities were not always included in this aspect of the Hatch Act.[19]

THE COUNTRY LIFE COMMISSION AND MOVEMENT

While reformers in the late nineteenth century were asking questions about socioeconomic inequality in cities, a new subset of reformers duplicated this approach, but with a focus on rural life. In the early twentieth century, The Country Life Movement, spearheaded by President Theodore Roosevelt and Cornell University's Liberty Hyde Bailey, expounded on new ideas about improving rural standards of living. In the introduction to the 1911 reprint of 1909's *Report of the Commission on Country Life*, Theodore Roosevelt wrote, "If country life is to become all that it should be, if the career of a farmer is to rank with any other career in the country as a dignified and desirable way of earning a living, the farmer must take advantage of all that agricultural knowledge has to offer, and also of all that has raised the standard of living and of intelligence in other callings."[20]

Essentially, these reformers believed there was a need to make "country life" more efficient, which would result in rural areas becoming more attractive places in which to settle. Yet, reformers continued to believe the yeoman farmer's morals were centered in the agrarian life. They believed modernizing agendas would be balanced by keeping some "traditional" aspects of rural lifestyles. Reformers also wanted to help farmers increase their production and to use scientific and technological knowledge to revitalize and uplift rural life. The ideal result was to create a progressive bucolic haven, which would encourage people to stay in the country, rather than seeking an urban lifestyle.

Theodore Roosevelt's decision to inspect rural conditions and affairs across the country was not surprising, given his support of conservation efforts and the use of systematic studies to improve food and drug production. A leading influence for this endeavor was Sir Horace Plunkett, who "intensified Roosevelt's interest in rural affairs and gave him, upon request, a famous formula for a sound agriculture, 'better farming' (the application of science), 'better business' (the organization of farm co-operatives), and 'better living' (mostly better schools and modern convenience)."[21] Another influence was Cornell University's Liberty Hyde Bailey, a pioneer in horticulture and botany. Bailey backed the "nature study" movement and even created a "nature study" program to teach in new York's rural schools, as well as hiring female professors in leading positions, including Martha Van Rensselaer, Anna Botsford Comstock, and Flora Rose. In 1907 Roosevelt heard Bailey's presidential address at the Association of American Agricultural Colleges and Experiment Stations, held in conjunction with the Semi-centennial Celebration of the Founding of Agricultural Colleges. Afterward, he chose Bailey to head the specially formed Country Life Commission, which was created in August 1908.[22]

Roosevelt charged the commission "to look into the 'deficiencies' of agriculture and country life and the means by which they might be remedied."[23] Funded by a $5,000 grant from the Russell Sage Foundation, the commission gathered a group of white men from a range of occupations connected with rurality or agriculture: Kenyon L. Butterfield, Henry Wallace, Walter H. Page, Gifford Pinchot, Charles S. Barrett, and William A. Beard. The Census Bureau helped the commission by distributing surveys with questions about country life to farmers and others in rural areas and received "an impressive 20 percent return rate."[24] The commission itself conducted correspondence and research on specific issues, held "public hearings designed to reveal the views and ideas of farmers and others on the state of country life," toured twenty-nine states, and called on country people "to organize meetings in local schools to discuss country life questions and then to forward the results to the commission."[25] By January 1909, the outcome was the *Report of the Country Life Commission*, which concluded that rural residents needed better roads, better education, ways to prevent social isolation, methods to increase crop yields, and mechanisms to improve overall health.[26]

Bailey believed that rural life was in peril. He reiterated his philosophy in *The Country Life Movement in the United States*: "The city sits like a parasite, running out its roots into the open country and draining it of its substance. . . . Many country places are already sucked dry. The future state of the farmer, or real countryman, will depend directly on the kind of balance or relationship that exists between urban and rural forces."[27] His solution, which was also the commission's, was twofold: first, to improve the physical infrastructure of rural communities, for instance, by paving roads; and second, to bring information to individuals through outreach programs. Soon, the Country Life Commission's report became a basis for its own reform movement, aptly called the Country Life Movement.[28]

Idealized versions of rural life and country ideals appeared in literature of the period, with narratives emphasizing the wholesome and beneficial aspects of living rurally. First published in 1912, William A. McKeever's *Farm Boys and Girls*, part of Bailey's Rural Science Series, was a how-to guide on building and attaining a proper country lifestyle. Chapter topics included choosing the correct education and vocation, properly socializing at school and church, and developing a country outlook. Advice reflected gender stereotypes. For example, in the chapter titled "The Farm Girl's Preparation for a Vocation," McKeever wrote, "The one-sided, classical college training has spoiled for life many otherwise good and happy women. Such a course tends strongly to draw the mind and affections of the young woman away from the home and from motherhood and other such matters so fundamental to the well-being of the race."[29]

Canadian professor O. J. Stevenson's *Country Life Reader* in 1916 contributed short essays, stories, and poetry aimed at young readers to foster a rural-based life, which, the book implied, would lead to tranquility and satisfaction. The sections were divided into seasons, with themed works from poets Christina Rossetti, Henry Wadsworth Longfellow, and John Greenleaf Whittier, as well as excerpts from Alfred, Lord Tennyson, Victor Hugo, Henry Ward Beecher, and Liberty Hyde Bailey. There were also short essays with such titles as "The Soil" and "Maple-Sugaring." The last pages comprised a letter debating the benefits of the farm compared to the deficiencies of the city: "What about the man's own life? . . . Does he have the better chance to develop his body and soul into the best sort of manhood? Let my forty years of city life speak on that point. . . . Stay in the country!"[30]

In her 1915 work *The American Country Girl*, Martha Foote Crow cautioned about rural residents who left for urban areas: "[They] rear their children in the hot, stuffy, unsocialized atmosphere of the town, leaving the happy gardens without the joyous voices of children, the fields without sturdy boys to work them, the farm homes without capable young women to—shall I say, *man* them? . . . Let us say to *woman* them, to *lady* them, to *mother* them . . . make them centers of wholesome interesting life."[31] Presented in an idealized light, a pastoral life was viewed as empowering, resulting in the making of a young woman. The "Country Girl" grew her home around her, and as education, service, and community were fostered and nurtured, she did not "feel called to go to the other side of the world to fulfill her mission." Crow continued, "In her own valley she can have a life work that will be full of the rich returns for well-directed, self-sacrificing service."[32]

The commission's report reinforced gendered roles and norms, especially with regard to keeping a "traditional" rural family unit in place. A farmer, it said, needed to realize that "the person who most needs consideration on the farm is his wife." At the same time, the wife "should [not] purchase ease at the expense of duty. . . . If the woman shirks her duty as housewife, as home keeper, as the mother whose prime function it is to bear and rear a sufficient number of healthy children, then she is not entitled to our regard. But if she does her duty she is more entitled to our regard. . . . The man should show special consideration for her needs."[33]

This reiterated a message that the happiness and well-being of women played a paramount role in keeping children and later generations engaged in rural life, rather than moving to an urban area. As Joyce Thierer writes, "Women were central . . . especially to the traditionalists who wanted to see the family farm continue as a way of life. . . . If the farmer was the backbone of the nation, the farm woman was the backbone of the community."[34] Unsurprisingly, though, "the country life movement just did not understand the roles of farm women. . . . [It] failed rural women by refusing to acknowledge their economic contributions or misreading those contributions as 'drudgery.'" Rejecting a rural life was seen as almost akin to "rejecting America."[35] The Commission's suggestions, coming as they did from an all-male committee, are fairly predictable, providing advice on what rural women could do within their homes and not recognizing some might want a different path.[36]

Nonetheless, the Country Life Movement also inspired other people, including Benjamin F. Hubert, who served as a professor of agriculture and a director at South Carolina State Agricultural and Mechanical College, chairman of the Department of Agriculture at Tuskegee Institute, and ultimately president of Georgia State Industrial College for Colored Youth. At the Massachusetts Agricultural College he had studied under commission member Kenyon Butterfield. He became an advocate for African American farmers and rural families and would go on to organize the Association for the Advancement of Negro Country Life in 1928.[37]

In recent years, the Country Life Movement has been criticized as being "misguided," "patronizing," and overly "romantic." On the other hand, William L. Bowers in 1974 saw it as "not radical enough." In a 2004 reconsideration, Scott J. Peters and Paul A. Morgan claimed that the movement reflected "an emerging ecological sensitivity and a particular variant of Progressive Era reform devoted to the pursuit and realization of key American civic and economic ideals in an increasingly scientific, urban, and industrial age."[38]

The Country Life Movement also spawned the American County Life Association, which was formed in 1919. This inspired other reform organizations to create their own committees focused on country life.[39] One such organization was the National Civic Federation, a prominent civic and reform group founded in 1900, whose goal was to "bolster public confidence in the free enterprise system by initiating moderate social and industrial welfare programs," including "protective legislation for workers . . . [and] restrained government involvement in business affairs."[40] In 1908 the federation established a woman's department, which six years later created its own country life committee, chaired by Marie Bankhead Owen of Alabama.[41]

An early goal of the committee was to create a partnership with the George Peabody College for Teachers in Nashville, Tennessee, home of the Seaman A. Knapp School of Country Life. Owen, along with Maude A. K. Wetmore and Anne Morgan, the respective chair and treasurer of the Woman's Department, headed the push to establish an endowed chair in rural nursing at Peabody. This would support the training of nurses to work with rural populations, as well as aligning with the Woman's Department's goals about rural health. The chair was to memorialize Ellen Wilson, the late First Lady, who had died in August 1914. Eventually, however, the idea was abandoned—possibly because the group was unable to raise the required endowment funds of $100,000—and the Ellen Wilson Chair of Rural Nursing was never realized.[42]

Seaman A. Knapp, after whom Peabody's country life school was named, was viewed as an agricultural innovator and "a bit of a hero in rural America." He was active in supporting agricultural experiment stations and establishing early demonstration farms, which helped lead to a regional, then national, effort to hire county and farm demonstration agents to teach more scientific farming methods.[43] In 1910, Hampton University's *Southern Workman* claimed that Knapp's demonstration-farm movement did "more in enriching rural life and in nationalizing the South than any other agency emanating from the Federal Government."[44]

Soon, Peabody College, and its Knapp School of Country Life, became a hub for southern rural education and a training center for teachers and educational leaders, with a focus on rural, agricultural, and home economic issues. As a result, many white home demonstration agents were Peabody graduates.[45] Seaman Knapp's influence and the respect he generated inspired "local Knapp Memorial societies" to begin thinking about "a school of country life in his honor" soon after his death in 1911.[46] Peabody had been chosen as the location for the school, and Wallace Buttrick of the General Education Board (an endowed philanthropy backed by John D. Rockefeller) helped secure a donation of $250,000 to get the project off the ground, contingent on funding of $150,000 from Peabody itself. One of the key features of the school was a demonstration farm, which would also be named after Knapp. The entire enterprise was intended "to help every school and farm in the South" and was "the first institution in America devoted exclusively to studying the problems of country life."[47]

A sampling of the academic course catalogs from 1916 to 1929 confirms a variety of classes (along with diplomas and scholarships) designed for future home demonstration agents (HDA)s. Courses were designed for training in marketing and organization, although those ebbed in the middle to latter part of the 1920s. Mary S. Hoffschwelle writes of Peabody's early years, "A generalized reform movement subsumed the multiple goals of training educational leaders and tackling the problems of rural life through special educational training, the Knapp School, and home economics."[48]

THE SMITH-LEVER ACT OF 1914

The Country Life Commission called for a more effective means of reaching farmers and promoting new scientific farming techniques, and Liberty Hyde Bailey asserted that county agents should act as this lifeline in farming and rural life. This idea was realized when the Smith-Lever Act passed on May 8, 1914, although reformers did recognize possible challenges in convincing farmers and their families to trust in the idea of one-to-one contact. Section 2 of the bill explained the Cooperative Extension Service's role: "[It] shall consist of the giving of instruction and practical demonstrations in agriculture and home economics to persons not attending or resident in said colleges in the several communities . . . imparting to such persons information on said subjects through field demonstrations, publications, and otherwise; and this work shall be carried on in such manner as may be mutually agreed upon by the Secretary of Agriculture and the State agricultural college or colleges receiving the benefits of this Act."[49]

The Smith-Lever Act was not met with immediate enthusiasm by everyone. It allowed for continued disenfranchisement of African American universities. In its March 1914 issue, *The Crisis*, the official magazine of the NAACP, discussed the legislation's effect on African American farmers, with a chief concern being the lack of provision for the equitable distribution of resources. Despite lobbying by the NAACP, it became painfully apparent this discrimination would be embedded into the bill. "Our fight on the Smith-Lever Bill was not successful," *The Crisis* reported:

> The colored farmers of the South might or might not receive any of the millions which the bill appropriated.... To insure colored farmers a fair share of the moneys appropriated, the Association persuaded Senator [Wesley] Jones to introduce an amendment providing for this.... A substitute, the Shafroth Amendment, was offered, passed by the Senate and then lost.... The fight over this bill brought the whole race issue squarely before Congress and before the country.... A letter of protest from [the NAACP] was read on the floor.... Our part in the fight was made clear ... by the press which gave it the widest publicity.[50]

Thus, it is not an entirely progressive piece of legislation, as it reinforced systemic racism and inequality with the allocation of funds, resources, and agents' employment. However, some African American Extension agents and HDAs were offered programs, professionalization, and employment, although those secured resources were not equal. Extension funding went through the white agricultural universities, so monies were not evenly distributed. For example, in the early years after Smith-Lever was enacted, the state of Alabama received $10,000 for Extension. The two African American land-grant universities, which are now called Alabama A&M and Tuskegee, received a total of $1,800, with the bulk of the designated money going to Tuskegee. By contrast, what is now Auburn University received the rest of the funds.[51]

Gender also played a role in the implementation of the Smith-Lever Act, because of the overlapping interests of home economics, early home demonstration, and Extension. As both men and women were involved in the management and operation of farms, land-grant colleges now had to consider ways to provide access to female students. As Alfred Charles True, a former director of the Office of Experiment Stations, wrote in an early history of agricultural education in the South, "[Where] agricultural colleges were not coeducational it was necessary to make special arrangements for the conduct of the extension work in home economics."[52]

In some states, home demonstration efforts began even before 1914 in the form of canning clubs, corn clubs, and the like. The Smith-Lever Act helped solidify and formalize HDAs and the Cooperative Extension Service. Many rural families were wary about applying science-backed techniques, whether in the field or the home. Shifting to modernity meant creating a new system of trust about the importance of new scientifically based systems, methods, and techniques. This meant farmers and rural residents adopting a new worldview, along with trusting governmental or university officials, as demonstrations and advice were usually replacing long-held or even familial traditions in how they operated their homes and farms.[53]

The impact of the Smith-Lever Act of 1914, as with later rural-focused federal legislation such as the Federal Farm Loan Act of 1916, the Smith-Hughes Act of 1917, and the Capper-Ketcham Act of 1928, included a dichotomy of successes and failures. However, by increasing the number of county and home demonstration agents, the Smith-Lever Act met its goal of spreading new knowledge to farmers and rural families. Farmers came to depend on the Extension Service, its agents and their new ideas about scientific farming. As times, techniques, and technology evolved, so did the Extension Service. The Smith-Lever Act played a significant role in expanding and systematizing home demonstration programs and in developing the science of home economics throughout the country.[54]

A BRIEF HISTORY OF ALABAMA AND FLORIDA LAND GRANTS AND EXTENSION SYSTEMS

The history of Alabama and Florida's land-grant universities and Extension Service systems helps in understanding how rural white and African American women would use home demonstration in these states.[55] Alabama is unique in that it has three universities participating and collaborating in the work of agricultural research: Auburn University, Alabama Agricultural and Mechanical University, and Tuskegee University. Auburn University was founded in 1856 as East Alabama Male College and received land-grant designation after passage of the Morrill Act. It was later called Agricultural and Mechanical College of Alabama and then Alabama Polytechnic Institute, before adopting its current name in 1960.[56]

Alabama A&M and Tuskegee received land-grant status retroactively after the Morrill Act of 1890. Alabama A&M, located in Huntsville, was founded in 1875 at the behest of William Hooper Councill, a former slave who had been a teacher and worked for the Alabama legislature and as a newspaper editor as part of his long career. The school began as the State Normal and Industrial School of Huntsville, was later called the State Agricultural and Mechanical Institute for Negroes, and finally renamed Alabama Agricultural and Mechanical University in 1969. A souvenir program marking the seventy-fifth anniversary of Alabama A&M's founding quoted the 1898–1899 course catalog in defining the institution's purpose: to "assist in supplying the public schools of Alabama with competent teachers, and the State with industrious citizens." This same program also celebrated Walter Gravitt, the first African American county agent in Alabama's Madison County, who began work with the Extension Service in 1918.[57] One of his colleagues was Luella Hanna, who became one of Alabama's first and most prominent African American home demonstration agents.[58]

Tuskegee University, located in Macon County, was founded in 1881 as the Normal School for Colored Teachers, the result of an agreement between W. F. Foster, a white Democrat who needed African American votes in an 1880 election, and Lewis Adams, a local African American leader who was formerly enslaved. Adams pledged support to Foster on the condition that an educational institute for African Americans be created and funded. Booker T. Washington was the head and first principal, modeling the institute on Virginia's Hampton University. Unsurprisingly, like its peers, the university has changed its name throughout the years: the Tuskegee State Normal School, Tuskegee Normal School, Tuskegee Normal and Industrial Institute, Tuskegee Institute, and, since 1985, Tuskegee University.[59]

The Alabama Cooperative Extension System, or ACES, is a joint research and professional partnership between Alabama A&M and Auburn University. The merger resulted from a court case, *Knight v. Alabama*, that challenged "numerous policies of the state's colleges and universities, including funding, on the grounds that they were racially discriminatory" and asserted that "most of its four year public universities . . . maintained structures, policies, and practices that . . . promote[d] segregation."[60] Tuskegee University was previously part of ACES with Auburn and Alabama A&M but now separately maintains the Tuskegee University Cooperative Extension Program (TUCEP), which cooperates with ACES. TUCEP continues its tradition as the home base for the first Cooperative Extension Service in the country for African Americans.[61]

For over a century, Tuskegee was a key site for African American county agents, home demonstration agents, and African American agricultural research. One of TUCEP's programs was the Farmer's Institute, a long-running educational and training event that highlighted the newest methods of agricultural production. TUCEP is also involved with research, workshops, and other initiatives. The Tuskegee Experiment Station was established in 1896, and Thomas Monroe "T. M." Campbell was appointed as the first Extension agent for the Cooperative Extension Service in November 1906. Campbell's efforts were critical for Tuskegee to be able to reach rural African American farmers across Alabama, as well as other southern states. Campbell is also connected to one of Tuskegee's most visual forms of outreach and demonstration to rural African Americans—the Movable School.[62]

T. M. Campbell employed the Movable School, or Tuskegee Institute Movable School, an innovative idea that started in 1906 as the horse-drawn Jesup Agricultural Wagon. Designed by the faculty and named for Morris K. Jesup, an early investor and benefactor from New York, the wagon was equipped to demonstrate the latest techniques, depending on the season, for improving farms and homes. By 1918, it had been replaced by the Knapp Agricultural Truck and soon included the services of a rural nurse, Uva Hester, who provided health and sanitation outreach. After five years of use, the Knapp Truck needed replacing. Thanks to donations totaling $5,000 from African American farmers and others, the new Alabama Booker T. Washington Agricultural School on Wheels was set into motion.[63]

This version of the Movable School was outfitted with demonstration items for men and women, including an inoculating set for livestock, milk testers, sewing machines, a bathtub for a baby, a playground, a lighting plant, and a film projector. The Movable School was both a "transitory school," providing one-day programs and demonstrations at a predetermined location for those unable to travel, and a "stationary school," which offered those attending three to five days of programs in one location. Both African American men and women took part in the demonstrations and lectures. In 1923, the Movable School spent "164 days in the field, held 22 extension schools . . . included all counties that had agents, and reached 67 communities in Alabama. The total attendance at these schools was 24,447 men, women, and children." The Movable School was retired in 1944. Along with the Farmer's Institutes, which are still conducted today, the Movable School helped in making Tuskegee University an early force in connecting African Americans with scientific farming.[64]

Over three hundred miles from Auburn University sits the University of Florida, the state's officially designated land-grant university and primary center for agricultural research. Founded in Ocala in 1853 as East Florida Seminary, the institution moved to Gainesville in 1866 as a male-only school. It was not, however, the first land-grant college in the state. That distinction belonged to the short-lived Florida Agricultural College, which opened in Eau Gallie, then moved to Lake City in 1883, and was ultimately consolidated with other colleges because of the 1905 Buckman Act.[65]

This piece of legislation merged Florida's publicly funded institutions of higher learning into four colleges and universities. Florida Female College (now Florida State University), in Tallahassee, was for white female students. Next was the all-white and all-male University of the State of Florida, whose name was shortened to the University of Florida in 1909 and was the result of combining four schools: East Florida Seminary, Florida Agricultural College, St. Petersburg Normal and Industrial School, and South Florida Military College. The third school under the Buckman Act was the State Normal School for Colored Students, now Florida A&M University, in Tallahassee, for African American students. Last, the Florida Institute for Blind, Deaf, and Dumb—now known as the Florida School for the Deaf and Blind—was established in 1885 in St. Augustine.[66]

The University of Florida (UF) began holding classes in 1906. The Florida Agricultural Experiment Station, which had been located in Lake City at Florida Agricultural College, also moved to Gainesville and became part of UF's College of Agriculture. Today UF, along with its Extension system, the Institute of Food and Agricultural Sciences (IFAS), "fulfills the university's land-grant mission, working to enhance and sustain the quality of human life through its research facilities, Extension services offered in every Florida county, and top-ranked education at the UF College of Agricultural and Life Sciences."[67]

In 1884, Florida legislated the creation of a "white normal school" in Gainesville and a corresponding "colored school" in Jacksonville. When the State Normal College for Colored Students was founded in 1887, its location was instead in Tallahassee. The name was changed in 1909 to Florida Agricultural and Mechanical College for Negroes, and the institution is now known as Florida Agricultural and Mechanical University. The state legislature gave the college university status in 1953, making it the only public historically Black university in the State University System of Florida.[68] Florida A&M's 1890 land-grant status led to an agriculture department, which "embrac[ed] the culture of all semitropical field crops, gardening, fruitgrowing, dairy husbandry, rearing of livestock, poultry, and drainage."⁶⁹ Soon, the university played a crucial role as the headquarters of African American Extension Service work in Florida.⁷⁰

In Florida, Farmers' Institutes and other educational programming, such as Mid-Winter Institutes, evolved into the 1910s. Such events could last as little as one day or as long as four days or more, providing valuable information for male farmers, women, and others. "In addition to activities designed to improve farming techniques, programs planned exclusively for homemakers and older children were also emphasized," writes historian Barbara Cotton. "Wives participated in doing needle works, cooking, preserving, and canning activities. . . . Mid-Winter Farmers' Institutes had become so popular . . . a special agent was appointed by [Florida A&M] to plan and coordinate them."⁷¹

Arthur Anderson "A. A." Turner, a graduate of Ohio's Wilberforce University who had worked at Tuskegee, was the first African American Extension agent in Florida, supervising male agents from 1917 to 1929, as well as female agents once they were allowed to join the Extension ranks in 1918. Julia Miller took charge of supervising all the HDAs in 1929. Miller, an Arkansas native and Tuskegee graduate, worked as an agent in Alabama and was appointed local district home demonstration agent for African American women on the recommendation of T. M. Campbell. A newspaper article about her appointment noted that "seven women agents" were employed, making "direct contact with rural women and girls. . . . Signs of their work can be seen in the homes and about the premises throughout the territory worked by the women, as is seen about the farms where the men work."⁷² Turner was instrumental in helping to implement "Project VI," which was to expand the "instruction of negro boys and girls living on farms," part of a "seven major priorities" list in Extension work, per the director of Florida's Agricultural Extension Service, Peter Henry "P. H." Rolfs. Issues of racism, discrimination, segregation, and lower funding persisted, but the overall "promotion and growth of the work conducted under Project VI" were because of Turner. He retired in 1948, having worked thirty-three years.⁷³

In the early part of the twentieth century, Florida A&M expanded its Farm and Homemakers' Clubs, marketing clubs, and other programs for boys and girls. The first short course for African American boys and girls was held in 1918 and brought young people from twelve counties to Florida A&M after "interested white and colored people" donated scholarships, which amounted to $245.00, to help provide "means of transportation and their fees while at the Short Course."⁷⁴ The home demonstration program was added in 1917, when six female agents were appointed. Because of World War I, the first African American HDAs "were emergency volunteer workers employed to assist rural Blacks in conserving food and improving home life in general."[75] Their work went far beyond canning demonstrations, however; as Barbara Cotton notes, "Despite an absence of centralized planning and supervision, black home demonstration agents nevertheless strove to provide rural homemakers with knowledge and skills needed to improve nearly every aspect of home life."[76] This was achieved despite continual issues with financial resources. A summary of 1923 Extension work with African Americans noted, "Owing to limited funds, a policy has been established of placing one agent, either man or woman, as local people may prefer, in every county having a large negro rural population before placing two agents in any one county. The agent, either man or woman, is expected to carry on all lines of work among negroes as far as practicable."[77]

In Florida, home demonstrations began several years before the passage of the Smith-Lever Act. Possibly as early as 1908 or 1912, Agnes Ellen Harris, a pioneering HDA who helped start tomato canning clubs, began conducting canning demonstrations in Ocala and Marion County. In 1908, the head of the Home Economics Department at the Florida State College for Women gave a demonstration on creamed eggs for the Florida State Federation of Women's Clubs. Early versions of canning clubs and other work for girls and women began when Alachua, Bradford, Columbia, Clay, Escambia, Hillsborough, Holmes, Leon, Madison, Pasco, and Walton Counties "organized" in 1912. Marion and Suwanee Counties were added in 1913, and the following year, programs were extended to Baker, Citrus, Dade, DeSoto, Duval, Gadsden, Osceola, Polk, Putnam, Santa Rosa, St. Johns, Sumter, and Volusia Counties. One historical retrospective agreed the work was established in 1912 and that only three counties, Leon, Escambia, and Hillsborough, had uninterrupted home demonstration work from 1912 to 1936. Another set of HDA notes, which contained a printed timeline, included Alachua County in this "since 1912" list.[78]

The home demonstration agents also faced a decades-long unique situation. Florida's system of higher education was segregated by gender, as well as race, at this time and as a consequence, the white Extension Service and administration were all located at the University of Florida campus in Gainesville, which is in central Florida. However, the University of Florida was an all-male institution. Therefore, any Short Courses, training, and events meant for women had to be held at Florida State College for Women, in Tallahassee, which is located in the Panhandle.

The half-century span between the first Morrill Act of 1862 and the passage of the Smith-Lever Act in 1914 emphasizes the long road toward helping to implement a modernizing rural foundation. The need to disseminate the latest in scientific research, which was met by employing men and women to work with farmers and rural individuals, coexisted with the reality of racism, discrimination, and gender politics. The establishment of home demonstration agents would ultimately foster new avenues that Alabama and Florida's rural women used to create new paths to economic gains.

CHAPTER TWO

RURAL ALABAMA WOMEN AND CULTIVATING COMMERCE

After the Smith-Lever Act was passed, home demonstration agents in Alabama hoped to play a vital role in helping rural white and African American women improve their dietary and health habits, conserve and preserve food, develop and enhance sanitary practices, and make aesthetically pleasing changes to their homes and personal appearances. While agents would be successful in meeting their objectives and goals outlined in their plans of work, before long, rural women engaged with home demonstration programming began using the knowledge they had gained from the HDAs and applying it to sell food and other goods through various marketing ventures.

Such ventures contributed to farm, family, or personal income. Rural women used the extra money to purchase new household items, engage in leisure activities, afford medical procedures, pay for school tuition, discharge debts, and buy cars and other tangible items. As a result, rural white and African American women became producers and consumers, creating an economically beneficial system of their own making. As one HDA later wrote, "The women have turned cabbage, beans, be[e]ts, etc. into Fords and have learned to drive them."[1]

For more than two hundred years, agricultural production has been a consistently dominant force in Alabama's economy. The impact of the agricultural industry, built on the five traditional crops of cotton, peanuts, corn, soybean, and wheat, maintained its hold even as coal, steel, health, aeronautical, and other business industries took root in the twentieth century.[2] Alabama's agricultural industry today is robust and diversified, thanks to an unlikely source—a beetle with a long proboscis, which altered the state's farming economy and became a turning point in its agricultural future.

In the early decades of the twentieth century, the boll weevil was the farmer's greatest fear. Cotton fields were rendered useless as the insect ravaged its way across the state; according to one writer, "The weevil has had no equal relative to agricultural pest status or impact on a rural economy."[3] However, there was a positive outcome of the boll weevil's relentless waste laying—to attempt to circumvent the weevil, farmers had little choice but to practice crop diversification. While the boll weevil was finally eradicated in Alabama in the 1990s, it was not forgotten. The town of Enterprise, in south Alabama, is the location of a famous boll weevil statue, in remembrance of the insect that brought the town from "despair to abundance."[4] The boll weevil is a marketing strategy for businesses as well as a school mascot.[5]

Because of the dependence on agriculture, a year with poor yields or outputs had far-reaching effects across the state, and as a result, any income women could earn became that much more important. In the early years of home demonstration, methods of creating this income for women and girls included canning clubs, marketing products and strategies, poultry raising, and club-based prizes. HDAs showed women how to can food, raise poultry, and make a variety of handmade products, as well as teaching them simple accounting so they could keep track of profits and overall finances. As an HDA in Clarke County wrote, "I plan to have each mother . . . keep an account of the home and the saving. That is one thing the farm women need. So often they don't have any system by which to spend their money, and the result is they spend more than they realize."[6]

In 1917, spurred by World War I, Congress passed the Food Production Act and the Food and Fuel Control Act, which urged fuel and food conservation, encouraged the growing of food and increasing crops, and urged Americans to eat less of certain food items through campaigns such as "Wheatless Wednesdays." Observing these conservation tactics was framed as a patriotic act, done for the good of the country and for service members fighting overseas. The Food Production Act also provided emergency appropriations for the Extension Service, which led to an increased number of HDAs and the creation of Home Demonstration Kitchens. A 1919 report looking back on the previous year describes these kitchens as "laboratories for the training of volunteer classes in War Time Cookery, and as schools of instruction for city housewives."[7] In addition, HDAs served as home economics directors for the newly established U.S. Food Administration, which made them more visible to the public and also created greater demands on their time.[8]

AFRICAN AMERICAN WOMEN AND HOME DEMONSTRATION

In the 1910s and 1920s, large numbers of African American residents left Alabama's "Black Belt," an area that consists of Russell, Barbour, Pike, Bullock, Macon, Montgomery, Crenshaw, Butler, Lowndes, Wilcox, Dallas, Perry, Hale, Marengo, Choctaw, Sumter, and Greene Counties. The name comes not only from the region's fertile black soil but also from the historically high concentration of plantations and enslaved workers. In more recent times, it also refers to the grim socioeconomic conditions of the region.[9] The echoes of enslavement and the bitter realities of sharecropping and tenant farming, combined with persistent discrimination, white supremacy, and racial violence, provided more than enough motivation to move away from a vicious cycle that included "rural isolation that was little better than slavery and offered no real economic independence."[10] Yet, as Valerie Grim explains, people also had reasons to stay, as they found strength in community and in sharing their experiences collectively. "Many felt oppressed, exploited, and in serious need of relief," she writes. "Opportunities for self-identity and expression of beliefs and values evolved, however, within rural enclaves throughout the South."[11]

According to one USDA report published in 1925 and written by James A. Evans, the aim of Extension and home demonstration programs for African Americans was "to influence them to adopt better farm practices, to help them increase their earning capacity, and to improve their living conditions."[12] At the same time, the report noted, it was "also to interest negro boys and girls in farm activities, and to train them in the use of improved methods in farming and home making."[13] While it was written with a paternalistic tone when discussing African Americans and the goals of Extension efforts designed for whites and African Americans may have seemed similar, there were certainly different motivations lying beneath the surface. African Americans were leaving the South, and part of the African American Extension agent's job was to "[check] the migration from the rural sections."[14] The Extension Service believed people were moving because of "poverty, dissatisfaction, and unrest."[15] Widespread systemic racism, persistent threats, and actual racial violence were noticeably absent from their list of reasons.

Leaders in the Extension Service hoped their African American division could stop the "Black exodus" of labor from leaving the South. In 1920, one USDA circular stated flatly, "The better class of Negro leaders foresaw that when wages were reduced and industries closed down it would be impossible for those who had recently gone to the cities to maintain themselves with any degree of comfort. These leaders have done what they could to bring back to the farm those who desired to return. They very properly recognize that while conditions may not always be what they should be on the farm, the average Negro, dependent on his daily labor, is better off there than in a crowded city."[16]

A few years later, an Extension circular from 1923 posited:

> The northward exodus of negro farmers embraced all classes—farm owners, tenants, and share croppers. . . . Thousands who had no compelling economic reasons for seeking new fields and employment caught the fever to go North . . .

and moved at once or began making plans to go. . . . Negro agents' work was partly successful in checking the rush of negro farmers to the cities. . . . The agents [pointed] out to them the possibilities of a profitable and satisfying life on the farm through the use of better methods and the adoption of a "live at home" program.[17]

Addressing the ramifications of husbands and older sons migrating north, Josephine Schooler Calloway, the wife of C. J. Calloway, head of Tuskegee's Extension Department, advised African American women to become a saving force. She argued how keeping a homestead going meant economizing, maintaining a budget that kept husbands out of debt, and having a "few dimes that you can spend for yourself and children."[18] Moreover, she said, "the responsibility rests on you. . . . Some women are better managers than their husbands. . . . Show what you can do to meet these hard times. . . . Be industrious: be economical. . . . Make your home and family the best . . . on this earth."[19] This emphasis on being the critical role in stabilizing the family economy was reflected in a 1919 Montgomery County report when an HDA commented, "Colored women . . . are interested most in money saving projects and are anxious to have things that don't cost much."[20]

In writing about Extension Service programming, historian Jeannie Whayne notes that "some means had to be devised to make conditions better for blacks in the South."[21] At the time, African American HDAs were focused on keeping families and babies healthy by teaching better nutritional and sanitary practices. "The work of women agents centers in and around the home," noted the Extension circular from 1923. "Their activities have to do with home industries through which women and girls may earn money, or with things that make for health, comfort, and better living of the family."[22] But African American agents had to achieve a difficult balancing act and avoid, as Whayne says, "the appearance of challenging the racial status quo."[23]

While a decreased need for labor, resulting from the growth of mechanization in farming, as well as other economic problems related to agriculture, received some of the blame for the Great Migration, the South's atmosphere played a significant role in why and how African American residents left. Unsurprisingly, African Americans sometimes viewed the government-based Extension agents with skepticism; as historian Susan Lynn Smith points out, "Based on previous experiences with local government and its history of upholding white supremacy, [African Americans] were reluctant to participate in programs for fear of being exploited."[24] Yet ongoing racial discrimination and violence are generally not mentioned in HDA records in Alabama and Florida. This time in the South was marked by violence against African Americans, especially males. The NAACP's *Crisis* tracked lynchings, murders, race riots, and other incidents of suppression, violence, and intimidation. By contrast, events such as the 1920 Ocoee, Florida, massacre and the 1917 lynching of the Powell brothers in Letohatchee, Alabama, do not appear in home demonstration reports.[25] During this period in the South, the threat of racial violence was always hovering in the background, and the omission in the reports might have been a conscious choice by both African American and white HDAs.

Most southern white women accepted segregation and other forms of discrimination by maintaining strict adherence to racial boundaries. Mrs. Samuel Fischer (likely Ida Stewart Fischer), president of the Woman's Community Club in Hope Hull, Alabama, wrote, about the growth of her rural club, which started in 1921, noting that "every white woman within a [radius] of five miles" had been invited to meet at her home to "organize a community club."[26] She wrote of the club's inclusivity, remarking that its membership included "old Southern families [while] some are real Yankees, some from the border states of Kentucky and Tennessee, one from far away California, one of our most faithful members is a Russian Jewess, and one a lovely cultured Scotch woman . . . all working harmoniously together, each one giving something and each one getting a great deal."[27] Some activities were viewed as normal, despite their overtones. One photo in an HDA report for Henry County highlighted twenty-five club girls at a Girls' Camp and what was described as "an interesting feature of the camp"—the girls holding "Negro Dolls" made out of "socks for the 'Baby Show.'"[28]

While white and African American agents interacted with white and African American populations through the Extension Service programs, the implicit and explicit bias remained; however, on the page, it was not expressed as anything beyond normal or routine within an already existing culture of pervasive racism. In an early 1910 farm demonstration report, a white agent described work with African American farmers and agents: "These men are all meeting with immense success and are transforming the slovenly negro farmer into a farmer who is able to produce his own living upon his place, independent and resourceful. . . . Some of the most successful demonstrations carried on under these excellent white agents have been worked out by negro farmers."[29] While the economic and living situations of white and African American rural people might have been similar, Jim Crow laws and discrimination made the home demonstration experience fundamentally different for the two groups.

AFRICAN AMERICAN WOMEN AND FINDING ECONOMIC POSSIBILITIES

The ways in which African American women in Alabama used home demonstration programming and skills to generate extra income both paralleled and differed from those of their white counterparts. For rural African American women, the added cash more often went toward the family income. As Margaret Murray Washington, "Lady Principal" at Tuskegee, the wife of Booker T. Washington, and a longtime advocate of domestic science who had been part of the home economics movement for decades, said in emphasizing the importance of modernizing domestic life, "The home and family is the starting point. . . . We women must meet the demands by making our organizations avenues of help to the better way."[30]

By 1919, participation in home demonstration began to show steady growth for both white and African American women. That year, a combined estimated 5,864 Alabama women and girls were involved with home demonstration work. A decade later, the number had more than tripled, to 21,567. For 1919, statistics for African American women indicated high numbers of attendees at club meetings, with ninety-one clubs, a total of 901 demonstrators enrolled in clubs, and individual demonstrators not in the clubs. Although it is not further clarified, it is noted by T. M. Campbell in a 1919 report that 3,780 African American women were influenced by demonstration work.[31]

Reports about early HDA work also reflect how agents sought to address people's basic needs. In describing her efforts in Macon County, Alabama, Nannie Juanita Coleman—a Tuskegee graduate hired as the first Movable School agent in 1915—wrote of the need for "Rest Room[s]" for women in rural churches, "to raise the dignity of the church" and as "a model for persons attending," because "too many of the farm homes are neglected because there is no money to buy furniture from [the] store."[32] "Health, home, and church" was a common refrain across the counties. Coleman noted women were interested in getting rid of houseflies, having "better" (healthier) children, cooking, and working with poultry. Coleman directed programs on home improvement, sanitation, sewing, handicrafts, soap making, bread making, and food preparation, which she incorporated into her 1920 Movable School demonstrations.[33]

One challenge Coleman faced in her work was widespread illiteracy. "The majority of my club women cannot read nor write," she noted, as she was focused on a plan of work that would help them learn to develop and follow household budgets: "I hope to work out a method that can be used by all."[34] Coleman described one such alternative method. "They are told that 4 teacups of flour will make a pound; knowing the number of cups used each day, they are able to determine just how long a 48-pound sack of flour will last," she explained. "The same method is used in handling meal and sugar problems."[35]

The status of the household purse was an increasingly important factor in the HDA's work. In 1919, agent Tisby Luella Ray reported that African American women in Clarke County had started making "cold water soap," which soon led to "some ladies who have stopped buying soap and are making and selling it to their neighbors."[36] Some women and their daughters doubled their work at certain times of the year or during different agricultural seasons and were described as "field hands as well as housekeepers."[37] In 1920, Rosa B. Jones, whose official title was "state agent for Negro women," noted women made a combined value of $1,370.50 from selling poultry, butter, milk, eggs, fruits, and vegetables using cooperative marketing. Some also sold baskets and handmade brooms. This prompted her to argue for more HDAs: "The outlook for home demonstration is hopeful. The people are anxious to be instructed."[38]

African American HDA reports reiterated faith in their work, especially because of financial conditions and response to the programming. Montgomery HDA Laura Daly noted, "Efforts are made to make the work educational . . . to fit itself to the needs of the people . . . inspire them with the hope of material prosperity . . . to get the most out of the things which they have right around them."[39] The Movable School drew as many as 250 people in one day, with emphases on stockpiling, food preservation, and home-based improvements. Salt and pepper shakers were made from Vaseline bottles, floor mops from rag strips and a broom handle, and bags and hats from corn shucks, in an effort of "keeping up the spirit among the rural people who had food, but little or no money." Some homes lacked kitchen cabinets or cupboards, so those were constructed using available materials, or "wall bags for knives and forks" were made instead.[40]

At the same time, agents recognized the importance of entertainment and leisure activities in not just raising the overall quality of life but also creating recreational time during Movable School or club meeting days. As HDA and Movable School agent Luella Hanna reported in 1923, "All work and no play makes children very dull [and] grown-ups less friendly toward each other." So, Hanna and her fellow agents introduced games including "volley ball, spud ball, dodge ball, various over-head relays, no mans land, tug of war, and radio." She added, "We all go home feeling like honest-to-goodness neighbors." In addition, there were movie nights, with "reels" from the USDA and Alabama State Health Department: "These pictures furnish wholesome, instructive, entertainment for rural people, and we have many white people to come in and enjoy themselves also."⁴¹ Bringing the community together also meant connecting businesses and organizations with Extension and HDA work. T. M. Campbell's work plan for 1927 included efforts "to acquaint the Negro organizations such as the state branches of the National Negro Business Leagues, Press Associations, Church organizations, etc., with Agricultural Extension Work."⁴²

African American women had the same home demonstration programming as their white counterparts, with health, sanitary practices, food preservation and canning, home improvements, and clothing as major focal points.⁴³ African American women also turned programming into profits. As historian Mary Waalkes writes, "For black extension women, the primary identity of a black woman included her ability to add to farm income. . . . Black farmers needed all the family members to survive."⁴⁴ Precise figures are not always easy to come by, however—as Rosa B. Jones, the state agent for Negro women, wrote in her 1923 summary report, "It is hard to get an accurate report of the amount of money earned, as a result of home demonstration instructions, but 1,570 women and girls report money earned from handicrafts, chickens, bees and other activities."⁴⁵ Women were clearly capitalizing on their newfound knowledge. Jones continued to explain, "One agent, not only influences boys and girls to earn and save money, but she also takes them to the bank and helps them deposit."⁴⁶ Individual HDA agents reported that African American women were focused on the health and economy of the home, as well as on creating items they could not afford to purchase.

Cooperative marketing was encouraged in Hale and Perry Counties, but apparently "little" had been "accomplished" in that endeavor in 1921. However, the girls' clubs had thirty-four bank accounts totaling about $200 resulting from club activities. Three girls used their money to help pay for school expenses.⁴⁷ They also earned extra money, prizes, and certificates through exhibiting in booths at fairs and participating in contests. One of Rosa Jones's reports reprinted a letter from Catherine Rogers, an Evergreen club girl, who won $13.50 for speaking at a 4-H conference. Her parents let her keep the money to encourage her.⁴⁸ Meanwhile, in Montgomery County, HDAs sought to improve rural diets by promoting peanut consumption and teaching people how to make peanut butter at home. Agents also focused on sanitation, soap making, and redesigning old garments.⁴⁹ A 1924–1925 annual report for the state of Alabama claimed that 747 African American women and 170 African American girls were "earning money" from making handicrafts and raising chickens.⁵⁰

As the Extension Service and home demonstration were working to improve the lives of the rural population, other entities were seeking to achieve the same goal but in a separate arena—that of public education. One notable effort was the Jeanes Supervising Industrial Teachers program, funded by a million-dollar endowment from Quaker philanthropist Anna T. Jeanes. The Jeanes teachers were generally handpicked by school superintendents on the basis of "leadership qualities and . . . skill in teaching the industrial arts." In her 1912 book, *Country Life and the Country School*, Mabel Carney, longtime head of the Department of Rural Education at Teachers College, wrote, "Two rural movements looking to the betterment of this class may be mentioned here. One of these, the Anna T. Jeanes Foundation, embodies a plan for the improvement of negro rural schools."[51]

There was some overlap between what Jeanes teachers taught and what HDAs provided. For example, a 1916 report noted that Jeanes teachers oversaw homemakers' clubs for African American girls, where students learned about making items from native materials, gardening, and canning food. General courses in subjects such as English, history, and music were also taught. A 1917 pamphlet from the Alabama Department of Education said of the Jeanes teachers, "[They] visit the negro rural schools, teach the industrial work in the classes, supervise the schools under the direction of the county superintendent, and hold patrons' meetings for the improvement of schools. During the winter months, their time is largely devoted to actual work in connection with the schools. In the summer they devote their time to club work and community fairs."[52]

A 1926 letter printed in the *Montgomery Advertiser* noted, "The Jeanes workers are among those supervisors who can and do contribute much help to the colored schools. The contact with rural school systems is immediate and first hand."[53] Like Extension agents, Jeanes teachers worked with adults as well as children, providing not "a systematic form of instruction but . . . functional adult education involving community coordination on problems of health, making a living, recreation, and home-making." According to a 1945 article about the program, "The major factor in the work of the Jeanes teacher is the large number of teachers who are her contacts with that portion of the community whose children they teach." The Jeanes teachers relied on their extensive network of educators who knew their communities well.[54]

Jeanes teachers appeared at larger Extension Service meetings and Farmer's Institute conferences alongside home demonstration agents, and sometimes workers moved from one entity to the other. For instance, in 1920, Luella Hanna, who was from Tennessee, became one of the prominent African American HDAs in Alabama after leaving positions as a Jeanes Fund worker and Smith-Hughes vocational teacher. While there was early overlap between the

Jeanes curricula and home demonstration programming, it was largely the latter that helped African American women and girls gain pocket money and attain a greater degree of financial independence.[55]

THE TENSION WITH TRADITIONAL GENDER ROLES

While they encouraged women and girls to participate in home demonstration, in some cases HDAs also supported their determination to complete or continue their education, especially when it could be paid for by the extra money they earned. In 1924, HDA Mary Strudwick intervened on behalf of Elberta resident Martha Haupt, who had been out of school for two years and wanted to finish her high school degree. Strudwick wrote, "Her father did not see the [importance] of her going to school. After my showing him Marthas ability and what she could make of herself if given a chance, he consented. Martha is going to make three years work in two by taking extra work each year and going to summer school." Once Martha returned to school, Strudwick concluded proudly, "she made the Honor Roll, and is quite happy over the priveledge [sic] of being in school." Martha Haupt earned her high school diploma and went on to college at Alabama Polytechnic Institute (Auburn University), where she was elected "Miss Personality Plus" in 1929. Upon graduation, she became an HDA herself, which had been her chosen career goal because of Mary Strudwick's influence, as well as working for the Farmer's Home Administration and supervising a federal meat canning plant.[56]

The majority of home demonstration agents were college educated, earning degrees from such institutions as Alabama Polytechnic Institute (API); Columbia University; Troy State Normal School/Troy State Teachers College; Alabama Girls' Technical Institute and College for Women/Alabama College, State College for Women (now known as the University of Montevallo); the University of Illinois; Florida State College for Women; Judson College; Cornell University; the University of Idaho; Peabody College; Winthrop College; and Tuskegee Institute.[57] Former Jeanes teachers and supervisors also became HDAs. The 1929 annual report noted that of the forty-one white HDAs, almost 70 percent had college degrees—three with master's degrees and twenty-seven with bachelor's degrees. Fourteen had no formal degree but were qualified instead by years of training. Nearly half of those degrees—fourteen out of thirty—were from API. The report did not note the educational attainment of African American HDAs.[58]

One HDA wrote in 1919 that the plan for the program of work was to train club girls to "increase their incomes . . . improve their present home conditions and to secure better educational advantages." The goal was to ensure that "girls are receiving that training which will fit them to become the future home-makers of Alabama."[59] Seven years later, Agnes Ellen Harris, the state home demonstration agent, wrote that "women frequently bring the produce to market" but then "return home in time to cook dinner for the farm hands. Thus farm work was not interfered with during the busy season." The HDAs had to delicately balance entrenched traditional gender roles while at the same time promoting the notion, in historian Ann McCleary's words, "that rural women and girls were entitled to accumulate and control their own income—and that they should have access to activities that would help them make money."[60]

The statewide 1920 report emphasized that women's participation nonetheless supported cultural norms. "The Club Girls and Women of Alabama have been better qualified as homemakers and have also been enabled to earn more money on the farm," it read, "thus contributing materially to the income of the farm home, and thereby making home life more pleasant for all its members." The 1925 Montgomery annual report noted that "the girls learned the value of native shrubbery and incidentally learned in some instances what a good 'pal' a father can be if a girl is interested in the right things."[61] A Hope Hull club member lauded the impact of demonstration work, saying that "it had removed the stigma formerly centered around the selling of butter, poultry, orchard and garden products by the women down South. It was not considered 'good form.' Now the best families do it with a perfect sense of propriety and many of them are aiding materially in running both home and farm by the sale of commodities."[62] In 1927, the agent for Etowah County noted, "[The] country woman is not ashamed to sell the things she produced." Many girls and women worked on farms and fields all across Alabama, but especially in farm-heavy areas. Clay County's agent observed, "A few of them, quite a few, even plough like a man."[63]

Yet women were still expected to fulfill their traditional roles as housewives. "During crop time," an HDA noted in 1927, "the women will come sell out and get back home to cook their husbands dinner."[64] Sometimes men regarded their wives' participation in home demonstration work with skepticism and suspicion. Initially, for example, the husbands of farm women selling goods at Montgomery curb markets "rather looked down their noses at this, off at a tangent, selling business," wrote Emmie Adams DeRamus, an active member in home demonstration programming. "Few men graced the market with their presence. Bless you, not so now! They are there with bells on!"[65] The HDAs expected such resistance, knowing that husbands' objections to their wives and daughters participating in HDA programming could stem from a number of factors, from mistrusting the government to concern over any time spent away from household duties. In 1926, Elizabeth DeLoney, Franklin County's HDA, wrote that one local woman stated her husband thought demonstration meetings were "foolish."[66] She continued, "The next thought was how to convince men that Home Demonstration work was essential to the growth of rural communities. [My programs] would play but a small part in convincing them my work was essential."[67] Thus initially dubious husbands or fathers could eventually be won over. One father reportedly stated, "When you told us about teaching the girls to can and cook, I thought my wife knew enough to teach our girls, but I have changed my mind for my little girl now makes better biscuits than my wife ever did and takes more interest in helping her mother. I am in favor of continuing that work!"[68]

Even as women were balancing traditional roles as wives and mothers with their newfound independence as entrepreneurs, as well as adjusting their attitudes about what constituted "respectability" and acceptance, women were also modernizing in any number of ways. Victoria Lingo, an HDA in Barbour County, wrote in 1924, "The rural people now buy better grades of material, technique improved, and when you see a car drive into a town, country is not stamped on the manner or appearance of the occupants."[69] In 1929, the Pike County HDAs wrote that rural women "[took] advantage of conversations to increase their vocabularies. . . . Mrs. Robert Whitehurst overheard a customer say, 'Pardon me for being so abrupt,' not knowing the meaning of abrupt Mrs. W. made a note of the word and soon as she reached home looked it up in [the] dictionary and now uses it as her own."[70]

Home demonstration programming played a role in and reflected greater societal movements that were transforming the lives of rural women and girls. While the programming offered outlets for educational opportunities and social mobility for rural girls and women, those offering the programs were working within traditional gender roles. However, by creating possibilities for better situations in life and education, home demonstration offered the means by which women and girls could assert another form of independence.

PROGRAMMING FOR PENNIES

HDAs held classes on growing gardens, animal husbandry, and how to can, jar, or brine food. They taught rural white and African American women scientific methods for raising chickens and making butter and cottage cheese, as well as new approaches to household tasks such as cooking and sewing. Results at home and in selling were quickly noticeable. Participating in canning clubs, making jellies and preserves, and producing eggs and butter were early ways rural women and girls started earning extra income, which encouraged them to continue.[71] For example, in 1915, an HDA's annual report noted that Gadsden, along with Etowah and Tuscaloosa, were becoming "an assured market" for girls selling canned fruits and vegetables, as well as homemade baskets and boxes.[72] A Calhoun County girl made "$10 selling spinach" in 1916, while "46 club girls attended city and county high schools, paying their expenses with canning club earnings."[73] Some rural women improved their kitchen equipment because they were "particularly interested in making good butter for market."[74] Over a span of six months in 1916, Lauderdale County women sold over one thousand pounds of butter at thirty cents per pound.[75]

FINDING PROJECTS FOR PROFITS

As HDAs developed programs to help rural women increase their income, one in particular seemed to consistently equal cash: poultry. As a 1923 annual report remarked, "The Alabama farm woman makes her greatest economic contribution through the poultry project."[76] One example was a Chilton County woman with an invalid husband, who stated in 1919 that "before she joined the egg circle she never had any spending money but that now she always has from ten to fifteen dollars in her pocket-book."[77] In 1925, Flossie Bonner Malloy of Smith's Station used 115 Leghorn hens to sell $409.90 worth of eggs and $60 worth of chickens.[78]

Crenshaw County's HDA noted, "Before country life can be made fully satisfying there must be an increase in the farm income. . . . The best way to increase their income is to raise poultry."[79] By 1927, in Tuscaloosa, there was an effort to create a canned chicken market, with the product "put up in glass jars . . . packed with a special variety of the meat and meat products."[80] HDA reports for white women frequently mention profits earned from selling poultry. However, African American women and girls also used poultry for extra income. In 1929, there was a combined total of sales of $18,436.25 from poultry and poultry products in fourteen counties. This led to the conclusion from the Extension Service's annual report, "Rural women are beginning to realize that there is more profit in poultry than in any other project on the farm."[81]

Home demonstration programming also ventured into smaller animal-based ventures, with varying degrees of success. Beekeeping produced honey, which was a sugar substitute, as sugar prices started rising in the early 1920s. Talladega County was one of the first areas to see a push to increase and refine beekeeping at that time.[82] Although apiaries were the bee's knees for a short time, beekeeping did draw periodic interest occasionally throughout the 1920s.[83]

Also in the early 1920s, HDA programs began encouraging rabbit keeping. One might expect rabbits to be easier to manage and care for than bees. But a 1924 Montgomery HDA report explained why rabbits were "discontinued" as part of children's club work: "After [children worked] with them, they became pets and they would neither sell them nor eat them. Consequently, they gave their surplus away. . . . They would not keep them penned properly and . . . the gardens suffered and the parents objected."[84] Children evidently preferred raising Peter Rabbit to eating him.

JAMS, JELLIES, AND PRESERVES

A consistently reliable way to produce extra dollars was to sell homemade jams, jellies, preserves, and marmalades. Figs were especially popular, as the trees were a common sight in Alabama's yards and gardens. Dallas County women created a fig preserve club, which sold "$2,400.00 worth . . . put up in Christmas packages, which sold for $1.00 per package," while three Bullock County women sold fig preserves yearly.[85] Macon County women sold blackberry jam, while Mobile women wanted to "manufacture" a marmalade for retail using not figs but satsuma oranges and kumquats.[86] Three women in Conecuh County made "a standardized product of strawberries and figs" and had orders "for 2 dozen pints." The HDA remarked, "This sounds rather small but we feel that we have really started a market."[87]

Grapes, such as muscadines and scuppernongs, and other vines were listed as part of demonstration programs at times or were mentioned in local newspapers. In 1920, Montgomery County's home demonstration received three hundred vines with the goal of starting an industry around making juice and other products.[88] That same year, the *Marion County News* reported that "many women and girls are adding materially to their income by the sale of [grape] juices."[89]

A Barbour County woman—unnamed in the 1924 report but later identified as Rosebud Baker Davis—owned an orchard of at least two thousand trees, some of which were probably peaches and figs. Her sales of preserves between January and November 1924 totaled $200. Her products, including canned meat, sold in Piggly Wiggly grocery stores in "different small towns" such as Eufaula and Columbus.[90] By 1926, she was known for making, canning, and selling Brunswick stew, fig preserves, pear preserves, watermelon rind, corn relish, and peach and pear pickles. A notice placed in Alabama newspapers claimed, "Starting several years ago with the Brunswick stew business in her kitchen, Mrs. G.H. Davis, of Eufaula now has a small canning plant in her yard where she makes a dozen or more products which she is selling under her own label." The 1929 HDA report noted that Davis had created a profitable canning business and had also made a small income as the curb market mistress. According to Barbour County HDA Victoria Lingo, Davis worked up a "considerable trade."[91]

Different demonstrations created new opportunities. In 1925 the Barbour County HDA, Victoria Lingo, taught women how to can Brunswick stew and make watermelon rind, while other HDAs continued to help women make fig or pear preserves, ostensibly for marketing purposes.[92] Agent Helen Johnston's 1922–1923 report noted that her plan for the months of April, May, and June included "plan[ning] a sale of baskets, preserves and rugs exhibited, in order to assist in obtaining markets for Home Demonstration club women."[93] In Clay County, a demonstration in cake making and decorating led to the sale of three cakes for seventy-one dollars, with the profits designated for school funds. Mertie Hudson took rolls, biscuits, and a butter cake to the Montgomery State Fair and won twenty-five dollars for her efforts.[94]

THE ART OF BASKETRY

Baskets—most often made out of reed, pine needles, and honeysuckle—became another important revenue source for rural women and girls. Baskets were useful and practical and added an aesthetically pleasing aspect of home decor. As early as 1916, HDAs were reporting about baskets being made from materials such as white oak and willow in Mobile and Lee Counties.[95] Throughout the 1920s, rural women embraced basketry and basketmaking demonstrations. Tallapoosa County women learned about pine needle, reed, and honeysuckle basketry, while in Henry County, reed basketmaking became so popular that HDA Martha McCall reported, "it was necessary to spend more time on it than planned."[96] In Pickens County in 1927, while there was no formal basketry club or ongoing basketry demonstrations, one unnamed woman took the initiative to make and sell honeysuckle baskets and trays.[97] The state HDA report for 1925 noted, "[Two] clubs sent a leader to the State Short Course in the summer of 1924 to learn to make baskets and to meet Mrs. Ripley of the Mississippi Basket-Makers Association. In 1925 they sent an exhibit to the Southern Exposition held in New York City."[98]

Baldwin County women in 1925 sold and exhibited pine needle baskets in Alabama and out of state.[99] Stella Arnold of Autauga County also made pine needle baskets, winning prizes at fairs while also selling $35.60 worth.[100] Two Baldwin County women in 1927 sent baskets to the "Farm Women's Market" at the Loveman, Joseph, and Loeb Department Store in Birmingham.[101] The following year, according to the Perry County home demonstration report, Annelu Hairston Mason made "57 reed flower baskets, one baby basket, two pair candlesticks, six fruit bowls, eight sewing baskets, and one lamp shade. Fourteen flower baskets sold for $16.75. These ranged in price from 75¢ to $2.00."[102] Houston County's 1927 report referred to women making a "neat income from the sale" of reed baskets and sandwich trays.[103] In Etowah County, meanwhile, women in the Whitesboro and Webb clubs "made a thousand pine needle baskets and sold $800.00."[104] Mary Lessie Beaty Bedsole in Barbour County also used basketry to increase her income, as she sold fifty dollars' worth in 1924 and 1925.[105]

CLAY COUNTY BASKETS

While baskets provided a viable source of income for rural women across the state, Clay County saw a cottage industry that thrived at the state, national, and even international level. In 1925 or early 1926, a group of local women presented a basketmaking proposal to their HDA and requested help in finding a market. According to the 1927 HDA report, the idea was "introduced from Georgia into Clay County, Alabama, by Mrs. J.B. Kelley [Anna Lee Goza Kelley] . . . who gave it to the Home Demonstration Clubs through. . . Mrs. J.E.S. Rudd [Janie Elizabeth Simmons Rudd, the HDA], [while] Mr. C.L. Akers of the Huckabee Hotel in Ashland, Alabama, suggested the marketing in large, wholesale lots, and assisted the agent in her first efforts of their marketing."[106] The "Ashland ladies" started marketing baskets in nearby towns and out of state.[107]

The Clay County Basket Association was formed and, in 1927, "the 4-H Basket Shop," which primarily sold pine needle baskets. Birmingham was an early test market, with local businesses—including the well-known department store Loveman, Joseph, and Loeb—partnering to help with advertising and promotion. Baskets sold out in the first week. Other stores, such as Piztiz and Saks, also sold them.[108] The pine needle baskets attracted interested buyers in Chicago, New York City, where they were on display on "Fifth Avenue, Broadway, and Savoy Plaza," and even Denmark, because of an "intensive sales campaign." One promotional tactic was "securing" space in stores and having women demonstrate making the pine needle baskets. Newspapers around the country also reprinted stories about the baskets written by Posey Oliver "P. O." Davis, an agricultural writer and editor who later became the state Extension director.[109]

In a 1927 HDA report, Clay County's HDA Janie Simmons Rudd noted, "Many women have sold baskets enough to save every dollar of the cotton money.... One merchant told the Agent yesterday a lady began payments on a forty dollar range with her basket money and contracted to pay it out same way." According to Rudd, another woman, who had moved from Alabama to Texas, was "a regular field hand under very unpleasant home conditions. She does not go to the field at all now. She makes a good 'salary' doing a little store work and making and selling baskets out in Texas. Her straw and burrs are shipped to her there and prices are superior and she gets retail for every one she makes." The woman later reported to Rudd that "the baskets the Clay Co Agt sold for her brought more than her years work in cotton" and she felt "her independence."[110] Baskets were seen as a gold mine: noted a 1927 account, "The payroll for November [1926] was more than $2,400.00 gross and $1,800.00 net for the women.... 207 women received [Christmas] checks; the smallest amount paid was 50 cents and the largest [was] $83.35.... The average check was above $20 and some were $40 and above."[111] The HDA claimed, "Basketry has taken the place of a curb market" in terms of income.[112] By 1930, the Clay County Basket Association reported $31,051.17 in sales.[113]

Working in basketry yielded far-reaching benefits, not all of them solely financial. The state annual report stated the program resulted in "an unmistakably stronger tie between the home town people and the country people." At the same time, it led to more children in school "since extra funds have been added to the family purse." Perhaps most importantly, the report said, "it has placed a confidence in the hearts of the rural women which will sustain them ... tide them over in moments of depression and link them together as a unit when a big piece of work must be done."[114] Rudd highlighted in her annual report for 1926 how local men participated in the basketry industry, from transporting the raw materials for their wives and daughters to attending demonstrations. In the Gum Springs community, she said, "the women can very easily get the most obstinate husband's cooperation ... in getting up the straw and marketing the baskets in town." As "people are needing money worse than most anything else," Rudd commented, "when the men see a prospect for cash they are *willing* to listen.... Most of the men have been *very* nice to their wives and daughters ... suggesting to them in the field that 'this is club day, its about time you went to the house to get ready.'" Finally, she remarked, "I am honored by most as many visits from men as I have had from women; in several instances I have taught the men and they have carried it to their wives who are semi invalids but can work from home."[115]

Despite all this, including promotions that featured silent film star Clara Bow posing with a Clay County basket—the basketry business proved to be tenuous, depending on the year.[116] For example, the goal for sales of $30,000 or more for 1928 was not achieved, because, according to the report, "we did not take into consideration this was [a] presidential election year and there is always a scarcity of money . . . during those years."[117] Previously, money had been borrowed from a local bank to ensure women received Christmas checks.[118] Expenses such as rent, shipping, and operating costs cut into revenue. Rudd explained, "People want our baskets; Being short of salesmen and money not circulating freely, sickness, and 'too high an ambition' make sales seem small."[119]

However, despite these ups and downs, women were not deterred and were determined to earn the profits they thought they deserved.[120] Mrs. D. C. Harris wrote, "My check for six baskets was eleven dollars. I thought I was flying! . . . I have painted my house . . . paid my taxes . . . fed and clothed myself, loaned my baby boy more than fifty dollars. . . . I am depending upon my basketry for my living."[121] Emma Mitchell Green earned $225, enabling her to help two daughters with a graduation outfit and class ring and put money in the bank for a youngest daughter.[122] Nora Mayo, an eighty-four-year-old with high blood pressure, who was unable to work "like I want or would like to," nonetheless made $176.73 from baskets and had "several dollars worth at the Basket Shoppe to be sold." The baskets were her "living," along with her garden and poultry.[123] Ashland's Essie Thomas's sales put money in the bank, paid for clothing, groceries, and "one milk cow [and] three pigs," and helped her father "to meet his financial obligations and start each year clear of debt. I have some money in the bank."[124] Meanwhile, Bessie Dean Jones took up basketry after leaving paid work as a classroom teacher to become a full-time mother. She declared, "My baby was nine months old and I could see that I must soon get down to business. The business of getting a new start in the business world. I, being like all enthusiastic mothers had begun to plan for the future life and education of my baby."[125] She sent the HDA a picture of her smiling daughter, Martha, wearing new clothes paid for by basketmaking profits. "Baskets did it," Jones wrote. Baskets also bought Jones a new Ford Sedan.[126]

THE WORTH OF HANDICRAFTING

Other forms of handicraft also brought in money for rural women. For example, leather tooling programs began to show up in HDA reports, as demonstrations taught women how to create pocketbooks, belts, card cases, and billfolds. A 1924 Madison County report stated, "The women all studied how leather articles were made," with some producing hand-tooled purses.[127] Limestone County was the site of a two-day leather demonstration led by HDA Blanche Heard, who had "studied the work in Paris and brought . . . with her many beautiful patterns from which each lady selected one for her trial work." In reporting on the demonstration, county resident Bertha Cox Hull noted that "each lady was justly proud of her handiwork, a genuine calf skin purse tooled and double laced."[128] Allie King took orders and made "a specialty on belts," while Inez McGraw Stewart won a state fair prize in Birmingham for her work. They were also listed as "assistants" in helping lead a "successful leadership school" in leather tooling.[129] Josephine Eddy, the state clothing specialist, noted one county's work in "tooled leather and glove making" sold enough "to pay for all supplies."[130] In 1926, Limestone and Jefferson Counties recognized women who had a "nice display" of bags, card cases, and "nice looking gloves" at a state fair in Birmingham.[131] One Tuscaloosa woman designed and customized leather billfolds for traveling salesmen, while a Jefferson County woman sold sixty dollars' worth of leather billfolds and purses and $150 in leather gloves.[132] While leather work was not as common an endeavor as basketry, rural women still saw the time spent at demonstrations and effort as worth it, once sales starting adding up.

Other handicrafts proved profitable too. In 1925, there was an "income-earning booth" at the state fairs in Montgomery and Birmingham, where bedspreads, baskets, dolls, and rugs were sold.[133] One report in 1929 noted the selling of wool blankets and feather pillows in Limestone County, rugs in Etowah County, woven rugs in Macon County, baby clothes in Coosa County, baskets made of native materials in Tallapoosa County, and hooked rugs, bath mats, "tufted" bedspreads, and feather fans in Bullock County. This was in addition to more leather work in both Jefferson and Tuscaloosa Counties.[134] Tuscaloosa women sent handicrafts including leather goods, tufted bedspreads, vases, and fire screens to be displayed for sale or to be specially ordered at a department store.[135]

The making of fans offered breezy business opportunities for women. Macon County's Martha Visscher Lightfoot, a former Montgomery dressmaker, was profiled in the *Southern Ruralist* about her achievements in selling feather fans. Made of turkey, goose, and peafowl, they were sold at tiered prices, from $2.50 to $10. She received orders from Omaha, Philadelphia, San Antonio, and overseas. The newspaper noted she "devotes her spare time to her fan business, making about twenty each month, or a little less than one each day. From her sales, she pays the expenses of her daughter in college." After the article was published, she received "over two hundred" inquiries about the fans, including one from First Lady Grace Goodhue Coolidge, who ordered a "handsome pea fowl" fan.[136] Eva Ingram Tompkins of Bullock County raised her own birds and used feathers from geese, turkey, peafowl, guinea, and other birds to make her fans. She exhibited them at fairs, where she sold them, won prizes, and took orders. It became a "regular business" for her, as she "realized $100" during 1928. Her obituary noted she "received a write up in National Geographic for her talent."[137]

Another home demonstration program rural women used for financial advantage was millinery. When HDAs taught mending or refashioning old hats into new styles, rural women employed their new skills as hatters to put silk, velvet, gingham, or felt hats on other heads. One Calhoun County woman "sold them at an average price of $3.50" and was "delighted with the information which has enabled her to make some spending money."[138] In 1923, so many women in Foley were making hats that allegedly no one bought a commercially made one that year.[139] Chamber County's HDA was a little surprised at her members' enthusiasm for making hats and hoped they would be equally interested in a planned program on dressmaking.[140]

Millinery also became a dividing line of sorts in programming. Some white women made hats and sold them to African American women. In 1924, a white woman from Montgomery County made "eleven organdies, four taffetas and seven ginghams" and sold them to African American women, "making for herself a neat little sum." According to the HDA report, this woman "did not have much wordly [sic] goods and no way to make any."[141] It does not mention the economic situation of the African American buyers. In Hale County, several women whose husbands had stores "made hats to sell to the negroes. They can sell the hats easily for $3.00 to $4.00, which the negroes gladly pay, and make them at a cost of $1.50 to $2.00."[142] Thus, it is not surprising African American women wanted to learn millinery for themselves, rather than buying hats. At a Calhoun County community fair in 1923, the HDA was approached by an African American woman who asked for instruction on making hats. The HDA referred her to "the white women of Wellington who were doing nice work and needed this practice. The white ladies were present and agreed to show them how to make a hat."[143]

In 1926, the Extension Service's state clothing specialist, Josephine F. Eddy, noted, "It has been our policy, to help with the negro work whenever a request comes in." However, when Rosa B. Jones, the African American state agent asked Eddy "to give the negro agents felt hats during their two weeks short course at Tuskegee," Eddy steered them in a different direction. "I had given them millinery before, and had never given them any other work," Eddy explained. Instead of hats, Eddy suggested "dressmaking, remodeling, or infants' clothing. [Jones] selected the dressmaking, and I gave them a week's work based on our work in the year's clothing program. . . . At their request we spent one evening discussing girls' clothing club work both as to subject matter and methods." Eddy's rationalization for not teaching millinery was that "it seemed to me inadvisable to spend so much time on one phase of clothing and that phase a less important one."[144]

Another product that rural women made and sold for profit was woven, hand braided, or hooked rugs. They used materials such as "old dresses, curtains, and strips," which they often dyed new colors. In 1926, Eddy noted, "4 counties report woven, braided, and hooked rugs made and sold."[145] One Cullman County woman sold rugs for five dollars apiece. Lula Brown Keller of Escambia County used the income from selling crocheted rugs to send her daughter, Helen, to high school. A member of Perry County's Pisgah Club did the same, taking the fifty dollars she made selling ten rugs to pay for her daughter's education.[146] In Bullock County, Laurie Pickett wove rugs to sell at Loveman, Joseph, and Loeb. Franklin County also sent their rugs to be displayed at the Birmingham department store, as well as at the Russellville Furniture Company.[147]

Whether they were making baskets or hats, fans or rugs, handicrafts played an important role in increasing the income of rural women. Demonstrations of new skills meant to improve a home became another way to help women fashion an economic path. As Josephine Eddy wrote, "There is great need for increasing earning power of our farm women, [HDAs] receive frequent calls for work in anything which will help the women make money."[148] Both white and African American women could participate in these programs to improve their financial circumstances. However, African American women had different experiences than their white counterparts, as they faced discrimination and racism, while African American HDAs tried to help in a system of inequality and underfunding.

Alabama's rural women used the money they earned to send children to school, buy cars, pay off debts, enhance their homes, buy farm animals, or add to the family account. With new home demonstration opportunities came creative ventures as the women made the HDA programming their own, thereby gaining an economic independence beyond the farm.

The Movable School, Tuskegee University. Thomas Monroe Campbell, *The Movable School Goes to the Negro Farmer*, 1936.

Tomato Club demonstration in Florida, 1912. State Archives of Florida via Florida Memory.

Group of students from Bullock County (Alabama) who are taking a short summer course at Tuskegee, July 9, 1925. On the extreme left in the front row is M. B. Ivy, Bullock County agent. Courtesy of Auburn University Special Collections and Archives.

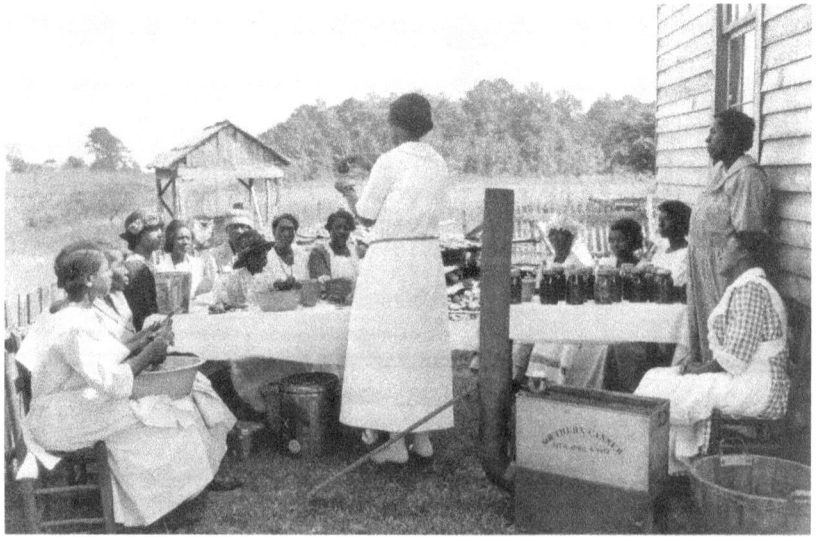

Home demonstration agent demonstrating canning methods at the home of Frank Taylor in Montgomery County, Alabama. Courtesy of Auburn University Special Collections and Archives.

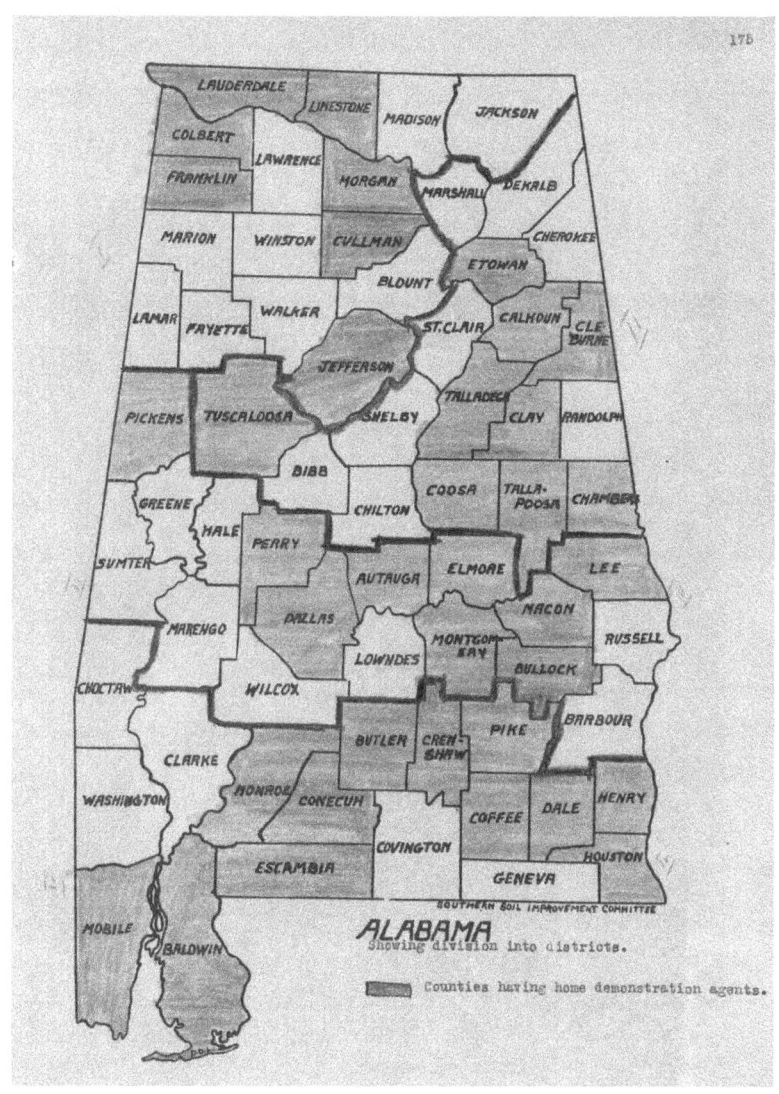

Picture of Alabama counties divided into districts, 1926. Courtesy of Auburn University Special Collections and Archives.

Clara Bow posing with a Clay County basket, 1928. Courtesy of Auburn University Special Collections and Archives.

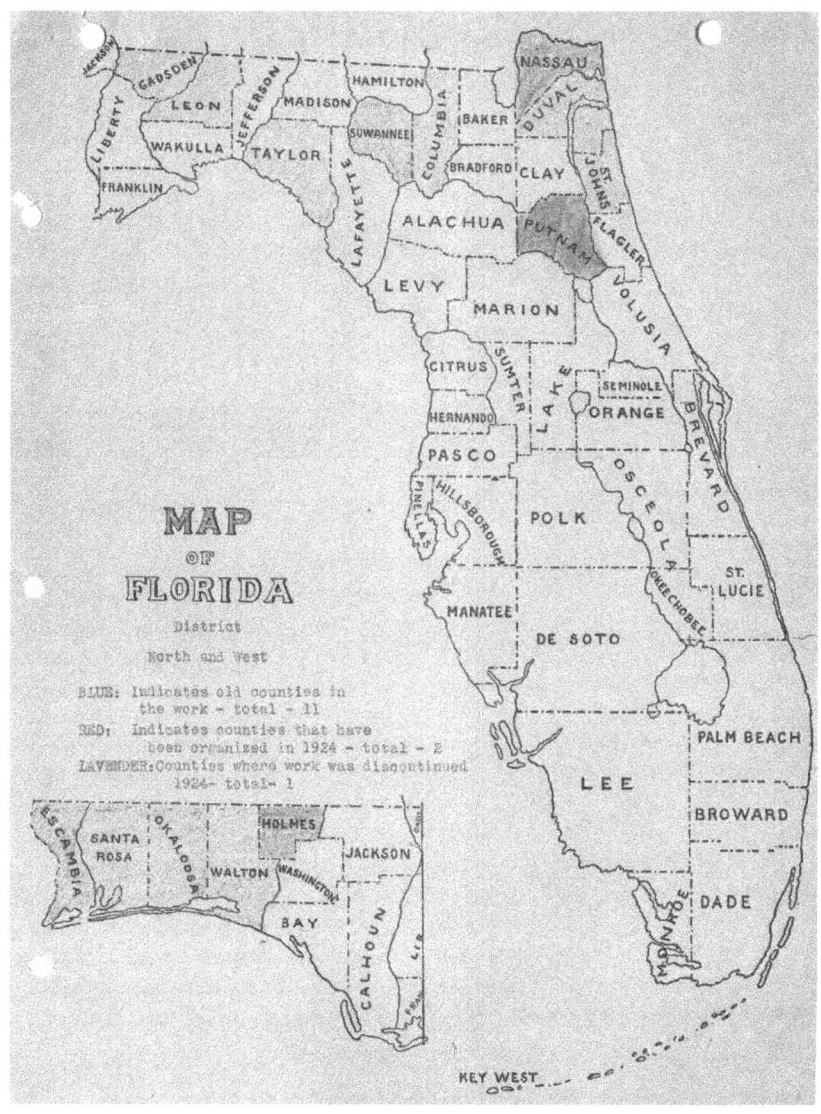

Map of Florida, 1924 or 1925, located in "Home Demonstration Annual Report (Including District Reports), 1924–1925." UF IFAS Extension Records, University Archives, Special and Area Studies Collections, George A. Smathers Libraries, University of Florida.

Home makers' club, Washington County (Florida), from *Farm and Home Makers' Clubs* bulletin by A. A. Turner, 1919. University Archives, Special and Area Studies Collections, George A. Smathers Libraries, University of Florida.

Image of a woman with caption reading, "One of the four steam pressure canners placed in Putnam County, 1917," from *Cooperative Extension Work in Agriculture and Home Economics: Report of General Activities for 1917 with Financial Statement for the Fiscal Year Ending June 30, 1917*. March 1918. University Archives, Special and Area Studies Collections, George A. Smathers Libraries, University of Florida.

CHAPTER THREE

> # GROWING DISPOSABLE INCOME THROUGH FLORIDA'S HOME DEMONSTRATION PROGRAMS

While Alabama and Florida are Southern siblings and share part of a state line, the Sunshine State is more regionally diverse, from the Panhandle to the Everglades, and from the Atlantic Ocean to the Gulf of Mexico. Home demonstration programming in the two states had some obvious similarities, but there were also important differences in how rural women created new opportunities for financial enhancement for themselves and their families.

CANNING EDIBLE ECONOMIC REWARDS

As in other states, Florida's early form of assisting rural girls and, later, rural women in making extra money was through canning and canning clubs. Even before the passage of the Smith-Lever Act in 1914, women including Agnes Ellen Harris, dean of the School of Home Economics at Florida State College for Women and state agent for home demonstration work for Florida, encouraged canning.[1] Canning clubs, which usually focused on tomatoes, started as a way to promote "the health and economic benefits of canning fruits and vegetables."[2] They also taught girls and women aspects of science, economics, and standardization of products. The Department of Home Economics at the Florida State College for Women became an essential participant in developing these types of programs for women throughout the state; by 1912, Harris "enrolled over 500 girls in 11 Florida counties."[3] The canning most women did in Florida was for home preservation and involved sealers, steam pressure cookers, glass jars, cans, and other equipment meant to speed up and ease the overall process. This small-scale production enabled women to fill their pantries and lengthen the time between purchasing certain groceries. Canning, though, also signaled cash, as canned food items could be easily sold. Some women created their own canning businesses, expanding their sales beyond smaller markets.[4]

Canning was seen as a modern, convenient way to preserve food, saving money in the process. However, saving money was not necessarily enough to keep wallets full. A 1914 "Canning Clubs" bulletin encouraged girls to preserve vegetables and fruits they canned for themselves or their families, as canning gave girls "an opportunity of earning money at home, thereby assisting them in helping themselves and others."⁵ Tomatoes made up most of the output but were not the only produce in the garden. The bulletin reported some girls marketed "marmalades, jellies, catsups, pickles and canned vegetables and fruits of such excellent quality . . . they are selling their products for better prices than the best commercial packages receive."⁶ However, canning and marketing were not to be limited to girls; as the bulletin noted, "There has been a great call from the women of Florida."⁷

Club girls were encouraged to plant a one-tenth-acre plot of tomatoes for canning. Agents taught girls how to prepare the tomatoes, sterilize the cans, and weigh, measure, and evaluate them for either home use or to sell. These demonstrations later expanded to include other fruits and vegetables or fruit, such as okra, beets, peppers, and beans. In 1916, one of the bulletins highlighted Yvonne Seckinger, who made $77.55 in profits from almost three thousand pounds of tomatoes, onions, beets, and peanuts on her one-tenth acre.⁸ Dade County's Mildred Adams "cleared" $100 and found a "ready market for all her products," which included tomatoes and sauerkraut, while India Alderman stayed with tomatoes, making over sixty dollars selling 340 "No. 3" cans at eighteen cents per can.⁹ Gladys Givens from Walton County generated $85.65 from chowchow, squash, relish, figs, preserves, peaches, and catsup (ketchup), while Duval County's Eula Trantham sold grape jelly, pear preserves, chowchow, and tomatoes, making $83.77.¹⁰ In 1918, Dade County's Anna Sykes reported one of the state's highest tomato yields on a one-tenth acre: 6,300 pounds, from which she earned a profit of $192.42.¹¹ Like many club girls, Hillsborough County's Pettie DeShong used money from sales and awards to put toward her education. She explained, "[One] reason I joined the club is that it gave me a way of making my own money at home, and in the club I may get the education and view point necessary for farm life." She later attended Florida State College for Women.¹²

Girls who were club members for a couple of years received the opportunity to "specialize in the manufacture" of a product of their own choosing.¹³ Examples included jarred fig preserves, made by Walton County members, and the two thousand glass jars of guava jelly prepared for marketing by DeSoto County girls. Floy Brown of Polk County "made a specialty" of canned guavas in tin, with this venture becoming so popular she was "unable to supply the demand for her product."¹⁴ This was not her first brush with canning success, as she had previously sold over a thousand cans of tomatoes at the price of one dollar per dozen. According to an HDA report, Brown was initially unable to afford a canning machine of her own and the Meridian Canning Machine

Company offered to send her a canner on the condition she demonstrate and sell their product. Brown sold six canners, which meant the company sent her a "splendid large canner" of her own. Thus equipped, she became a leader in the demonstration program for her canned products.[15]

Club members also learned that when economic circumstances change, one has to pivot. In 1918, for example, in the south and east district of Florida, one county's canning club had to "abandon" tomato shipping because prices were low. But the girls still needed a way to earn extra money, so an HDA arranged for them to earn a dollar a day helping to can a farmer's forty acres of surplus tomatoes. The girls were permitted to board in the farmer's home for free, under the care of the farmer's wife.[16]

The 1918 influenza outbreak also required home demonstration agents to shift their focus. During this public health crisis HDAs sprang into action by organizing soup kitchens, especially in bigger cities under the direction of urban demonstration agents, providing food, going into homes to nurse the ill, providing support for caretakers, acting as drivers, delivering medicine, helping find doctors and nurses, making and distributing masks, and coordinating food deliveries. One agent, Alice Dorsett of Suwanee County, assisted a family in preparing a deceased member's body for a funeral.[17] In addition, HDAs responded to the challenges posed by World War I. The Florida State College for Women held a ten-day program, "War College for Women," in September 1918 to discuss women's roles in supporting those fighting overseas.[18] Representatives from different agencies, including HDAs, discussed topics that ranged from rationing to suffrage. Materials were distributed regarding food conservation efforts such as canning, wartime cookery, and dietary changes. Participants learned about the "uses of cottage cheese" and "the wheat situation and bread making in war time."[19] HDA programs also discussed how women could use conservation and preservation to contribute to the war effort and combat food insecurities.[20]

After the war ended, rural women continued to take what they learned about canning and conservation and capitalize on these skills. Women in the early 1920s had standardized canned products "placed with leading hotels, with the Pullman company and shipped on individual orders into distant states."[21] While tomatoes remained an important commodity, rural women and girls participated in other activities they hoped had marketing potential. As in Alabama, beekeeping and, to a lesser extent, the raising of rabbits made appearances in HDA programming. In 1920, there were thirty-three demonstrations on beekeeping and twenty-four on Belgian hares. Osceola County was the first to start with bee work, which continued as a small program with some honey yields in Taylor, Palm Beach, Orange, Gadsden, and Suwannee Counties.[22]

The agents developed creative ways to get girls engaged in home demonstration programming and keep them interested as they grew older. For example, in 1920, girls who went to the state prize winners' short course in Tallahassee were asked what club work meant to them. Answers included "If I should have to earn my own living, I would know how to do so" and "I bought some furniture for the house and have paid for my own clothing."[23] Years later, at a state short course in Manatee County, one team demonstrated how to make different citrus products by appearing on stage as the "Orange Blossom Special," the conductor of which was a young girl dressed as an orange blossom flower. During the pumpkin and squash portion of the course, an Okaloosa County girl took the stage dressed as a mammoth pumpkin.[24] Taylor County took a different approach for their younger members. To encourage good habits in children about personal hygiene, Cho Cho the Health Clown was invited to perform for more than five hundred children over two performances and was apparently a hit with the audience.[25]

THE CANNING OF FISH

Florida was a natural place for home demonstration in canning seafood. Some accounts credit Mary Keown, the HDA in Pinellas County, as the first to do work in canning meat and fish, in 1917.[26] One report noted, "Two commercial canning factories for putting up fish have been established and many women who went to resorts for the summer were able to buy fish at reasonable prices and can them."[27] The same 1917 report also told of two women who successfully canned fish and other types of seafood—Mrs. Burleigh, who "canned 23 No. 2 cans fish, bass, mullet, and others; 10 No. 2 cans shrimp, and 10 No. 2 cans crab," and Miss Preston, who "filled 250 cans with coquina soup, mullet, shrimp, scallops, and red fish."[28] On Anna Maria Island, also on the Gulf of Mexico, a section of dock was built and equipped "for doing this work on a commercial scale."[29] By 1920, HDA Sarah Partridge claimed, 1,055 cans of fish and oysters were put up, at a value of $212.[30]

In 1922, the director of the Agricultural Extension Service, Wilmon Newell, and Frantz P. Lund, Extension agent for food preservation, discussed plans for a fish canning demonstration. "There is great need in Florida for information as to the preservation of fish," Lund believed, "especially when there is occasionally a large surplus of fresh fish that cannot find a ready market as such."[31] Canned fish and seafood saw upticks in usage and marketing. A district agent reported the Pinellas County Fair of 1922 had an exhibit highlighting conservation, including "sea foods, fish, oysters, clams, crabs, etc."[32] Pinellas and Pasco Counties were well situated for seafood and fish canning. In 1923, agents at a Cedar Key meeting noted that "eighteen fine products were made from nine varieties of fish. Among the fish used were some for which there is no market."[33] Pinellas County had three canning demonstrations in 1926, which resulted in canned Florida stew, Pine Bark Stew, chowder, and fried fish.[34] A year later, agents in Pinellas and Citrus Counties were reportedly smoking and canning fish.[35]

Fish was not the only type of protein rural women learned to preserve. In Putnam County, "sixteen beeves and sixty hogs" were canned by club members in 1920.[36] The next year, a couple named the Browns gave a meat canning demonstration in a private home using "the whole carcass."[37] The instructors baked, stewed, pickled, spiced, and fried the meat, while also canning Hungarian goulash and soup. Those in attendance left "planning to can beeves now."[38]

As in Alabama, the early years of home demonstration in Florida reveal how rural women were creating conduits for adding extra income to their bank accounts, usually by canning food. Women continued to use knowledge gained from home demonstration programming for their benefit. One Leon County woman who was working alongside her daughter to learn about raising grapes and poultry, canning, sewing, and baking bread told the HDA of her gratitude that "her daughter has the opportunity to learn while she is young the things she had to learn after she was a middle-aged woman."[39] Throughout the 1920s, rural women kept building on their progress and money already made. An HDA narrative in 1924 recognized a "need" for marketing surplus home products: "Much attention has been given to establishing curb markets, women's exchanges, egg circles and poultry associations . . . in marketing of dairy, poultry, garden and canned products . . . basketry and other articles made from pine needles, honeysuckle, wire grass and palmetto and home cookery."[40] Both white and African American women in rural areas were eager for home demonstration support, but African Americans faced issues of discrimination and inequality that made it more difficult for them to navigate the spaces with white HDAs and white rural women.

AFRICAN AMERICAN EXTENSION AND HOME DEMONSTRATION WORK, PART I

In 1916 and 1917, African American women asked to be taught food conservation, and HDAs obliged. Soon, fifteen African American HDAs were hired to work under the supervision of white HDAs and African American Extension agent A. A. Turner.[41] Agnes Ellen Harris's 1918 report noted that two unnamed agents "equipped canning sheds in their yards and allowed the negroes to come and use their canners, bringing their vegetables and putting them up under the Agent's supervision."[42] Soon, the fifteen African American HDAs had enrolled 1,629 women and girls, organized 140 clubs, and, importantly, bought 417 canners. The white HDA also remarked on their "excellent work" in the areas of soap making, home improvement, sanitation, and clothing. Harris's report reiterated that the "Demonstration Staff of the Florida State College for Women act in an advisory capacity to the negro work, and will continue to supervise it, and give it careful study and assistance. It is being directly supervised and splendidly handled by the negro Agricultural and Mechanical College."[43] In 1918, there were eighteen African American HDAs, but the number was reduced to nine after World War I ended.[44] Sarah Partridge, one of the district HDAs, said of the African American HDAs, "The plan of having [them] appointed as assistant to the white home demonstration agent has proven a wise one. It has enabled us to give much closer supervision to the negro work than we could have done otherwise." She also explained that a "white agent . . . O.K.'s [an African American agent's work plan] before it is sent to our office at which time the negro worker in conference with the white agent works out the plan of work for the following week."[45]

Much like the HDA and Extension programs in Alabama, many of the programs developed for Florida's African American women focused on creating conditions to convince people not to leave and migrate away from the South. HDAs in Florida also sought to work with other minority groups, namely Latinas. In a June 1920 report, Hillsborough County was singled out for having three specific clubs for the Cuban population, one for women and two for girls. The HDAs started this work after the 1918 influenza pandemic, which opened up an outreach opportunity: "We were able to get in sufficiently close touch with the Cubans to get into their homes and carry on this work with them," noted HDA Sarah Partridge. "Fortunately our agent . . . has a sufficient knowledge of Spanish and through a former residence in Porto Rico, a knowledge of their habits of living to enable her to do most excellent work with them."[46] The report provides little in the way of detailed discussion beyond stating, "These clubs have devoted much of their time to a study of food and its preparation. This work is greatly needed. Good results have followed."[47]

The HDA in question, Edith Young (later Barrus), had previously taught home economics in Puerto Rico under the auspices of the United States Bureau of Insular Affairs. According to home demonstration documents, she had her headquarters in Tampa and was in charge of the work in Ybor City and West Tampa "among the Latin population." She helped conduct "two cookery classes weekly at the Rosa Valdez [a settlement house] and Wolff Settlements, and [met] the Woman's Club at the latter place for practical nutrition work one night each month."[48]

One way in which HDAs tried to engage African American residents was in developing programs related to community institutions such as schools and churches. A "Farm and Home Maker's Short Course and Prize Contest" was offered in 1920 for African American farmers, club members, and housewives given in different cities and towns around north Florida and the Panhandle. The short course lasted throughout September and October, starting at Water Oak Plantation at Bradfordville in Leon County and ending at a public school at Quincy in Gadsden County. The all-day event included Extension and HDA demonstrations, exhibits, and contests.[49] Also in 1920, there were two home demonstration projects aimed at African Americans that HDA Sarah Partridge considered "far reaching in its affects."[50] The first occurred after the Columbia County school superintendent "gave $10.00 to be used in the demonstration of what could be done in improving the condition of a room in the school building." An African American HDA from Duval County traveled to the area and "taught the girls to make soap and directed them in cleaning the room used for chapel. The district agent had the boys varnish and finish the window and door facings, a piece of work the carpenters had left undone, and moresco the walls of the room."[51]

The second project involved improving the homes of tenant farmers. In Leon County, a resident gave $200 "to be used in developing the work" and offered the use of a "small and rather dilapidated house on the plantation" on his land where the demonstration could occur.[52] Club members whitewashed the house, cleaned the area, and planted a garden, which was "done during the three day short course." This generated interest from "other negroes in the community," leading to a decision that "the demonstration [would] be repeated in part in some of their homes." The "plantation owner" himself offered "appropriate funds to purchase materials for similar work among his tenantry."[53] One report, written by a white agent, explains the rationale for financially supporting such efforts: "This branch of our work is accompanied by some minor difficulties, as you can all realize, but we are thoroughly convinced that the interested, industrious colored man, with a good home, is never a 'bad negro' and that the solution of the negro problem, if there be such a problem, rests in just such work as we are doing, instruction in industry and the making of good homes by the colored people."⁵⁴

From September 1920 to June 1921, topics of African American HDA work included growing grapes and fruit trees; producing eggs, butter, soap from fats, and shuck and pine straw hats; caring for cows; and more.⁵⁵ HDAs also promoted programs about acquiring a financial safety net. The Home Makers' Club included a "Savings Club" for adults and children and advocated "the habit of thrift and the ability to make profitable investments . . . [as] the direct route to the high ideals of life."⁵⁶ In addition, the club taught ideas about increasing profits. In 1921 "club members reported $480.15 in Savings Clubs" with the demonstrators "reporting $273.50."⁵⁷ In her study *The Lamplighters*, Barbara Cotton points out that "agents taught homemakers to put away as much as possible from their household funds. . . . To increase profits, agents lectured . . . on the value of buying and selling poultry, dairy, and garden products cooperatively."⁵⁸ In 1922, the Home Makers' Clubs summary highlighted extra income earned from milk and cream sold ($376.60), values from pine straw, shuck, and wiregrass items (8,290.25), and the value of poultry raised ($4,808.54).⁵⁹

Seeking out ways to earn extra money was a common goal of African Americans involved in home demonstration. According to one report, "In Leon County the negroes have been especially appreciative of the opportunity given them for marketing their products at the curb market. In St. Johns County . . . one club member marketed from a small planting of strawberries 114 quarts."⁶⁰ An African American HDA, Amanda Parrish, also in Leon County, noted that one of the demonstrators "reported. . . she had already made forty dollars on her winter garden and it was not yet exhausted."⁶¹ In another quarterly report for 1922, Sarah Partridge ticked off a list of success stories: poultry work in Jefferson County; canning centers that were equipped, maintained, and operated in Duval County; "better development" in work in St. Johns County after the agent "purchased a Ford"; and the announcement that "nine negro agents will be employed the coming year."⁶² A. A. Turner's account for the Farm and Home Maker's Clubs in 1924 noted that African American HDAs "have confined their activities mainly to the home and making better living conditions. . . . The women have been active in stimulating interest in poultry raising."⁶³

As one might expect in the Jim Crow South, African American Extension workers were careful in what they said in their official capacity about systemic racism. Duval County agent Minnie E. J. Washington wrote in 1924, "Home Demonstration work is met with a most cordial welcome in every part of the county, and most people are eager to cooperate in any way they can. The Preachers, and teachers are very active in the work. My people appreciate the work.... The White people are pleased over it too. I think there is better understanding between the races in the rural section."[64] In a report to his supervisor, a white Extension director, Turner made a point of saying, "Racial difficulties have never entered the work in Florida and it is at[t]ributed very largely to the ... relation of the white and Negro workers."[65] An article in the *Modern Farmer* recalling the history of the Extension Service for African Americans lauded county and state fairs:

> Under the direct supervision of race members ... to show the progress of the race each year ... the Negro Departments of the various fairs throughout the state have proven a great aid in contributing its bit toward "Better Race Relations," for the community in which this work is carried on and where these fairs are held, as the occasions offer equal competition between Negro and white citizens alike in their own Exhibit Halls which are inspected by the entire public, therefore a closer observation and a better understanding of the races results through this medium and each year better circumstances for all exist.[66]

In a 1922 report to A. P. Spencer, Turner addressed the Great Migration without identifying racism as a cause. Instead, he stated, "The increase in earning capacity and improved living condition of Negro farmers" and "the solution of the problem of educational opportunities for Negroes engaged in agricultural pursuits" could help reverse the trend, since the "very great exodus" from rural areas "may be traced to these two general conditions."[67]

MAKING MONEY IN THE LAND BUST

In the early 1920s—during the midst of the Great Migration—Florida's land and real estate market experienced a rapid boom. The bust came just as swiftly and was over by 1925. While the economic and ecological implications lingered for decades, HDAs and county agents were most dismayed by the immediate consequences. The boom dramatically reduced arable land, so when the unsustainable economic bubble burst, residents were left to deal with the aftermath.[68] The HDAs and rural women felt this aftershock keenly and turned to home demonstration to aid in easing the financial downfall. During this period, wrote HDA Mary Keown, the work of home demonstration "met its second great emergency situation which affected the homes of this state. In rapid succession came devastating storms in south Florida, the bank failures, crop losses, and other difficult situations.... Gardening, canning, and remodeling of clothes again were matters of necessity in order to feed and garb the family under the trying financial conditions."[69]

Another agent noted, "During the period of high values in lands thousands of acres were sold for real estate development, some of it at many times its production value." The impact, according to the agent, was "in that part of Florida that is more agricultural, [where] conditions have been disturbed by real estate activities."[70] The economic downturn hit East Florida especially hard, Keown believed: "No section of the country has been more disturbed physically or economically, during the past year. We have had the collapse of the real estate boom, and its economic aftermath that bore down heavily on the women and girls."[71] HDA reports began to note a lack of funding, which sometimes led to programs being suspended or agents becoming unemployed. Between this financial crash and two hurricanes, southern Florida continued to have economic difficulties into 1929, and women throughout the area looked for ways to gain extra income. Home demonstration programming responded, helping rural women capitalize on existing moneymaking ventures and creating new ones, as they confronted external economic forces far beyond their control.

FOWL WAS NOT FOUL FOR BANK ACCOUNTS

For many women, selling poultry products was an easy way to increase income. Hotels in St. Augustine, Jacksonville, and Miami bought capons from women at prices ranging from fifty to seventy-five cents per pound for live weights.[72] Egg circles also helped ease monetary burdens. Hernando County's egg circle—which had forty members in 1919, making it the state's largest at the time—received $4,788.34 from marketing 7,292 dozen eggs and 3,882 pounds of poultry in six and a half months in 1922. It was considered the "best county egg circle."[73] Poultry was a significant income generator for African American women. Flavia Gleason, the state home demonstration agent, noted in 1925, "Our egg circles [in St. Johns County] are doing a splendid business through the curb market." They were a "means for quick sales," she said, adding, "Poultry is a money maker [in Leon County]. . . . I have ten girls with bank accounts from the same." By Gleason's account, poultry brought in $4,036.44 that year for women, girls, and boys.[74]

Poultry turned girls and women into entrepreneurs. Two Hernando County sisters had a "pure bred flock" and used a small building next to their home to sell eggs, chickens, and groceries in 1923.[75] Juanita Lawrence, a high school girl, paid for her clothes and had $177 in the bank thanks to her standing agreement with an Orlando buyer to purchase "all of her baby chicks she can hatch in her incubator at 20¢ a piece."[76] For the Edge family of Crestview, chickens were a family affair: Bertie Leah Edge and her mother, Fannie Lee Kaley Edge, both raised and cared for the birds. Bertie Leah's father had taken her and her mother to assess different poultry farms and then helped them build a poultry house. They made enough money to pay the educational expenses for Bertie Leah and her younger siblings and to buy a Ford.[77] Some women created business contacts with hotels, ice cream parlors, and restaurants by supplying them with fresh eggs.[78] Mrs. H. K. Thompson of Manatee County raised white Leghorn chickens, selling them, along with eggs, to Tampa's Hillsborough Hotel and other markets, saying, "It isn't a question of markets with them—but a question of producing enough to supply the market." Her chickens paid expenses for her family's citrus grove, as well as the cost of the chickens themselves, as she plowed some of the profit back into the poultry business.[79]

BY THE ROADSIDE AND IN CLUBS

In addition to marketing through customary routes, HDAs helped women set up new ventures to take advantage of infrastructural improvements, including paved roads. For example, home demonstration agents helped set up a roadside stand in Daytona, which was "conducted more along the line of a stall market, each woman selling her own products." According to HDA Flavia Gleason, "One woman reported earning an average of ten dollars a week, selling for three hours on Saturday mornings."[80] Although Gleason did not specifically mention tourism in her report, it is reasonable to assume tourist traffic accounted for some of the profits. (For more on roadside stands and buildings, see chapter 5.)

In New Smyrna, the Home Demonstration Club planned for a "cooked food sale and fancy work bazaar," to be held two weeks before Christmas 1925.[81] Also in 1925, 408 women (this figure is inferred to be a statewide statistic) made over $13,545.29 in surplus income from curb markets, egg circles, the Home Demonstration Shoppe, and the Women's Exchange. According to the HDA, these "income earning feature[s]" allowed "rural women to supply themselves with comfort and luxuries they could not have otherwise hoped for."[82] Mrs. Herman Nordman, president of the DeLand Home Demonstration Club, described results of her eight-month home industry project, which amassed $24 from jellies and marmalades, $27 from "hand work at spare time," $116.75 from crystallizing, and $900.45 from home cooking, which included cakes, candy, meats, bread, and pies, for a total of $1,068.20.[83] In 1926, the Fort Myers Home Bureau added a monthly bazaar, and club members of "good standing" could sell there, with 90 percent of the proceeds going back to the sellers.[84]

STARTING AT HOME... AGAIN

In her 1927 annual, Flavia Gleason noted that "fifteen counties report[ed] standardization of special products for market" and "423 homes are reported as adopting improved practices in home marketing this year."[85] The women, Gleason continued, marketed "poultry products, canned goods, dairy products, fruits, vegetables, [and] baskets made of pine needles, wire grass, and palmetto, or honey suckle or rag rugs."[86] While the business of preparing and selling homemade goods obviously created extra work for these women, home demonstration agents sought to teach labor-saving techniques to make their lives easier. Virginia Pearl Moore, the assistant state HDA, noted in her report, "Women seem to feel there is a certain wifely devotion to be always tired out, and to always do things in the hardest and most laborious way. I often tell them they are only saving for the second wife."[87]

Isabelle Thursby's 1926 food and marketing report revealed how women used their local fare to create disposable income, especially after the land bust. One Holmes County resident planned to use her four acres of beans to can and sell at a later market.[88] An unnamed woman sold $15.60 worth of Easter lily bulbs in west Hillsborough County, while another sold eight dollars in canned onions.[89] In DeSoto County, Margery Thomas Buchans made thirty-eight dollars selling peas and corn from a garden truck, adding to the fifty dollars she made from "fresh greens" and turnips.[90] In Columbia County, women prepped for a basket and cake sale for Christmas. A year later, they planted over one hundred acres of pimento peppers in the hopes they would become a new "money-making crop."[91] Pimentos were also grown in Nassau County, because of the "ready market for them."[92]

Lois Ellis, a club girl in Holmes County, sold $106 of okra in 1927.[93] Meanwhile, in Okaloosa County, Josie Lee Harrelson Hicks, who lived with her husband, four children, single sister, and two aunts, described how she spent the profits from her garden: "I bought some cloth, cooking oil, flour and just any kind of groceries... a half year tag for the car, as we had not been able to get one all the year, then gas and oil, and anything that a housewife needs in the way of house keeping, even some medicine."[94]

AFRICAN AMERICAN EXTENSION WORK PART II: AFTER THE LAND BUST AND MIGRATION

A. A. Turner's report on African American Extension and home demonstration activities for 1924–1925 focused on profits gained from truck crops, particularly in Alachua and Marion Counties, where fifty-nine loads of spring vegetables were shipped "cooperatively to Northern Markets" and brought in $63,600 for the farmers.⁹⁵ To be sure, migration altered the strategies of HDA programming. There were dwindling numbers of African American farmers, and Florida's "extensive road building programs" prompted an "unusual demand for common labor" that drew people away from farming areas. One report explained:

> This condition has taken much negro labor and many tenants from the farms of Florida. . . . Many thousands of acres that were formerly farmed . . . [and that] produced cotton, are not in use. There remains . . . a substantial number of negro farmers in most of the north Florida counties. . . . [As for] the work . . . principally, of staple crops, poultry and to some extent dairy products and hog raising . . . the negro farmers of three counties have made progress . . . by shipping cooperatively . . . particularly [in] Alachua, Marion, and Putnam counties.⁹⁶

In 1925 and 1926, agents were optimistic, and they predicted a "decided increased interest in agriculture" for the coming years, with "undoubtedly . . . a larger production of vegetables, hogs, poultry, tobacco, dairy products, and feed crops."⁹⁷ Agents also knew they had a critical role to play in aiding with the sale of agricultural goods. "The farmers . . . are asking for help in the marketing of their products," observed the state Extension director's annual report, "and it is proposed to work with every possible cooperation with the Florida State Marketing Bureau in the marketing of these."⁹⁸ The report noted the crops growing in the state's western section, were "grapes, strawberries, blueberries, and satsumas" which had been "planted pretty generally all over the territory," and that citrus and vegetable properties, most likely in the southern part of the state, would be put back into agricultural production.⁹⁹

In two 1926 reports from local agents to A. A. Turner, L. A. Hamilton described her efforts to help African American residents in Hillsborough County. "Many hampers of beans, crates of tomatoes, cucumbers, cars of melons and other produce are being sold," she wrote, "with the outlook very bright." Hamilton also reported that women and girls had put up 3,500 cans of fruits and vegetables, 300 jars of fruit juice, 300 jars of pickles, 200 jars of meats and fish, and 1,500 glasses of jelly. Poultry was another area of focus, as over "6,000 dozens of eggs" were sold at forty cents per dozen on average, and six thousand chicks were hatched and sold at forty-five to forty-eight cents per pound.¹⁰⁰ Proceeds went to purchase more cows, home improvements, and clothing. Women also made hats and hat boxes, brooms, pine needle baskets, various textured styles of rugs, and moss mattresses.¹⁰¹ Meanwhile, in a report that spanned January to July 1926, Leon County's agent observed, "The dairying and poultry are the most outstanding, or ready money industries. . . . Having individual and co-operative milk lines operated in the county enables the farmers to get their produce to a daily market."[102]

By the end of the decade, African American women were still marketing their extra goods. In 1928, African American HDAs were encouraged to create local markets "for surplus home products such as poultry, vegetables, and fruits."[103] Nonetheless, in 1929, Julia Miller, the newly hired district agent in charge of Negro Home Demonstration Work, reported most African American women used the HDA programs to enhance their home supplies.[104] The calculated numbers of participants were "1,028 women and 1,565 girls living in 97 different communities and sections of the State."[105] Miller noted the need for an "increase in production of home grown foods and an adequate supply for family meals."[106] This would have been preferable to relying on truck marketing. Home gardens and community gardening projects were undertaken by club girls, such as in Windermere, where members of a club planted a community garden, sold what was grown to the community via a local store, and used the profits to reinvest in their club.[107]

Miller highlighted other African American women who made an income from participating in HDA programs. When Tallahassee's Mary Speed remodeled her home, her "garden and poultry paid for the paint which amounted to $52.25."[108] In Greenland, a community in Duval County, Ella Mahue reported having sold from her home garden "115 quarts of butter beans [at] 35¢ per quart, 20 dozen ears of sweet corn [at] 25¢, 128 quarts of string beans [at] 15¢ and 15 dozen bunches of greens [at] 1.00 receiving a total of $88.55." In Jacksonville, Arimentha Morall sold $72.55 of eggs from forty-five hens.[109]

Also in her 1929 report, Miller discussed her visit to the Southern Sugar Mill Quarters, or the Sugar Mill Negro Quarters, in Canal Point, in Palm Beach County. The business was associated with the Southern Sugar Company, which had operations at Canal Point and Clewiston. She described it as a "very beautiful place" and the area as having one hundred cottages for married couples, a mess hall for single men, a barracks, three public bathhouses, a modern washhouse, and a school building. Miller made note of home sanitation, aesthetic appeal, and the eating habits of residents: "There are no gardens in the community. . . . [I] found most of them were eating meat and fried bread and a few had rice. I noticed that most of the women fried bread." Miller demonstrated to the female residents of Sugar Mill Quarters how to make bath cloths and gave lectures on typical home demonstration objectives. Miller wrote of the community, "[It] is just what one finds in the average Negro community. I think the people in the majority are as fine as will be found in any Quarters. I will not hesitate to say that Sugar Mill Quarters is the best Negro Quarters to be found anywhere."[110]

In contrast to the reports about programming for white Florida women, the overall plans of work and programs for African American women reveal the more pressing needs of creating better and more varied food options for a family. This included canning, preserving, and juicing to meet nutritional needs, as well as the importance of home improvements, sanitation, and other familiar topics. Even when the topics were the same, the way women used their new knowledge varied, as racial segregation was firmly in place.[111]

PUBLICIZING THE RURAL HOME LIFE IN FLORIDA

In 1927, the state Department of Agriculture published a bulletin of over two hundred pages entitled *Rural Home Life in Florida*, which praised the virtues of home demonstration, women, and the ideal rural life and thus echoed the Country Life rhetoric from two decades prior. Unsurprisingly, the bulletin distinctly focused on white women and their home demonstration work. Flavia Gleason wrote the overview, where she reinforced the importance of home demonstration activities such as raising poultry, growing vegetables, tending to dairy, making clothing and baskets, investing in home improvement—which also meant planting various fruit and nut trees for aesthetic purposes—and enhancing home sanitation.[112]

Rural Home Life in Florida also provided accounts of the ways women used the surplus they created. "Many girls and women," the publication pointed out, "in all sections of the state are setting aside a certain number of chickens, a certain garden space and a certain amount of jellies, marmalades, or gift packages to get 'home improvement money' with which to make the home more attractive."[113] Some examples throughout the publication reinforced ideas about putting extra money toward educational purposes. Ellie Ruth Bryce of Nassau County built a "permanent garden by starting grape-vines. . . . [She] will have more money to improve her home, and will no doubt have a college fund by the time she is ready to enter college."[114] Gadsden County's Ruth McKeown sold over fifty dollars' worth of chickens and vegetables and found an eager market for her soup mixture and canned peaches, putting her earnings toward education.[115] One story of resourcefulness came from Santa Rosa County, where Ethyl Holloway—faced with the prospect of dropping out of college because her family could not pay the tuition—used tomatoes to make a deal with the college president. She would provide the school with canned tomatoes for a year, as long as she could return as a student. On less than an acre, Ethyl "handpicked the bugs from the vine" and grew enough to can four hundred gallons of tomatoes, some for the college, the rest to sell. In a twist of fate, she later became the HDA for Santa Rosa County.[116]

OTHER FLORIDA-MADE PRODUCTS

As in Alabama, not all home demonstration–inspired cottage industries involved food. An unnamed Taylor County girl made a small business from millinery and was reportedly "delighted with her new money making scheme. . . . [She] has made a hat for most every wom[a]n of her community."[117] Club girls exhibited hats in Sumter County store windows, which led to some orders.[118] Clara Townsend sold handmade hats for a total of $180, while Mrs. J. W. McKown made $147 and Ruth Walker brought in $125.10 for their homemade hat blocks.[119] The "primitive craft" of making Florida sun hats from palmetto was a program topic in 1926 Polk County.[120] One canning club girl sold palmetto hats to women in her unnamed town, who adopted the hats as "morning wear." So it was that women and girls sought to establish a "business for themselves for the marketing" of homemade products.[121]

As they did in Alabama, baskets generated income for Florida women, as they claimed their own position in the marketplace. Claudia Haynes, a dressmaker in Citrus County, was pictured in *Rural Home Life in Florida* sitting on porch steps with numerous baskets. The caption reads, "Upon learning how to make baskets out of native materials [honeysuckle, wire grass, pine needles, and reed] [Haynes] found that she could make more money by making and selling baskets than by sewing."[122] Haynes switched careers from dressmaker to basket maker, doing "a profitable business along this line."[123] In 1922, Lee County women learned how to make vases, baskets, candy boxes, and jardinieres from natural Florida products—bamboo, coconut, palmetto, pine cones, and pine needles. This particular demonstration was requested to be put on "for the tourists."[124] Later, baskets made in 1925 were used as Christmas gifts and sold "at a good profit."[125] One fourteen-year-old Holmes County girl sold six dollars' worth of baskets after a single lesson in basketry.[126]

By 1929, Flavia Gleason noted, "1,065 women and girls in five counties did definite work in rug making and 1,060 women and girls . . . learned the art of turning such native materials . . . into baskets, trays and other articles. . . . Many of these articles have been marketed individually and in home demonstration shops."[127] Twenty-eight Fernandina women made six baskets and twenty trays at one meeting, leading an HDA to comment, "Quite a bit has been realized from baskets made by the ladies. Most all have been sold."[128] Meanwhile, Mrs. T. J. Boswell sold handcrafted articles, tiles, leather, and other items to generate $249.56 in profit.[129] Jacksonville Beach club girls made felt purses, which they sold "to raise money to be used towards next years short course expense."[130]

Some women and girls found still another, more fragrant source of income—flowers, on which Florida's name is based. In 1927, Hannah E. Palmquist King stated she made a $25 profit in her first attempt at selling flowers. This was a real achievement, since Osceola County, where she lived, was experiencing a drought at the time. According to Gleason, King was "assisting" her disabled husband "in finishing their new house of five rooms." The extra money came in handy, according to the HDA: "They have done all except $30 worth of work on the house, which is practically finished."[131] In a 1928 report, home demonstration agent Meade Love noted that Whitlock Fennell, of Homestead, was "working toward entering the florist business with her father who specializes in the growing of orchids."[132]

THE 1926 AND 1928 HURRICANES

Exacerbating ongoing economic and ecological issues was a hurricane that directly hit Miami in September 1926. Later referred to as the Great Miami Hurricane, it caused death and significant damage, with flooding in and around southern Florida, up to Lake Okeechobee.[133] HDA programming quickly included storm relief. Girls' clubs from communities around the state, such as Duval and Nassau, sent pine needles to provide women with free raw materials for making baskets. The Fernandina Women's Club sent money for help in rebuilding Palm Beach club houses, while Volusia County's women sent clothes.[134] The hurricane, which "wrought havoc to counties in the southern part of the district," damaged fruit trees and crops, prompting the Dade County Council of Women to encourage local women to plant fruit trees. Local women also created a small fruit exchange.[135] In Lee County, Mabel Williams, who had previously learned to make bags from silk scraps and hooked rugs, witnessed how the hurricane "wrecked the family income," so she had to "earn her money by the sale of her rugs."[136]

Recovery had barely started when two years later, in September 1928, the so-called Okeechobee hurricane made landfall, causing even greater devastation. A category 5 storm, the hurricane killed thousands of people, mostly African American workers who lived near Lake Okeechobee. It decimated livestock and poultry, damaged homes and crops, created massive flooding, and caused millions of dollars in damage, likely billions in today's dollars. The Okeechobee storm is still viewed as one of the deadliest hurricanes to strike the United States.[137] As with the Miami hurricane, women quickly responded. Edith Young Barrus, the HDA who had earlier moved from Tampa to the Palm Beach area, traveled by boat to visit women and their homes. The local home demonstration shop, which had opened just a week before the storm to provide a space where products could be marketed, transitioned to provide a completely different service. Fortunately, the only damage the shop sustained was a fallen ceiling, which allowed for quick cleanup.[138] The space was turned into a clothing center, where women brought in sewing machines and material to create garments for those who had lost their belongings.[139]

For the women who were picking up the pieces of shattered lives, the shop also became a place of encouragement and support. Barrus wrote, "I then later interested some of [the women] in home industries to occupy their time and some small amount of money. Many women's and children's garments and home furnishings were made by women and sold at the Home Demonstration Shop."[140] Within two years, women made close to three thousand dollars at the shop.[141] After the shop closed, some women used the skills learned there to pursue new business options. Barrus mentions a Mrs. Olson who became a seamstress and opened her own dress store, presumably because of her participation at the home demonstration shop.[142]

CONCLUSION

At the close of the decade in 1929, a major economic depression had begun, which compounded the environmental and business-related economic downturns already present in Florida. Thus, the ensuing plan of home demonstration work called for continued efforts of providing participants in their programs with a means by which to raise revenue through marketing. According to Flavia Gleason, the goals of programming in 1929 were creating "high grade, uniform products for sale . . . establishing curb, roadside, and home industry markets," and promoting the use of home demonstration items "locally in hotels and other eating places."[143] Over ten thousand girls and six thousand women participated in more than seven hundred clubs throughout the state by the end of the decade.[144]

Rural women recognized that having disposable income would be critical to improving their circumstances. As one report stated, "Home demonstration work helps the farm woman and girl with her poultry, dairy, garden and marketing problems, so that she may have more money with which to buy the things she wants—things for the house, things for the children, things for herself."[145] An HDA report summed up the objective neatly: "The 1929 motto is 'Produce more, sell more.'"[146]

CHAPTER FOUR

CURB MARKETS, FINDING CUSTOMERS, AND RIPENING BANK ACCOUNTS

On one Decatur curb market day in Morgan County, Alabama, a sign highlighted the available offerings: chow chow, (sauer)kraut, "side meat" (a type of bacon or pork, usually from the side of a hog; cured, but not brined), black walnuts, peanuts, "chile" sauce, radishes, eggplant, spare ribs, hominy, pickled beets and peaches, pork, chicken, corn, potatoes, cucumbers, parsnips, okra, squash, and greens.[1] Another photo, this one from an unspecified curb market, shows a Mrs. Mitchell in a fashionable, but practical, coat and wide-brimmed hat, holding a small purse and standing behind a table with displays of what appears to be onions, turnips or radishes, small baskets of other food, and additional varied items. Under the photo is written "in 22 months she sold $2000 worth of produce."[2] The presence and prevalence of curb markets in Alabama and Florida offered women new opportunities to earn income from what they had cooked, crafted, grown, or sewn.

In Alabama, curb markets first appeared in home demonstration reports in 1919, alongside mentions of farmers' exchanges and marketing booths.[3] Curb markets found support from the Farm Bureau, county councils, the Alabama Federation of Women's Clubs, and the Alabama Council of Home Demonstration Clubs, the last of these becoming a major force in backing the development and synchronization of the markets. By 1929, curb markets developed into a vital way for rural women to earn disposable income, which helped them achieve a measure of financial independence.[4]

In 1923, a male district Extension agent and Elizabeth Mauldin, an assistant state HDA, visited curb markets in Georgia and South Carolina. In November of that same year, Alabama's first curb market opened in Gadsden, followed by one in Tuscaloosa in May 1924.[5] A third market was added in Anniston, and a fourth in Selma.[6] Gadsden's opening day was considered successful, with a newspaper recounting, "More than 25 produce vendors were at the opening. . . . Ten wagons and trucks parked on the curb with produce. . . . Almost one side of the curb was lined with vehicles. . . . A large number of [Gadsden] women . . . were all pleased . . . and promised to be regular customers in the future."[7] Vendors purchased permits, usually costing from ten to twenty-five cents each, with all sellers required to "pay the market a commission of 5 percent of their receipts." In Montgomery, a seller could pay ten cents for the day, or fifty cents annually.[8] In Calhoun County, each seller paid a ten-cent fee, which paid the salary of the market master. Markets were open two or three days a week, depending on the season.[9] They were usually outside but sometimes transitioned to permanent buildings or moved inside during winter months.

In some counties, establishing curb markets required a long period of planning. In Tuscaloosa in 1924, it took months of preparation to get one going. First, a curb market committee was formed that included representatives from different organizations, including the Merchants Bureau, the Grocery Men, the Farm Bureau, women's and girls' home demonstration clubs, Federated Clubs, the Women of City, and the city Health Department. The committee helped set rules and regulations for the market. Discussions were also held with "peddlers who were opposed to the market."[10] Ultimately the City Commission backed the need for the market and on May 1, 1924, it successfully opened.[11]

Tuscaloosa's population grew steadily in the 1920s, partly because it is home to the University of Alabama, and this growth contributed to the market's success. In 1924, the market saw its highest estimated attendance (4,500 people) during the months of May and July and its lowest (1,725) in October. In the six months from May to October, sales totaled over $14,500. The Farm Bureau and donations provided additional support.[12] Sellers from surrounding communities such as Jena, in northern Greene County, traveled to Tuscaloosa to be part of the market.[13]

What was offered at the curb markets depended on the location, but generally buyers had their choice of a variety of fruits and vegetables, such as melons, apples, cherries, pears, peaches, eggplant, grapes, and cucumbers, as well as hogshead cheese, cracklings, walnuts, berries, butter, eggs, peas, potatoes, pickles, dried fruits, cakes, hams, other meats, live chickens, dressed chickens, cane syrup, leafy greens, cheese straws, and peanuts. Sellers also offered nonfood items, including flowers, trees and shrubberies, and bedspreads. Among the more unusual items found in the records were a "chicken snake," sold to a merchant who "wanted to rid a storehouse of rats," and "pussy willow flowers" for a teacher to use in her classroom. Later, curb markets sold wool, collie and terrier puppies, ax and hoe handles, wood, and even "home cured" ham sandwiches.[14] Many sellers cleared $100 to $500 in profit. Curb markets offered other benefits too: providing community members with fresh foods and the chance to socialize, while at the same time creating a system for grading and standardizing products. But the importance of earning income cannot be overstated. This "market money," Isadora Williams, the home demonstration agent pointed out, was used to buy "cars, rugs, refrigerators, clothing, foods, expenses of keeping the children in school, hired help and . . . other things."[15]

In Conecuh County, in south central Alabama, an HDA identified the pressing need for a curb market. "We have no systematic market for anything," she wrote. "[The women] are very anxious for a systematic way of marketing their surplus vegetables, butter, eggs, and chickens."[16] In Cullman County, in north Alabama, Elizabeth Striplin, who was the HDA, explained in 1924 there was "a desire to organize a Curb Market," but "the housewife [in the county] must first be educated to the value of the curb market."[17] A year later, Striplin stated that there were "not enough vegetables grown and the variety is not large enough" to support a market.[18] She also believed they needed "more cars in the county," as the only mode of transportation for some women was walking.[19] Nonetheless, the HDA saw the presence of "very few peddlers in the town each morning" as evidence it had potential to be a "fine town to begin curb marketing."[20] In Calhoun County, the subject arose in 1923 because "any means of securing money interests the average person." The idea was to begin with "two trial Curb Market days"—a plan that was "satisfactory to producer and consumer, but objectionable to the retail merchant who fought it strongly."[21]

Despite interest, obstacles and resistance emerged in some areas. In Limestone County, on the Tennessee state line, discussions in 1924 about bringing in a market ended with the decision that it was "not advisable because of the home gardens, cows and small flocks of poultry in the county seat."[22] People in Chambers County, in east central Alabama on the Georgia state line, echoed the same worries. "Our marketing is done principally through hucksters," wrote HDA Zelma Gaines Jackson. "We have not attempted the curb market because our towns are small and the majority of families have gardens."[23] Similarly, in central Alabama's Elmore County, one report noted local women "are vitally interested in some form of curb market. . . . It was decided to appoint a group of rural women as a marketing committee to study the subject and make recommendations . . . but our county seat is too small a town to warrant a curb market."[24] An examination of Alabama curb markets, using defined districts of clustered counties, helps to highlight their successes, failures, and efforts.[25]

DISTRICT 1

In Lauderdale County, a local seller at the curb market, Caroline Powell Delano, wrote that Florence's market was successful on its very first day, with eleven sellers, an estimated two hundred visitors, and profits of $90.14, which "surpassed

[her] expectation."[26] In fact, sellers were "so pleased" with the results "they all came back the next market day and a number of additional ones too." Over the course of fifty-seven market days, Delano reported $736.01 in profits for herself and $6,370.20 for other vendors. She sold, among other items, "krout [kraut]," "sweet and Irish potatoes," grapes, peaches, radishes, carrots, strawberries, and jellies. "I consider my curb market work a most pleasant feature of my home demonstration club work," Delano wrote. "The curb market has been a great blessing to the farmers and to the Florence house wives as well."[27]

Colbert County's curb market, located in Sheffield, was a community effort. A city commissioner, Allen Roulhae, donated the lot on which the market sat, and local lumber dealers and merchants gave money for lumber. A committee—which included the presidents of the Colbert County Woman's Council, the Farm Bureau, and the Kiwanis Club; two merchants from unspecified businesses; the farm agent; and the HDA—was created to set the regulations and path forward for the curb market. Once it opened, it made roughly $85 a market day, or $2,940.05 over a six-month period.[28] Farmers from neighboring Franklin County sold strawberries in Sheffield, since they had no market of their own.[29] In 1927, over a six-month period, Limestone County's market put $2,100 "into the hands of sellers". Their market's success was especially remarkable considering that three years before, the HDAs had reported, "The question 'would a curb market be the project to undertake with the club members?' has been discussed at length but not advisable because of the home gardens, cows and small flocks of poultry in the county seat."[30]

Recognizing the financial benefits of curb markets prompted rural areas such as Morgan County, located in north Alabama on the Tennessee River, to establish their own. The relief for many was fairly instantaneous. One woman recounted how she and her husband had tried and failed to sell vegetables and fruit door to door in a mule-pulled wagon. Because of the market, she wrote, "we go in a car and we know exactly where to go, straight to our new Curb Market, where there is a demand for everything that we have.... In the month of June I made $106.84." One couple drove thirty-five miles to the curb market, making $125 in their first month.[31] Another couple sold over 1300 pounds of butterfat from January to mid-September 1927, resulting in $504.50.[32] One woman made $16.80 from her sales of cakes, pies, and doughnuts and even more—$23.30—from radishes alone.[33] Audrey McGlathery expressed gratitude for the extra money: "I have been selling since the first day the market opened... eight days a month. My sales have amounted to $96.20 to date.... The money has been used, generally, for what ever we needed in the home." The report also included the statement, "Getting a little money . . . kept us from having to draw on the bank so much. . . . The market is the best help the rural people have had. I can see a great future for it."[34] When discussing the Morgan County market, one person noted, "We think the curb market a grand thing."[35]

DISTRICT 2

Once a curb market was active, it became a community affair.[36] Farmers and others donated bags, change, and other items to market sellers. And as profits grew, so did the number of sellers. The first six months of Tuscaloosa's curb market saw both men and women traveling as far as thirty miles each way to sell. One woman (likely Ada Marlow Pate), who was "thoroughly disgusted with [the curb market] at first," became a successful vendor, clearing $632.76 after driving expenses. These profits came from her sales of butter, poultry, honey, chestnuts, melons, peaches, grapes, meat, flowers, berries, beans, and other items.[37] Some women asked the HDA for extra demonstrations in making cottage cheese, as more "city people" were demanding it at the curb market.[38]

In 1925 Mada Windham West sold flowers, vegetables, fruits, butter, and chickens on the market and netted $259.41 in profits. With the money she "painted, put in a mantlepiece, finished [a] floor and bought a rug, and three pieces of furniture for her living room."[39] West reappeared in the HDA report the following year, when she was described as a "typical industrious farm woman of the South," who "st[ood] behind her table and offer[ed] her merchandise from her own farm and her garden for sale."[40] Her sons, who accompanied her to the market, also helped. The curb market became critical to the family's economic well-being, as they were $4,000 in debt after purchasing a farm.[41] Her husband found a job as a mail carrier, using their one vehicle for mail delivery, which "did not daunt her." He drove her early to the curb market and she either found a ride back or walked the four miles home. She stated, "We have . . . paid for our farm . . . painted and furnished my dining room and my dining room suit is of walnut . . . partially furnished my kitchen, living room, a bed-room and bought a suit of porch furniture. . . . I have bought much food and clothing keeping up the home generally." West noted she financially assisted in putting up a lighting system in their barn and potato and poultry houses, as well as adding running water to the house. She hoped to install heating and other "minor improvements" in the future, creating "a model country home, one of which any one would feel proud."[42]

Over the first two and a half years of its existence, profits at the Tuscaloosa curb market totaled nearly $83,000, with 11,539 sellers and 59,000 customers.[43]

In June 1926, the market received a visit from Herbert Hoover, then U.S. secretary of commerce, and his wife, Lou Henry Hoover. Hoover was impressed by what he saw and spoke to the HDA about maintaining and extending such ventures. Tuscaloosa's market drew other visitors, as well as vendors, from outside state lines. One farmer traveled from Tennessee to sell baskets and chairs. Two farmers selling apples came at least five times from Cornelia, located in northeast Georgia, a distance of roughly 280 miles.[44] The curb market also attracted sellers who were not part of the farming profession, including public school teachers.[45] An HDA report related the story of "one man (a broken, tired teacher) who had become tired of his profession and life generally [and] was urged by the marketmaster to try the market." The tale has a happy ending: "From May 1 to November 1 he took in $160.00, selling only once a week. [He] is cheerful and interested and enthusiastic."[46] This unnamed teacher also sold hickory nut and black walnut fudge, along with carrot and banana marmalade that his wife made. A University of Alabama professor who visited the market explained that it had "been good for [him] physically, mentally and spiritually." According to HDA Isadora Williams, this professor left his customers and table one market day to help another seller, a "young student," with geometry homework. The market master took over the professor's table and sold his produce for him until he returned.[47]

One woman reportedly sold $400 of angel food, Mary Ann, devil's food, and chocolate cakes.[48] Mary Maddox Robertson, of Northport, "motored in 23 miles over bad roads" and "arrived at the market at 6am" to sell butter, eggs, and other produce. She took her daughters, Clara May and Irene, ages eight and six. The girls helped their mother by gathering flowers, including sweet William, sweet peas, yellow daisies, mountain laurel, and phlox, "enough to come to four dollars, most of which came from the woods. [They] gathered the eggs and were on hand for the selling. They were given a share of the proceeds."[49] Kate Neighbors Spiller, one of the original curb market organizers, took her youngest daughter, Mary, to sell items out of their car—mostly flowers but also fruit, vegetables, poultry, and dairy. As with Mary Maddox Robertson's daughters, the youngest Spiller learned the importance of marketing and earning extra money early. One report for 1926 indicated Spiller made $1,000 from one acre of land, on which she grew vegetables and "a fine production of flowers" such as zinnias, sweet peas, and rose. Spiller also advertised figs that were "ready for delivery . . . [with] orders being booked now . . . at curb market or phone."[50]

In 1929, Bessie Stephens Smith wrote she had been selling at Tuscaloosa's market three days a week, for 1,633 "successive curb market sales days."[51] She earned over $3,000 from milk, butter, vegetables, flowers, and other farm surplus, allowing her to cover family expenses and help pay her four daughters' educational costs, including college tuition. When asked about the market, she spoke about "regularity and system," because in her opinion "those two words count for success in business and that applies to the curb market business."[52] She explained, "I have never failed to fill each new order regularly and at exactly the time agreed upon, and found that doing this and giving good measure, the customer would always return for more!"[53]

The experiences of three women vividly illustrate the impact of the Gadsden market. Lula Bankson made $112.80 from selling flowers. Dora Callan Aldridge sold at the market once a week to "put light and water in her home." Over the course of eleven months, but not selling every market day, Minnie Millican Anderson made an average of fifty dollars per month—even more during strawberry season, when she brought in thirty dollars a week and sold "$75.00 worth of berries off of eight little rows." She also sold cakes and dressed hens for extra Christmas money. Thanks to her profits, she paid "running expenses of her home, had dental work done for her children, bought casings for her car, [and] gave two of her children nice trips this summer," the HDA reported, adding, "It ha[s] been a great deal of help to her."[54]

The Gadsden market maintained consistently high sales numbers, attendance, and sellers' participation. It held special events to garner attention and draw in even more business. January 1924 featured a "Turkey Trot," in which the plan was to "turn loose several turkeys, geese, guineas and chickens and the rule will be 'keep what you catch.'"[55] In 1927, an HDA account reported the market had "sold at least $70,000 worth" of products, which included dried hams, fish, rabbits, fresh meats "of all kinds," geese, flowers, cakes, syrup, baskets, buttermilk, berries, and fruits.[56] In 1928, HDA Diana Williams wrote that sellers from other parts of Alabama were traveling to the Gadsden market, as were vendors from Georgia, who brought peaches since the Alabama crop was not available. She also noted that two smaller markets had sprung up in Etowah County—one in Alabama City and one in Attalla—but the former was not thriving because of its proximity to the Gadsden market.[57]

In 1928, Fannie Bellenger made $1,006 in profits, mostly from selling flowers, having found an outlet "where she could turn them into money."[58] Irene Griffin Freeman was delighted with her success at the curb market. "Myself and others have really made our principal expenses entirely from the sales," she wrote. "The wives and daughters do all the marketing, leaving the men and boys at home to do the field work. This division of labor is a wonderful financial help and keep[s] [us] out of the credit stores."⁵⁹ A Mrs. Kelly sold vegetables, earning $1,866.66 in ten months, which allowed her to install "home delco lights" and running water—the HDA noted, "[She] was so modest did not want to tell me the things she had done for fear of bragging."⁶⁰ One HDA's collection of newspaper clippings for Etowah County included an article observing how the curb market "has been giving the farmers and their wives . . . an opportunity to turn their products into cash [which] has saved waste, and has furnished the people of the city much greater quantities and varieties of wholesome food."⁶¹ Catherine Dempsey Satterfield used the $2,128.10 she made to reroof her house, buy "better" clothes for herself and her daughter, extra cows, and a car.⁶² As an added bonus, she had spending money "when [she] did not have it before."⁶³ Previously, she had lacked money to buy a cow, so the HDA loaned her money, and Satterfield sold milk and butter to pay the loan back. As her daughter was "thinking of going to work," Satterfield stated, "I am going to learn to drive the car, so that I can continue coming to the market."⁶⁴

In 1928, Talladega County's curb market was "small, but successful." The home demonstration agent reported, "The sales amounted to $3521.60 for the year. Special features are advertised from time to time to draw customers."⁶⁵ It followed the same pattern as other markets—opening early in the morning, encouraging all to attend, and advertising a space for African American vendors—and also placed special emphasis on "home income earning." Thanks to the market, four women were able to sell items on consignment at Loveman, Joseph, and Loeb Department Store in Birmingham. At the curb market itself, the Home Income Earning Committee's booth offered items ranging from "handpainted novelties" to baskets and canned products.⁶⁶ Sue Wallis Carpenter stated she sold "33 cakes to one customer in as many weeks at $1.50 per cake. I averaged three cakes a week . . . during the winter months. I sold 20 sunbonnets, in the early spring for $0.75 each."⁶⁷ All told, her sales generated $465.50, leading Carpenter to say, "I find the Curb Market one of the best things for the farming people. . . . I am for [it] now and always."⁶⁸ In its first seven months, the Talladega market saw 2,300 visitors patronize 688 sellers for a total of $2,559.79 in receipts. Daisy Jane Brown London noted it was "the best way to make money since I've lived on the farm!"⁶⁹

DISTRICT 3

The Montgomery curb market opened on May 21, 1927, and, according to one report, operated three days a week.⁷⁰ In seventy-six market days, there were two hundred sellers and close to $26,500 in sales.⁷¹ The curb market served as a hub of sorts for sellers from surrounding counties: a 1927 report indicated that since Elmore County did not have its own market, "an average of 10 people per day" sold in Montgomery instead.[72] One of those vendors was "the meat lady," who sold "sausage and meat the year round and everything else that the human mind can devise." She earned up to $105.60 in one day.[73]

Items sold at the curb market even included live animals: Persian cats "of great beauty, at $10 to $15 each," as well as "common" cats and "little" dogs.[74] An ad in the local paper taken out by C. E. Douglass touted, "Everybody who likes babies [will] be at the Curb Market celebration . . . to see the Pinehurst babies, baby chicks, baby rabbits, baby dogs, baby cats."[75] For women like Julia See Claire, Montgomery's market provided a much-needed financial boost. The family had moved to the area from Missouri and "bought land about a mile from a gravel road in the midst of sticky black mud." Claire continued, "For four years we lived off to ourselves. . . . I began [going to the market] with four products: butter, eggs, chickens, and cottage cheese. . . . I have sold three days in the week . . . averaging between $35.00 to $40.00 a day. The marketing end is managed entirely by me with the help of my sixteen-year-old son." She concluded, "Our work of selling is a pleasure."[76]

Although she had to contend with drought, Mrs. T. C. Thompson was also positive about the Montgomery market. "I . . . paid my way on a neighbor's car, and averaged $30 in sales per month," she explained. "Today I go in my own conveyance, sell $50 worth per week, owe no debts and have some cash on hand. . . . I have set my goal for this year's at $100 per day." During one period of drought, she had to pivot her marketing plan by turning "to the forest" to find local plants and trees to sell. Although this venture was profitable, the State Department of Agriculture had to "put a stop to this" practice until the woods could be properly inspected.[77] One unnamed woman underwent surgery and "had money enough in the bank to pay for it" because of the profits from her sales.[78] Teenager Louise Smilie sold her own canned huckleberries at her mother's booth. One day at the market she wore a smocked, pink gingham dress she had made herself, with the intention of advertising her dressmaking services, and "announced" she was taking orders, at two dollars per dress. "I earned sixteen dollars in this way," she declared proudly, "and best of all earned confidence in my work." According to the report, she hoped to earn more money through rug making and put it toward music lessons.[79]

In her 1928 annual report, Luella C. Hanna, the state agent for African American women, noted that $155.53 had been "collected from products sold at the colored curb market."[80] This might have been an African American curb market located in Montgomery, according to the date given by the county's African American HDA, Annie Mae Boynton—the future sister-in-law of civil rights activist Amelia Platts Boynton Robinson, who started as an HDA for Dallas County in 1929. This market opened June 16, 1928, "for the farm men and women to sell their products at market prices." Boynton noted, "They sold fruits, vegetables, chickens, and eggs. The following was realized: for June, $57.81; July, $64.54; August, $10.49; total, $166.63." The director of the Alabama Extension Service, L. N. Duncan, later referred to the existence of two curb markets specifically for African American patronage.[81] However, this particular curb market had not yet started when Mrs. Turner, a widow, drove her one-horse wagon or sent her daughters in her stead to Montgomery in 1926. According to Rosa Jones, the state agent for African American home demonstration, "One [of Mrs. Turner's daughters] pulls an express wagon, the other carries a basket . . . filled with green corn, butter beans, English peas, carrots and other delectable products from their little garden. Mrs. Turner brought the first [locally grown] English peas . . . [and] has a bank account for the first time."[82] Meanwhile, a Mrs. Rollins created a vegetable garden with her husband's help, surrounding it with chicken wire and plowing and fertilizing it. The plot gave her "an abundant supply of fresh vegetables" and she made "pin money throughout the summer by selling to her neighbor."[83]

Hanna's 1928 report recounted that African American women sold "fruits, vegetables, chickens, and eggs" over a period of three months at "market prices" for which they received a total of $166.63.[84] Mrs. Rosa Dale, a member of the Oak Hill Club in nearby Wilcox County, used her profits of almost a hundred dollars to buy a vanity case table, two chairs, a "good" cook stove, and a phonograph.[85] According to the report, Mrs. T. H. Taylor (likely Emma Jackson Taylor), of the Oakwood community, "planted four rows of collards and has sold $16 worth, enough to pay for her garden wire, saying nothing of supplying the family." Sadie Jordan sold twelve dollars' worth of eggs, fifteen dollars in milk and butter, and three dollars in collards.[86] After earning money from selling vegetables, Mary Greene bought a porch set and rocking chairs, while Eva Jones saved $30.90 from her lima bean sales to eventually "present herself with a refrigerator."[87]

In Selma, the county seat of centrally located Dallas County, the HDA reported that when she offered "Method Demonstration," "the women would say, 'Don't teach us how to do any thing more, until we get a market for what we already have.'"[88] The response was the same, according to the HDA, "when a drive for money for any purpose was put on in [Dallas] County": the women would state, "'Give . . . chickens, turkeys, pigs, hay, or produce of any kind, as we have every thing, but money.'"[89] Unsurprisingly, when the curb market began, the first nine months of operation saw "361 sellers, value of products sold $7820.00, and estimated profits 35–40%."[90]

The Selma curb market, which opened on March 15, 1925, owed part of its success to the publicity push by citywide organizations such as the Chamber of Commerce and Kiwanis Club. They assisted in promoting the market both as a way "housewives can secure the best and freshest vegetables" and as a means to "help the out of town sellers, which in turn helps Selma's merchants."[91] The curb market gave women "a chance to stand by the producer and help foster the agricultural program of the Farm Bureau in a practical helpful way."[92] These organizations believed women would put money they made at the market back into local businesses. HDAs, too, assumed women would spend "surplus cash through the county."[93] In addition to ceremonial addresses by local leaders, the opening of the market was celebrated with band music and viewed as a draw for the "housewives of Selma."[94] Indeed, one Saturday market day featured a play called *The Vegetables Entertain*, in which seventeen children from the Tyler School dressed as vegetables talked about having a healthy diet.[95]

African American residents sold at the market in a segregated section. The market manager, Pearl Stanfill Hain—referred to as Mrs. John Hain—was reportedly "anxious to have the negro hucksters bring their fresh produce to the market to sell" and appointed Gertrude Callier, an African American woman, to be in charge of the "colored hucksters."[96] African American sellers were given tables near the courthouse and Selma Marble Works and asked to pay ten cents a day for their slots, the same fee required by those selling at the market.[97] An article published in the local newspaper, likely in 1925, noted visitors to the market "can take advantage of the splendid facilities. . . . Negro truck raisers will be given places in the curb market line, and every effort will be made to [e]nsure equal opportunities for sale for all who sell at the curb."[98]

By 1927, the Selma curb market had become important to the county, as it was a smaller area in terms of population and economic growth compared to neighboring Montgomery. Sales from November 1926 to November 1927 equaled $17,555. The curb market was "entirely handled and practically supported by women," and the report indicated "every homemade product mentionable is being sold at this time."[99] One local woman expressed her appreciation of the market for fulfilling a "long felt need" and helping farm women "supplement their income."[100] Among the women who benefited from the curb market was Emma Price Thornton, who used money from the local sales and out of state orders of cakes and cottage cheese to pay for household items, a car, and a yearly summer vacation for herself and her husband.[101]

Union Springs, the county seat of Bullock County in south central Alabama, opened its market on February 5, 1927. It was smaller than the one in Selma, and the HDA report noted it "began with sales amounting to $9.75." However, thirty-five sellers helped those profits rise as the year continued.[102] As a local paper noted about the curb market's opening, "women of [Bullock] county [had] the opportunity of placing their wares and handiwork there for sale" for the initial two market days a week. As one local paper wrote, "The curb markets have proved most successful in a number of Alabama towns and a need of such a market has long been felt in Union Springs."[103]

In some counties, there were concerns about whether there would be enough items to sell. For example, it took until April 21, 1928, for Macon County to open its own curb market, for just that reason. However, once the market opened in Tuskegee, those fears proved unfounded, as sales within six months reached $2,821.50. One woman made over ninety dollars solely from angel food cake sales, while another sold canned chicken, as well as eggs and live chickens.[104] In Autauga County, Emmie Adams DeRamus used her $1,714 profits from butter, dressed chickens, pork sausage, eggs, and flowers to buy living room furniture and a cream separator and to give $250 to her college student son.[105] Daisie Wright Smilie, of Montgomery County's Grady community, spoke for many when she described the curb market as "one of the greatest helps the rural people have ever had."[106]

The 1927 HDA report included accounts from four women about their financial successes at the Opelika curb market. Ermine Watson Orr said that between the business she did at the curb market and her sales of eggs to the local hatchery, she received $1,697.76. According to the report, she and her husband sought to sell "enough . . . to pay for the household expenses, clothes and other little things without using the crop money" for the members of her family, which included three sons. The money they earned paid for "[school] books, tuition, clothes, gas and up-keep of their car and also another family car." The profits came from fruits, such as apples, plums, watermelons, and peaches; vegetables; butter, milk, and cream produced by her cow; and eggs from "nearly [a] thousand chickens."[107] Florence Ellington Robertson of Waverly sold cakes, chickens, eggs, and some vegetables two days a week and averaged one hundred dollars a month, creating a cumulative total of $1,134.35 by November 1927.[108]

Opelika resident Mrs. J. D. Allen sold two days a week for over eighteen months, netting $963.01 in one year. She wrote, "I have been able to buy almost every need for our little family. It made me happy to give my daughter her spending money while at college. I am planning to buy a new Buick Coupe next year."[109] At first Auburn's Mrs. Newton was not, by her own admission, the best seller. She recalibrated and made improvements after poor sales—mainly buying higher priced seeds, ostensibly for tomatoes. She increased her sales to $264.64 over eight months.[110] One 1927 newspaper report noted that "sixty-nine growers from all sections of the county" sold at the market.[111] In her 1928 yearly HDA report, Mary Bailey expressed the goal of seeing twenty-five family incomes increased by the curb market. She surpassed that goal when forty-five families had their incomes go up.[112]

DISTRICT 4

The Mobile curb market opened on May 1, 1927, after Tuscaloosa's HDA, Isadora Williams, who had been the "market master" and director of operations for that city's curb market, traveled to Mobile to talk about the value such a market could bring.[113] Representatives from fifteen communities in and around Mobile were involved in preliminary discussions. However, according to an HDA report, there was not a unanimous desire to see a curb market. The home demonstration report noted, "On account of some disaffection on the market caused by people who desired to destroy it, some of these leaders changed." Eventually, "each community ha[d] excellent leaders working for the good of the market." The home demonstration agent did not identify reasons for this initial conflict but explained she helped find a leader for the market, as she did not want to assume that "responsibility directly for the conduct of the market," since it had taken all her time "to keep this leadership"—between city and county officials—"bolstered up and functioning."[114] Instead, the HDA held a demonstration called "Curb Market Cookery," which led to "the women selling superior baked goods, for which there is still an increasing demand."[115]

Once it was in business, the Mobile market—whose location was on Broad Street between State and Congress Streets, or Adams Street, depending on the news article—was advertised with prominent signs. Some mornings it opened with music and bands. It was even the topic of a local school essay contest sponsored by the Chamber of Commerce. Students from all thirty district schools were invited to write about the market, and the winners were to be celebrated on May 14, two weeks after its opening. The prizes were a free sightseeing trip, which included a boat ride around the bay and harbor, lunch, and tickets to a movie and vaudeville performance at the Saenger Theater, which had opened in January 1927.[116]

These attention-grabbing measures proved to be a success, and the curb market was a profitable venture. According to the HDA, $44,862 worth of products were quickly sold after the market opened, with profits estimated at $32,000 to $35,000.[117] She noted, "The women in almost every case are better sellers than their husbands. . . . [Women] have made outstanding successes as sellers on the curb market."[118] One news report asked whether the "housewives" of Mobile would even want to visit the curb market, because they were accustomed to "the practice of ordering over the telephone," but then explained that the experience of other cities and states "proved that housewives will patronize a curb market when given the opportunity." In response to such concerns, the HDA held more demonstration lectures on "curb market business" and "curb market specialties."[119] The Chamber of Commerce held a celebratory event for the one-year anniversary of the curb market, complete with speeches and prizes that included items sold at the market.[120]

There were also discussions about building a structure to house the curb market, which would help expand the amount of products sellers could provide and allow the market to remain open in bad weather. This helps to illustrate how successful Mobile's curb market was becoming. Newspaper articles from May 1928 indicated that a second curb market had been established on nearby Jefferson Street and a special Easter market had resulted in $350 in sales of flowers, baskets, homemade candies, cakes, rabbits, poultry, plants, and novelties.[121]

In a letter to the HDA Louise Riley, Mrs. F. A. Tucker (likely Lucy Brawner Tucker) of Mobile's Crichton neighborhood described the financial and social advantages of the curb market. She explained that she "never missed a Saturday" and "have never cleared less than $10," and as her husband would also join her at the market, she noted, "our sales have been over $300." Tucker created her own thriving business selling a range of products from chickens, eggs, butter, and various other dairy items to vegetables, fruits such as Japanese persimmons, and marmalades. Her sales also extended beyond the curb market: "I now have a staple trade for my home made products, and I receive also orders for delivery on days on which the market is not held. I now deliver special orders for parties and other functions, such as church suppers, etc."[122] By 1929, the Mobile curb market was described as "an area of fine buying power."[123] As with other curb markets, to shop local meant to keep money circulating within a community's economy.

From March to November 1927, the Houston County market generated $10,780.14 in profits, with three market days a week, 187 issued permits, and the support of local clubs and businesses.[124] Milbra Kelley Halstead of Dothan used her profits to purchase a refrigerator, have an eye exam, and purchase glasses, as well as paying to have her husband's "teeth pulled and a new set made."[125] Houston County's Effie Waddell Holland used part of her profits to support a son who was in optometry school.[126] Pike County did not organize a curb market until May 1927, but it quickly experienced rapid growth, as membership increased from 10 to 152 members and brought in $17,777.23 in sales within a year.[127] One member, Shirley Wilson Smart, wrote that once she started selling, she was able to pay for "[a year's worth of] carbide for lighting purposes, most of the groceries, clothing, refrigerator . . . expenses of two girls in high school for two years and one in training school."[128] However, success stories were not universal. For example, Escambia County was slower in developing its curb market than other communities. The female rural residents sold canned goods, hats, baskets, and rugs, but not at the same level as other communities—"we have not yet developed the marketing industry as we hope to do in the future," admitted home demonstration agent Mary Segers.[129] Butler County held a one-day curb market on November 5, 1927, a precursor to a more permanent market, with profits of $150.[130]

OVERVIEW

Profits from curb markets expanded throughout the mid- to late 1920s, prompting one HDA to quote a University of Alabama dean, "A most encouraging study can be made in watching the people become happy as they improve their economic situation."[131] For example, Selma's curb market in 1926 had $16,000 in sales, with 35 to 40 percent in profits going to 162 sellers. At Gadsden's market, four hundred farmers from Etowah County sold $70,000 in products. Meanwhile, profits at Anniston's curb market totaled up to $18,000, as individual sales increased up to 50 percent for some sellers. Opelika's market opened with twelve sellers and eighty-four dollars in produce, growing to seventy sellers with almost $4,000 in overall sales, prompting the Chamber of Commerce to find the market a winter location.[132] As one headline noted, "Curb Markets Are Paying in Alabama."[133] The latter half of the 1920s saw an expansion of markets crisscrossing the state, as the number increased from three to eighteen, thirteen of them opening in 1927 alone. There were major financial incentives for counties to open their own curb markets. Rural areas that likely depended on cotton or other single crops needed to secure alternative revenue sources. The success stories spoke for themselves: Gadsden's market earned $156,380 from November 1923 to November 1927, while Bessemer's curb market, starting in August 1927, earned $33,195.[134]

As the 1920s ended, the curb market became a reliable source of income. By 1929, Alabama had twenty-one curb markets, with five closed for unstated reasons. Over six years, the total sales from these markets amounted to a reported $1,206,892.46.[135] The original Gadsden market alone brought in $104,805 between 1928 and 1929.[136] L. N. Duncan summarized the importance of the curb markets to home demonstration in his 1929 annual report. He calculated the number of women's clubs for home demonstration was 374, with 9,535 women enrolled, a 17.5 percent increase over the previous year and an enormous jump from ten years prior, when only 2,457 women were enrolled in HDA activities.[137] "The development of marketing among women continues to be one of the outstanding features of home demonstration work," Duncan asserted, and he singled out curb markets as the "most conspicuous examples of the marketing activity of women," stating that in 1929, over 1,300 women in 21 curb markets brought in sales of $401,316.11.[138] However, these figures are for white women only.

Duncan's report indicates poultry and dairying were the most profitable moneymakers for African American women and girls in 1929. While some curb markets had designated marketing areas for African Americans, he noted only two unnamed counties established markets solely for African American vendors and patrons, with one assumed to be in Montgomery. Also, in 1929 "droughts and floods wrought havoc with the gardens" and so there was less to sell.[139] Instead, African Americans marketed "most of the farm products produced by women and girls" to "hotels, private homes, and peddled through the streets." He added, "Sometimes the grocery stores buy them cheaply and sell them at one hundred percent profit."[140] However, the total sum of sales was just $1,793.85—far less than that made by white women.[141]

For rural Alabama women, although more so for white women than for African American women, curb markets proved to be a key method to earn extra income. HDAs could adjust their programming plans as women learned what was profitable to them as sellers. Alabama did not necessarily have the same natural environmental advantages as their neighbor to the southeast. Montgomery marketer Emmie Adam DeRamus, in a slightly mocking tone, wrote, "We hear that Florida is the Garden Spot of the world. We merely look over our green fields to be dazzled by what we see on the other side of the fence."[142] DeRamus then declared in her home state she found "a little bank account and a contented mind. A great combination . . . Alabama should take off their hats to the curb markets. They lead in sales; they are waking up the farmers to the fact that cotton and corn are not the only things that bring in money. Long may they live and grow!"[143]

CURB MARKETING IN FLORIDA

Curb markets began appearing in Florida starting in 1918, becoming more prevalent around the state throughout the 1920s. Rural women became steadily more active in these spaces, especially in urban areas such as Miami, Orlando, and, later, Tallahassee.[144] Orlando's market was started not by home demonstration agents, but by members of the Women's Council of National Defense, who went before the Board of Trade Directors and requested that a market, along with a "liberty kitchen," be established within the city. The curb market began with a monthlong trial basis and was initially located on a vacant lot owned by the mayor, Braxton Beacham, near the former Orange County jail and San Juan Hotel. The local newspaper soon reported, "All housewives will be asked to liberally support the curb market from the start to insure its continuance."[145] Within days, a letter appeared in the *Orlando Sentinel* from George Harris, an African American man, who raised concerns about possible racism at the newly established venue:

> I am respectfully asking the consideration of the leading citizens of the curb market.... I feel that the plan is a very good one, but I ask that there be no discrimination. I desire to be loyal to the Government and obedient to our city and county laws and I do not mind being obligated to the buyers, but I do not want to feel that I am taking a chance in a gambling game when I carry my little produce to the market ground. I want to feel that there will be no discrimination made and ask that this notice be considered.[146]

MIAMI'S MARKETS

The Miami HDA, along with the head of the Women's Club, created the city's curb market after hearing from people that there was interest in it. The Miami Metropolis supported the effort, asserting, "If all housewives would endeavor to patronize the market it would soon be demonstrated that there is a way for Dade County farmers to sell their products in Miami. It has been a sorry business, the importing of vegetables for the Miami consumers from 'up-state' when the Dade county products were rotting in the fields."[147] Two weeks later, the *Miami Herald* reflected on the increasing variety of goods offered: "[Soon] there will be some choice Bombey mangoes in the market. Kumquats are to be a Saturday feature, also. Many dozen ears of Dade county corn were sold ... as well as fine watermelons."[148] The Red Cross's canteen committee sold flowers one day to fund a lunch for the men who worked in the "aero-gunnery school."[149] In early September 1918, the curb market items for sale included grapefruit, sugar apples, mangoes, lemons, okra, and homegrown and home-canned tomatoes.[150]

At the time of a 1921 HDA report, the curb market was praised for its produce and for the response of patrons.[151] The market had become so popular the police commissioner, J. K. Fink, voiced concerns about its proximity to the police station, which resulted in traffic issues and other difficulties, and asked the city council for the market to be moved elsewhere. The city council members warned him, "The curb market is an institution which has proved desirable and popular, and if Mr. Fink is not careful he may bring down around his ears a storm of protest from its patrons."[152]

By 1922, the Miami curb market boasted over one hundred stalls for people to sell their wares.[153] The *Miami Daily Metropolis* described it as an inviting place: "Clean and fragrant, fresh from the dew, the fruit and vegetables and flowers on the curb market these days make a beautiful picture in the early morning. . . . It will be well worth your while to get up early."[154] The curb market was also a space for holiday shopping. At Easter time, the market was featured on the front page of the local newspaper. Fresh corn, potatoes, summer squash, tomatoes, pies, and candied fruits were all offerings for Easter Sunday dinner, along with "gaily colored eggs arranged in fancy baskets" for sale.[155] Meanwhile, at Christmas time, Ellythe Lowe of Davie had a "rare display" of tatted and crocheted lace and embroidery, in "delicate" shades of yellow and lavender, made of a linen material she purchased before World War I, as the material was still considered scarce a few years later. The *Daily Metropolis* noted Lowe's goods served as excellent Christmas gifts and were an "innovation to be a feature of the market in the future."[156]

In 1920, one article recounted that a weekend frost prompted a lower than usual supply of vegetables from Miami sellers, but the Redlands—a well-known agricultural area—had been "untouched" by the frost. Growers boasted about "enough tomatoes and beans ripening in the Redlands now to take care of the entire city of Miami." The paper also highlighted the local citrus crop, observing that the "tourists and home folks vied with each other in relieving the groaning trucks and automobiles, laden with the golden fruit."[157] The following year, children from Orange Glade sold items to raise money for their school grounds.[158] The area's newspapers continued to spotlight the curb market. In 1921, *the Miami Daily* Metropolis took special note of Nellie Mahan's fruit, honey, candy, and cakes; the Oakes' poultry, citrus, and avocado products, much of which was grown on their five acres in Redland; two sisters selling preserved fruit under the name of Carter and Wilkerson; the Pinellas, who moved from California and sold avocados and pears; and the Bernick family, originally from Estonia, who sold Rhode Island Red chickens off their five-acre farm in Davie.[159] In 1922, Biscayne Park's curb market sold berries, radishes, and other goods, leading the *Daily Metropolis* to ask, "Why buy vegetables that have been in a store an indefinite length of time when you can get them fresh from the soil at Biscayne Park?"[160]

When *Florida Grower* magazine published an article in 1923 about curb markets, specifically on establishing one in Tampa, it neglected to mention Miami's curb market. The *Daily Metropolis* responded with exasperation, pointing out their five-year-old market, also called the Growers Curb Market, was open three days a week, had its own building, and was "increasingly popular with the growers and with the patrons."[161] It maintained its popularity with sellers and buyers from the Miami suburbs, including a Mrs. Ritchie, who sold fifteen gallons of relish in ten days—"a remarkable record"—and Bertha Benson Kjorsvik, who sold "fancy candy fruit," which she colored with fruit and vegetable juices and cut into "various flower shapes."[162] The high attendance and sales were still evident in April 1924, when the *Miami Metropolis* reported on the offerings during one of the market days that month, which included pawpaws, chayotes, okra, and bananas grown at Hialeah.[163]

In 1921, Mrs. Frank Young and her daughter Edith introduced the market to handmade "clever dolls" modeled on members of the Seminole Tribe.[164] They were constructed from local coconut or palmetto palm from Allapattah and Orange Glade and were described as "representations of the Seminoles seen on Miami streets daily. . . . The garments . . . have the full gamut of Seminole color including red, white, black, yellow, orange, green and blue. . . . Soft fiber corresponding to bark is peeled off the trees and rolled into the correct shape . . . sewed together and then dressed."[165] The Youngs came to the market weekly and sold over three hundred dolls, along with homemade miniatures of geese, dogs, cats, and elephants. They also sold the Seminole-based dolls at the 1922 Dade County Fair.[166]

CURB MARKETS AROUND THE STATE

Tallahassee likely had an earlier market in 1918 but saw a reenergized push for a new one in 1921.[167] An appeal to the City Commission in August 1921 stated, "Why can't we have one! Leon County farmers can and will produce the stuff if they get the cooperation of the consumer. Now is the time to talk it, to work for it, and to boost it."[168] These appeals and encouragement were effective, as the market opened early on a Saturday morning in the first week of April 1922.[169]

The June home demonstration report noted that Tallahassee's curb market was "specially appreciated by the farmers of the county and the housewives of the town."[170] One farmer selling mutton found he had "orders in advance for more than he could supply," while "those who had strawberries from the home garden could not meet the demand."[171] Tallahassee's market also created a space for African Americans sellers.[172] The local paper promoted the market, promising, "It will enable you to turn many of the things that go to waste on your farm into cash."[173]

Another early curb market was in Fort Myers. According to one source, discussions to form a market began in the latter half of 1921, after some previous attempts failed to materialize; and home demonstration sources give the starting date as January 7, 1922.[174] The first week, "four wagons of produce" were brought in and sold out after two hours. At one point, eighty people frequented a single wagon. The second week saw fourteen wagons, with new items including bamboo vases. Again, everything sold out in hours, with sellers profiting from palm bead boards, cakes, pies, homemade goods, candies, preserves, and dressed chickens. There were some complaints about high prices, but the market implemented regulated prices.[175] In January and February 1922, market sales totaled $1,790. The highest single-day total for those months was $380, on February 11.[176] One woman reportedly made forty dollars in one morning, all from baked goods. Another home demonstration report noted $385 of items were sold in one day in April 1922.[177] Some of the Fort Myers curb market sellers included P. John Hart, who sold beef and sugar cane; Mrs. M. M. Farely, who sold cottage cheese and radishes, and R. Manuel, B. Miles, Hampton Watkins, and Joe Summers, all African Americans, who offered vegetables, sweet potatoes, greens, beets, and other produce.[178]

Palm Beach's curb market was initially discussed as a way to help with food conservation and the Liberty Kitchen measures from World War I.[179] The first market day at the old courthouse on Clematis Avenue, in 1918, was successful, with a high volume of patrons and the selling out of products.[180] In its first month, sellers raised funds for the Red Cross, selling peppers, mangoes, and pineapples, among other items.[181] However, the market did not reorganize after the 1928 Okeechobee hurricane, and the building was leased to the National Guard.[182] Elsewhere, "in Pasco, Lee, and Pinellas counties," HDA Lucy Belle Settle wrote in 1927, "curb markets [were] established through which club members dispose[d] of their marketable articles."[183] One Pinellas woman found a "ready market" for her canned fried chicken. Each of her one hundred "No. 2 tin cans" contained an entire chicken, which was of "splendid quality."[184] Also, five girls from the Keene club sold a small table of vegetables one morning, making ten dollars.[185] Nassau County's curb market brought in $3,892 from the sale of garden products in 1927.[186] Sanford had a curb market in 1917 and 1918. According to the local paper, "People are well pleased with the innovation and wonder why it was never done before."[187]

"Ten club women" went to Washington County's small Caryville market twice a week, making from six to ten dollars each market day.[188] Meanwhile, the Suwannee County HDA "secured an appropriation of $150 each from Live Oak and the county for a curb market."[189] Escambia County's Council of Home Demonstration Women hosted a Thanksgiving sale that included turkeys, eggs, chickens, cured hams, pies, cakes, jellies, pickles, butter, and flowers. The women resolved to "try these sale days out and eventually work up a regular market which will be open each Saturday."[190] Even the small markets created major benefits. Gadsden County's market offered fruits and vegetables every Saturday, as local women found it better to use their garden's surplus than to grow solely for the market. They economized by sharing table space and generated a profit of $200 monthly. The HDA wrote, "Even this small amount seems large to these women from the farm."[191] Walton County women had a similar experience, selling roasting ears of corn, butter beans, honey, carrots, buttermilk, eggs, butter, figs, pears, and berries, totaling $500 over four months. The HDA recognized this was a "small sum" but observed "the women have said they would not have had this [money]" if not for the market.[192] In Ocala, people were urged to visit their curb market, which had been organized by the City Council, the Rotary Club, the Woman's Club, and the Chamber of Commerce.[193]

From Ocala to Tallahassee, and from Miami to Fort Myers, curb markets were another important aspect of Florida's HDA programming, allowing women to earn extra income. That was particularly true in Miami. However, while curb markets are mentioned less prominently in the home demonstration reports than in Alabama, the markets in both states still served as a primary mechanism for producing revenue and helping rural women improve their lives. Alabama's and Florida's curb markets helped in reinforcing the symbiotic relationship between home demonstration programs, the women involved, and the economic benefits that resulted.

Price list board, Decatur Curb Market, Morgan County, Alabama, 1927. Courtesy of Auburn University Special Collections and Archives.

Mrs. Mitchell Lives 21 Miles from the Curb Market; in 22 Months She Sold $2000 Worth of Produce (1927). Courtesy of Auburn University Special Collections and Archives.

The Vegetables Entertain, a show performed by children at the Dallas County curb market, 1925. Courtesy of Auburn University Special Collections and Archives.

Young Woman Weighing a Cake at a Curb Market in Montgomery, Alabama. Alabama Department of Archives and History.

"Buyers Displaying Their Purchases at the Montgomery Curb Market" (1928). Alabama Cooperative Extension Service Photographs, courtesy of Auburn University Special Collections and Archives.

This photograph's original caption reads, "Mrs. J. E. Spiller and daughter. At Tuscaloosa curb market, the Spillers sold $240 worth of flowers planted on 1/10 acre. Also sold fruit, vegetables, dairy, poultry worth over $2000." April 13, 1928. Alabama Cooperative Extension Service Photographs, courtesy of Auburn University Special Collections and Archives.

City curb market on the corner of First Avenue and First Street, Miami, Florida, July 30, 1923. State Archives of Florida via Florida Memory.

COOPERATIVE EXTENSION WORK
IN
AGRICULTURE AND HOME ECONOMICS,
STATE OF FLORIDA.

JULY – AUGUST

GARDEN SERIES NO. 17.

Dear All-Year Garden Contestants:

Fall in the garden really begins in the summer, as the land that is to be planted in the fall should be kept well cultivated even if the early crop of vegetables has been harvested. This cultivation conserves the needed moisture, prevents weeds from seeding and keeps soil in mellow condition. Or, planting a field-pea crop for soil enrichment, as well as to extend the food supply for the family, is a splendid practice.

ATTENTION! Don't fail to consider your planting tables for the fall vegetables and flowers that you may not go astray. To repeat: Planting for the fall and winter garden begins in August and September. Cabbage and their kin, lettuce, celery, endive, spinach, carrots and beets, all thrive best in cool weather. Therefore, these vegetables should be planted at such a time that most of the growing period will be in the cool months of the year.

WE BROADCAST ON OKRA —THE OLD STAND-BY: No garden deserves to be called a garden without its row of okra. It grows luxuriantly from the southern-most to the northern-most counties of Florida. In fact, it is beloved of the entire South.

Isabelle S. Thursby, Garden Series No. 17, "Helping Florida Feed Herself," 1929–1930. University Archives, Special and Area Studies Collections, George A. Smathers Libraries, University of Florida.

Cultivate the Garden-Sandwiches (date unknown). UF IFS Extension Records, University Archives, Special and Area Studies Collections, George A. Smathers Libraries, University of Florida.

Grove of coconut trees, Key Biscayne, Florida, August 1928. State Archives of Florida via Florida Memory.

Grapefruit trees in Florida, as taken by a "family's Tin Can Tourists vacation trip from Fargo, N.D. to Florida." State Archives of Florida via Florida Memory.

CHAPTER FIVE

HARVESTING TROPICAL FRUITS AND MILK AND USING FLORIDA GROWN

When it came to home demonstration programs, women in Florida had a few advantages over their Alabamian counterparts. These included tourism, agricultural diversity, and the commodification of items seen as unique to Florida. In the 1920s, women capitalized on the ever-growing tourist economy, as marketing connections to Florida boosted sales for distinctive products both in and out of state. Fruits such as guavas and figs, Florida-fashioned dairy products, and vegetables grown year-round formed part of the foundation for how rural women used home demonstration programs for their dinner tables and beyond. Rural women in Florida benefited from the abundance in their own backyards, evidenced by how they sold "Florida" as a concept and took advantage of the state's agricultural diversity.

THE SUNSHINE STATE AND SUNNY PROFITS

Throughout the 1910s and 1920s, as noted in HDA reports, tourism in Florida was big business, attracting everyone from early "tin can tourists" and so-called snowbirds who headed south to avoid cold winters, to sporting communities, artists and writers, and those seeking entertainment in the pre–Walt Disney World decades. As historian Karen Cox wrote, "Florida was considered the most exotic of southern landscapes and often the destination of many northern tourists, especially the wealthy."[1] Florida's name and branding were reliable, especially with food-based tourism and marketing.[2] According to Nicolaas Mink, tourists and travelers to Florida in the 1920s "encountered the sweeping tropical Eden they had both sampled in their kitchens and read about. . . Eating local foods from local landscapes represented the keystone of their traveling experience. . . Visitors relished the guavas, mangos, papayas and coconuts they had first encountered in their local markets and in literature . . . straight from the Florida Garden[which] reified the tourist experience by reinforcing the fact that Florida indeed epitomized a tropical paradise on a plate."[3] This influx of tourists and visitors meant a wider audience of consumers who would help rural women further their income-based objectives.

The importance of promoting Florida foods was still evident in the home demonstration reports of the late 1920s.[4] These reports noted there were demonstrations on food preparation with titles such as "The Use of Fresh Florida Fruits and Vegetables in Salads" and state contests encouraging the consumption of local produce.[5] Although the emphasis was on the nutritional value of a healthy diet based on these foods, these Florida food–based campaigns were not limited to fruits and vegetables. The HDAs also encouraged the act of drinking or selling Florida milk because it was healthy milk from Florida. While there were certainly Alabama farmers and gardeners who grew unusual vegetables and fruits such as chayotes, dasheens, Chinese cabbage, and kohlrabi, these crops are mentioned more frequently in the Florida HDA records than in Alabama's.

FLORIDA GASTRONOMIC GIFTS AND SELLING FLORIDA-CENTRIC

At first, many of the main HDA programs taught women methods for keeping poultry, the science of canning, and techniques for home management. Records show Florida's women became increasingly involved in marmalade, jelly, and preserve clubs. Women "developed and improved upon" recipes that minimized waste: a 1916 bulletin section entitled "Products Developed from Florida Fruits" mentioned "the use of the white portion of the orange peel in making mint, strawberry and other jellies . . . sour orange for marmalades . . . grapefruit peel for candy, and new uses for many other products."[6] However, as in Alabama, Florida women increasingly used home demonstration programming ideas for creating more profitable ventures, for example, adding the Florida name to their own label for marketing and selling. This was still being promoted in 1927, when the U.S. Department of Agriculture publication *Rural Home Life in Florida* proclaimed, "There is a world-wide demand for high grade citrus products, for guava jellies and preserves, for fig products. . . Magnificent opportunities exist for women . . . in establishing and developing self-sustaining industries that would make Florida famous. . . [Many] have already made splendid utilization of these fruits."[7]

Savvy women used an already established name recognition of "Florida" to further their own economic goals. A 1916 Extension bulletin noted, "Many women are becoming skillful in putting up the products from Florida citrus fruits . . . not only to producing a perfect product, but also to putting up these products in attractive packages. A package of 'Sweets from Florida,' has been put on the market by one woman, and her work has proven that there is a demand for these attractive packages."[8] As home demonstration agent Sarah Partridge explained in 1919, "Florida with its great abundance and variety of fruits offers one of the best fields for the development of special fruit products and fancy packs."[9]

One Lake County club girl, Roberta Shepherd, found her calling by making and selling gift boxes filled with her own guava jelly, kumquat spread, and grapefruit preserves. She also put fresh kumquats in her "South Florida gift package," selling them at home, in a local café, and in Minneola and clearing close to twenty dollars.[10] At a DeSoto County demonstration involving citrus products, "six ladies were present and they all thought it a fine idea to organize themselves into a club and do a definite piece of work. They were delighted with the idea of making orange marmalade to sell."[11] In 1925, HDA Flavia Gleason wrote, "Much interest prevails in standardizing 3 fig and pecan products in north Florida and 3 citrus products in the southern part of the state for 'Florida Gift Packages.'"[12] This proved so successful among the women that the following year, Gleason wrote, "a continuation of the Florida Gift Packages will be encouraged," with the gift boxes varying by region: "For North Florida these packages consist of fig preserves, fig conserve, and salted pecans; for South Florida they contain kumquat butter, guava jelly, and grapefruit preserves." Nonedible items were also available. "Native materials such as wire grass, honeysuckle, palmetto, and pine needle, will be used in making baskets and trays for sale," Gleason noted.[13]

Women proudly embraced selling these Florida products, and many of the HDA reports reinforced the consumption and marketing of local foods. A 1927 report from Mary Keown stated that for eastern Floridian counties, "our program of foods and nutrition . . . has as its object intelligently selected foods, Florida grown as far as possible," while the Palm Beach County HDA echoed, "We are stressing Florida products."[14] In Lee County, two women in 1926 standardized candied citrus peel, "finding a sale for all they can prepare," with uniform packaging and containers—one of the women sold $700 worth, while the other "succeeded in marketing successfully the Florida Gift Package."[15] Women in both Lee and Marion Counties viewed gift packages as a sure thing, "because of the quick sale on the market." The only thing holding women back was making enough supply to meet the demand. "We have found it one of the best sellers," an HDA reported. "We could sell three times the number we had."[16] A Miami paper published recipes from the HDA's office for candied orange, lemon drops, and popcorn balls, encouraging the reader to, "as far as possible, use Florida products, products made at home. They are just as good and will be found cheaper in the long run."[17]

Some women took the initiative to create their own Florida-themed gifts. Tallahassee resident Ruby Geddie Richardson chose local, north Florida produce, including watermelon rind, grapefruit peel, kumquats, pineapples, and pecans, for her own "Florida Goodies." She sold her products for $1.25 a pound at local markets and gift shops, as well as at the "State and South Florida Fairs." She said that marketing at these locations helped "supply a great stream of tourists every year with gifts to 'send back home.'" "My little package of 'Florida Goodies,'" she added, "has helped to fill the bill." Richardson stated, "From November 15 to January 1st, my receipts were $250 [and in] December 1925, I made sales amounting to $150." She also made sure her packaging was Florida made, stating, "Even containers may be produced from Florida material," by which she meant using wire grass or longleaf pine needles for the baskets. She attributed her success to the "standardization of my products and of my packages." She believed "this land of fruit" held ripe possibilities for women: "With the figs and nuts of North Florida and the guavas, oranges, grapefruit and kumquats of South Florida . . . [as well as] the ready market Florida women have for gift packages, there is a good business for those willing to standardize. Business management is necessary. Supplies must be purchased with good judgment; skill and patience in preparation of products are required."[18]

Florida as its own brand lent itself well to the marketing strategies of Richardson and other enterprising women like her. As food historian Joy Sheffield Harris observes, "Florida products have long been recognized by their geographical region: Key limes, Zellwood corn, Ruskin tomatoes, Plant City strawberries, and Indian River citrus. Tupelo honey from northern Florida and mangrove honey from Central Florida."[19] Floridian women were taking advantage of the state's natural food sufficiency for currency and using the Sunshine State's name as it grew into a widely recognized marketing option.

BROWSING AT FAIRS AND SHOPS

Regional, state, national, and even international fairs and exhibitions became important spaces where rural Florida women could market the products they created out of Florida's natural agricultural resources. The two 1920 state fairs, for example, featured booths highlighting milk and preserved fruits and vegetables. The booth with fruits and vegetables reportedly had a space of "40 feet, eight rows high" that could hold "two rows of quarts, two rows twelve ounce and two rows pints, one row of jelly glasses, and one row of bottles."[20] The fair also featured an exhibit about muscadine grapes, because at the time in the HDA programming, girls and women from north Florida counties had muscadine grape demonstrations, which produced juice, vinegar, jams, and butter. This fair's exhibit included "nursery cuttings, plants, small models of plantings and methods of cultivation; a pyramid made of muscadine grape products, shown under a white pergola entwined with wild grape vines."[21]

At the 1921 state fair in Jacksonville, women and girls created "most attractive gifts" of pine needle, wiregrass, and palmetto baskets—using skills they had learned from HDA programming—that were filled with "guava paste, orange marmalade, grapefruit jelly, grapefruit marmalade, sunshine marmalade, Roselle jelly, fig preserves, pear preserves, apple jelly, [and] crystallized fruit."[22] The 1922 Pinellas County Fair highlighted "beautiful crystallized fruits and many jars of fruit preserves" with another display of "sea foods, fish, oysters, clams, crabs, etc. . . . prepared for the same purpose." Guavas—in which "the county abounds"—were also exhibited.[23] Visitors and buyers did not have to worry about missing out on buying a product at one of the fairs or whether they would have the option of buying an item again: "Persons desiring to purchase products on display were given the name and address of the producer [so] that direct sales may be made."[24]

Soon the marketing of Florida-made products expanded to the national and even international stage. In 1924, items were exhibited at the All-Florida Exposition in New York City, the All-Florida Show at Madison Square Garden, and the Canadian National Exhibition at Toronto.[25] In October 1925, Beulah Felts of Palma Sola represented Florida as the "champion in home demonstration work" at the Boys and Girls Club Congress in Chicago, where—with help from home demonstration agents Lucy Belle Settle and Isabelle Thursby—she was to present "Florida dainties made a la Manatee [County] style." These "dainties" consisted of kumquat preserves, candied grapefruit peel, marmalade, and jelly. The *Bradenton Herald* hoped that by showing off some of the "appetizing products of Florida" Felts would "tell the world at Chicago just what good things this country is 'starving' on down here in this benighted land to which so many northern newspapers are pointing scornful fingers of editorial diatribes."[26]

Promoting the state's products was also popular at home. Polk County's HDA reported the "Federation Finance Committee [was] making a great hit with sale of Sundaes at Orange Festival—the secret to the success was likely because the sundaes were made with 'Polk County tangerines and grapefruit sauce.'"[27] The 1925 Farmer's Week event at the University of Florida featured an "All Florida Soda Fountain," supervised by Isabelle Thursby and other Extension specialists. The Fountain was to be a delicious way to combat the concern that the state's homes, hotels, and other eating establishments "were failing to make use of Florida products to the extent which the character, quality, and supply of these products merit." Since this omission might have been because of "[a] lack of acquaintance with the local products and of ways to prepare them," Thursby, along with her colleagues, realized a demonstration was in order.[28]

The All-Florida Soda Fountain opened the Friday during Farmer's Week, with frozen treats, drinks, and baked goods made from a variety of Florida-grown products and Florida milk and dairy goods. The menu included avocado and guava ice cream, grape sherbet, rose julep, elderberry juice–based "Duval foundation," "Pride of Pinellas" punch, orange smash, "Palm Beach coconut dulcie," the roselle juice–based "Volusia Venture," sun-gold coconut crush, "Perry Peach panada," mango malted milk mix-up, mint sparkler, lime cooler, "Gleason's Cheer-up" (which was a grapefruit sherbet), nut bread, and sweet potato bread. Another demonstrator showcased the "Pride of Pasco," a guava ice cream. The items were represented by the "farm woman," or the HDA from a particular county, who explained how the desserts were made and standardized.[29]

While the All-Florida Soda Fountain was a one-week event, rural women needed long-term or permanent spaces where they could market and sell their products. Home demonstration exchanges or shops helped to fill this role. DeLand, in Volusia County, had two cooperative markets in 1925—one for eggs and one for other products, such as cooked food, fruits, plants, and canned items. The second market, open only two days a week, garnered $3,869.23 in a year's time. One of the sellers, Jennie B. Cady, saw profits of $1,070.36 over the course of a year, which helped her take "a vacation trip of two months."[30] Adah Stanley made $29.97 from her garden, adding to $34 in profits she earned from selling milk. In 1927, she reported making $237.96 from selling dairy and meat from her cow.[31] In 1927, Dade County's Home Demonstration Shop had 182 members, who sold baskets made from pine needle, coconut fiber, and wiregrass; jellies and preserves; small craft items; and cooked food—all for a profit of $2,642.42.[32]

By 1929, per one annual report, 533 women in five counties sold through home demonstration shops (Volusia, Dade, Palm Beach), curb markets (Volusia, Nassau, Dade), and the poultry sales market (Alachua), with combined total profits of $13,122.54. In Dade County, Lena Ritter Link earned $572.52 from poultry and garden products and crystallized fruit. Florence Gazzam Kosel gained $161 from small fruit plantings and crystallized fruit. She and her husband, George, owned and developed "Jungle Grove," which had "rare tropical fruit trees," and grew strawberries, mangoes, citrus, and avocados in Redland.[33]

Women from twenty communities sold through the Hillsborough County Home Demonstration Shoppe. At a December 1924 meeting, the proceeds representing three of those communities were noted: "$38.00 at Sulphur Springs, $13.50 at Limona and $26.50 at Jackson-Heights, making a total of $78.00."[34] Finding markets to sell products became commonplace. In 1928, 627 Florida women used the exchanges, home demonstration shops, and curb markets to make $22,394.27 of extra money for their wallets.[35] In Palm Beach, the shop had members of the Home Demonstration Club make and sell Christmas gifts, grapefruit products, guava and orange jellies and marmalades, clothes, baskets made from native materials, and other items. The shop also gave customers the option of having clothes repaired or custom made.[36]

CRYSTALLIZING FRUITS

When it came to preserving and selling Florida's fruits, the women found ways to make the fruits appealing. One of the methods they used for aesthetic and edible purposes was crystallization. Ida Smith became "skillful" in preserving and crystallizing fruits such as guavas, mangoes, and citrus, as these and "other interesting tropical and subtropical fruits were abundant" around her Manatee County home. She deposited the $184 she made in profit—$90.85 of it from crystallized grapefruit peel—in her "Go-To-College Fund."[37] Pinellas County's Edna McMullen Kirkpatrick sold twenty-five to fifty dollars' worth of guava jelly and crystallized grapefruit peel; when she needed tax money, she also sold kumquat preserves, orange marmalade, and guava jelly. During the holiday season, she sold small gift packages for one dollar each, consisting of a square Christmas box filled with two guava jellies, two roselle jellies, and one kumquat jelly. She made $150 over the year, allowing her to pay off her taxes.[38] In Volusia County, Mrs. John Martin sold eighty-five whole crystallized grapefruits for $1.25 each, while another woman supplied a local candy store with crystallized fruit as part of a yearlong contract. Meanwhile, in Orange County, crystallized fruit brought in $1,200.[39]

One issue rural women faced was finding space to take advantage of these marketing opportunities. Many Pinellas County women used the former emergency home demonstration kitchen in City Park. In 1926, women sold six hundred pounds of crystallized kumquats, oranges, grapefruits, Ponderosa lemons, and pink shaddock to those visiting the park. They were especially successful "on the days when tournaments [were] held on bowling lawns and hundreds of visitors throng[ed] the park." Over the course of a week, Jessie Lorenia McEwen Shaw sold forty-five pounds of crystallized fruit for one dollar per pound "each day" for one week. It is no wonder that in the 1930 U.S. Census, she described herself as a "manufacturer" working on citrus products.[40]

In Homestead, Mrs. H. C. Camp demonstrated crystallizing whole grapefruit, which women made to sell at Christmas. Camp herself sold seventy-five of the crystallized treats over a two-month period.[41] In Dade County, Cena

Stromstadt Stewart started selling tropical candies and fruit punch, coconuts, and other citrus from her front porch. She earned enough profit to hire employees and build a shop, with a space for making candies, a short distance from her home. When Stewart contributed 125 boxes of tropical candy to sell at the home demonstration booth at the Fruit Festival in Homestead, they quickly sold out. It was not an uncommon sight to see women selling from roadside stands on their own property—some HDAs encouraged the practice.[42]

Women in Dade County found the Fruit Festival and similar events highly useful for selling their tropical fruit creations. When the HDA exhibited 312 containers of canned fruit in a large, fifteen-by-ninety-foot booth, one man bought "the entire exhibit [for $119] . . . except 36 containers which were asked to be retained"—likely because the exhibitors wished to keep some of their work for display. Tropical fruit juices and ice cream brought in $150 for the girls selling them, while a Mrs. Calkins of Homestead "could never get through expressing her appreciation of the check which she received from her exhibits sold." Calkins used the fifty dollars she earned to "t[ake] care of a debt that was due at that time, which she did not know how they were going to meet."[43]

Of course, not all rural women and girls used crystallized fruit for extra money. Etta Spear Huff Weed of Putnam County took the skills she learned in making grapefruit juice and used them to make sour orange juice. She created a "little cold drink stand" on the local highway and found it generated extra cash and helped her "dispose" of the fruit. Delaware Short Kraemer of Lake County canned orange juice, even though "most people consider[ed] it unnecessary."[44] Winnifred Cannon so impressed Estelle Bozeman, the conservation specialist, with her marmalade that Bozeman found "good markets" for the products, which enabled Cannon to build a "special kitchen" to expand her business.[45] Hazel Tipping used her grandfather's citrus groves as her own store: "When tourists were flocking to Mandarin for citrus fruits, Hazel sold . . . enough citrus marmalades, guava jelly and candy to buy a winter coat and hat."[46]

Among the club girls making a profit was Vera Alderman. She lived at a "station place," next to an "old store building," and one summer she "took some of her money and started a cool drink stand." According to a home demonstration report, "most every day someone would call for bread and a small line of groceries." So Alderman used the profits from her drink stand to purchase a larger stock of groceries to sell to her customers. She soon rented the store building for her small market. "All from one little idea, just something to do to pass her summer months away," noted the HDA. "She sews when not busy, and is banking $50.00 per week (an average)." Alderman also planted tomatoes on her tenth acre, which earned her $161, as well as beans, which "brought in a good price."[47]

DIVIDING FLORIDA IN TWO

As in Alabama, agriculture has historically been a driving force in Florida's economy. The state developed a reputation for growing particular crops, including citrus fruits, tomatoes, strawberries, watermelons, blueberries, guavas, avocados, herbs, and greenhouse vegetables. The state was traditionally a major contributor in the cattle and seafood industries, as well as producing the agronomic crops of peanuts, cotton, tobacco, and sugarcane. For rural women, agriculture was, in some capacity, usually part of their everyday lives.[48]

And while "Florida" itself was a selling point, regional diversity also mattered. In HDA reports, Florida was divided into districts, with Gainesville roughly serving as the line between the Panhandle and northern Florida and central and southern Florida. Having different growing seasons for crops and produce became an advantage for rural women to capitalize on certain foods. In a 1914 report, the head home demonstration agent said that "Florida products are so varied and excellent" because of the agricultural differences between the two regions: "In the South, the splendid Citrus fruits, the guavas . . . Jamaica Sorrell which makes a beautiful jelly . . . mangoes, sapodilla, pineapples and fruits and vegetables of every description, give the girls a chance to make a splendid variety of products. The great variety makes it difficult to specialize on any one product. In the Northern part . . . the figs, the watermelon, and the mayhaw are the three fruits in the greatest abundance."[49] With regard to the Panhandle and northern Florida, one discussion claimed the region was "ideally suited for general farming, dairying . . . poultry, lamb, and sheep" and the climate conducive for "blueberry, satsuma oranges, prunes, grapes, pecans and figs."[50] The area also grew specialty crops, such as the datil peppers of St. Augustine and St. John's County, which abound to this day.[51]

In *Rural Home Life in Florida*, HDA Virginia Moore paid tribute to northern Florida's agriculture history and included elements of an Old South and Lost Cause romanticization minimizing the role of slavery in that agricultural legacy:

> This was a wonderfully developed agricultural section, rich in rural life with its stately mansions, and beautiful grounds and well-tilled plantations. Slaves were plentiful, the land yielded bountifully and the country homes were of the ideal

Southern type. North Florida suffered with the whole South in the Civil War and the Reconstruction . . . the man power killed off in the war and the slaves freed, the proud and poverty-stricken landowners sold off to rich men who still maintain great hunting preserves and give little thought to agricultural development. . . . Large tracts of land have been sold, have had the timber sold off, the land has been cleared, and the small farmers, the "native born," are gradually getting a new foothold and making the "best better" with their little farms.[52]

In another report, she continued this look back into Florida's past, specifically the state's northern half, while omitting its African American residents: "There are rich agricultural possibilities and many of these Anglo-Saxon settlers have tilled the soil and settled back in the valleys and on the hill sides in this oldest yet newest part of Florida. Their homes are often crude, and [reflect] every characteristic of the far-famed mountaineers of this same 'stock' who settled in the mountains of Virginia, Kentucky, Tennessee, and the Carolinas."[53]

The *Rural Home Life in Florida* bulletin listed recommendations for Florida gardens "north of Ocala," which included different leafy greens, cabbage, watermelon, okra, eggplant, "cowpeas," cantaloupe, carrots, spinach, squash, pecans, peaches, pears, figs, and grapes.[54] Rural women's marketing output reflected many of these suggested gardening items, plus experimentation with "new vegetables." For example, in Calhoun County, women grew chayote, brussels sprouts, Chinese cabbage, parsley, and dasheen, a cousin variety of the starchy taro root. Kohlrabi, roselle, endive, and parsnip also made appearances in Panhandle and northern Florida gardens.[55] Women and girls in Volusia County grew and marketed grape vines, persimmons, orange trees, pineapples, guavas, loquats, chestnuts, English walnuts, and Venezuela nuts.[56] One home demonstration agent in St. Johns County demonstrated different uses of grapes for commercial purposes, while in Citrus County, grapes were also grown, along with Marvel blackberries, pears, strawberries, and figs.[57] Roselle—sometimes called "jelly okra," "lemon bush," "Florida cranberry," or "Jamaican Sorrel"—has a family tree relation to okra and was grown throughout the state. To create interest among sellers and buyers, the jam and jelly were described as "unsurpassed in flavor and of a marvelous color."[58] Soon, these plants became typical in average Florida gardens, depending on the area.

Of course, the gardens grew more than food—thanks to enterprising women who learned from home demonstration programming, they also grew money. Margaret Nicholson of Nassau County described her five acres, which had melons, grapes, bananas, English peas, horseradish, butter beans, corn, parsnips, (sugar)cane, celery, onions, Swiss chard, chayotes, pimento peppers, and more. She sold onions in Hilliard, which brought her $200, but because of limited market opportunities, she made the hour-long trip to Fernandina Beach fourteen times in four months, earning $300 in sales.[59] Leon County's Estrella Smith found a market "at her own door" for one thousand cans of meat, vegetables, and fruit and two hundred quarts of pickles, jellies, preserves, peanut butter, sauerkraut, and fresh items.[60] Two women in Taylor County planted large vegetable gardens so they could do "canning on a large scale" and then sell to the local sawmill stores.[61] Suwanee County's Bessie Sperning found a "ready market" for the cans of peas, butter beans, string beans, and tomatoes she and her family had put up.[62] Pearl Tyner sold seventeen dollars' worth of canned eggplant and peppers in Okaloosa County.[63] In Lake County, one home had thirty acres of Kieffer pears, using its "over supply" to can for market, while a Taylor County club girl earned seventy-five dollars from her first crop of onions.[64] Marion County's Fannie Pilkenton won a trip to the "State Short Course" at the Florida State College for Women after sending the "ten best" of what she had canned, jarred, preserved, and pickled to the local Marion County Fair. She also earned $100 from canning and gardening.[65]

The HDAs conducted demonstrations on how to work with squab, rabbits, seafood, and fowl, as well as techniques for developing products from citrus and other fruits, nuts, berries, peppers, beets, tomatoes, and beans. Women and girls learned new approaches to making vinegar, bread, ketchup, pickles, relishes, syrups, pastes, and cheese and other dairy products, as well as crystallizing and candying fruit and making macédoine, a mixture of chopped-up vegetables, fruits, or both, served raw or cooked. HDA plans included information on soap, flowers, various textiles, baskets, rugs, and articles of clothing. Rural women could market and sell items directly at curb markets, through "parcel post or express" under the 4-H brand or via other organizations, or by other means.[66] While rural women did sell to customers out of state, it was important to develop and nurture local markets.

In Suwannee County, four women whom the HDA called the "Mesdames"—Ettie Hatcher Weaver, Stella Williams, Teresa Madden Sperring, and Susie Lee Henry Childress—"sold seven dozen jars of preserved figs, 1 dozen quarts of cucumber pickles, 100 cans of tomatoes, 50 cans of peas, 18 cans of California beans and 30 cans of lima beans" over the course of a month. Individually, Williams sold thirty-two dollars' worth of preserved figs, while Sperring made eighty-four dollars from her canned acre peas and baby lima beans.[67] Meanwhile, one Holmes County resident shipped fifteen barrels of collards at four dollars a barrel.⁶⁸ Club girls sold $64.80 of chickens and eggs, along with canned products and "hand work," through a "Saturday Club Market" in Gadsden County. In Taylor County, Mrs. J. D. Johnson (Miriam Victoria Johnson) sold sour orange, which supplemented the ten to fifteen dollars a week she made from vegetables and canned goods.⁶⁹ Meanwhile, Hattie Fletcher of the Juniper community "successfully canned a 200 pound beef," reported the state home demonstration agent Flavia Gleason, adding, "[She] had an order for this and was glad to fill it. . . . Hattie also sold two dozen number 3 tins of soup mixture made from vegetables she had grown in her club garden."⁷⁰

At one time chayote squash was a regular staple in the home demonstration programs.⁷¹ In the 1920s, HDAs promoted chayotes for consumption and for their aesthetic appeal as an ornamental vine. Margaret Nicholson, who grew chayote, said, "We have a fine vine loaded with fruit and think it is going to be a great success." Chayote was versatile, which meant it could be sold cooked, fried, or raw, with immature chayote being used for making pickles. Encouraging the consumption and selling of chayotes became a regular feature of the HDA reports. For example, a contest was held to persuade women and girls to invest in the plant "because of its interesting growth as well as the financial reward that comes from its fruit."⁷² The contest became a specialized part of the 1927 plan of work, in hopes the chayote would become "a valuable supplementary food to the Florida table and make regular growers and users."⁷³ The HDA calculated chayotes sold in Volusia County for twelve to fifteen cents a pound. According to a 1929 home demonstration report, Holmes County alone boasted 155 vines in 1929. One particularly productive vine had six hundred chayotes "and was still making fruit," with the women involved selling "from this one vine this fall $10.50."⁷⁴ HDA Ruby McDavid expected the chayotes to continue to grow through the winter, with the hope that women could sell one thousand more of them, for ten or even twenty-five cents each.⁷⁵

For those living in the Panhandle, north Florida, and part of central Florida, agricultural conditions made it possible to grow a large selection of marketable products. While there was overlap in fruits and vegetables raised in north and south Florida, the northern landscape then, as today, differed from the state's southern half. South Florida had longer growing seasons, the ability to produce winter fruits and vegetables, and favorable conditions for growing tropical produce for consumption and for selling.⁷⁶

"The fruits of Florida," according to Isabelle Thursby, the marketing agent for the state, "especially those of south Florida . . . present a fascinating subject for the preserve maker." She explained that while "canned mangoes and guavas" were "not yet sufficiently appreciated," they were "easily the equivalent of canned peaches." At the same time, she argued, "tamarind butter is equal to any butter in the same class from northern fruits and superior to many." Other South Florida favorites Thursby highlighted were "Surinam jelly or preserves" ("so unique in flavor and so attractive in color") and "preserved ginger" ("a delicacy of unusual merit," which despite "grow[ing] well in the state" was "still unknown in Florida").[77]

In central and south Florida, the HDA reports mentioned quite a few crops that were considered advantageous to cultivate, including citrus such as oranges, grapefruits, and mangoes and Florida familiars such as coconut, pineapples, guavas, strawberries, papayas, and bananas. To a lesser extent, HDAs promoted growing Surinam cherries, star apples, and Monstera deliciosa. They also touted fruits that originated in specific areas, such as the Florida Marvel blackberry and the Ormond persimmon (Daytona) and the Lue Gim Gong orange, the Norris seedless orange, and the Enterprise seedless orange (Volusia).[78]

In central Florida, residents took advantage of the climate to grow distinctive items for home use and for sale, including French artichokes, asparagus, horseradish, and rhubarb, along with mulberries, grapes, pears, and avocadoes. In "extreme South Florida," HDA recommendations were sapodilla, rose apple, sugar apple (sweetsop), tamarind, coco plum, and carambola (star fruit).[79] A 1924 advertisement touting Orange County's "unusual opportunities" for agricultural production featured bananas, ferns, dairying, grapes, and poultry.[80] To encourage rural women to diversify their gardens, and to use the resulting products to their economic benefit, HDAs distributed brochures with titles such as *The Fig: A Prize Package of Food and Medicine* and *The Succulent Peach*.[81]

In 1921, conservation specialist Estelle Bozeman went to south Florida and demonstrated how to crystallize—and jelly—citrus, pineapple, and other fruit common to the area. She helped to convince women who were reluctant to participate in these demonstrations by promoting the financial opportunities from these preservation techniques: "Wherever I have found a woman who has been selling her products, I have tried to encourage others by having her tell of her project." Bozeman had already found women selling guava jelly and citrus marmalades, for which they "have a ready sale." Many women were eager to sell with the support of the Home Industry Project, which was designed to promote south Florida fruit. "It is gratifying to hear reports of the women as to the amount of money made last season and what they are planning to do during the coming season," Bozeman reflected. "One woman reports $200 worth of products sold during the past season. . . . She sold twenty whole crystallized orange cases filled with small crystallized fruits to one customer."[82]

Around the central and southern areas of the state, women made economic strides due to their ingenuity and initiative. In 1925, the Woman's Club of Arcadia made $105 at its bazaar, and the local HDA also made and sold thirty dozen doughnuts.[83] Since pineapples were one of the major cash crops for Palm Beach and St. Lucie Counties, women in West Palm Beach made pineapple and mango products, which went along with their "pickled pears and peaches in fancy packs, guava jelly and butter."[84] In Broward County in 1929, a celebration of the one-year anniversary of home demonstration work included a "special feature"—a display of "work done by the women during that time." Mary Keown, one of the district agents, reported that "more than five hundred articles made by the women and girls were displayed," which included a birthday cake, "made from county grown produce, iced with the snowy fresh coconut and decorated with golden preserved papaya." According to Keown, a "thousand visitors" saw the exhibit.[85]

THE TASTY ECONOMIC BENEFITS OF GUAVAS AND OTHER "EXOTIC" FRUITS

Guavas were a staple of the southern Florida landscape in the early part of the twentieth century and, in the 1920s, a frequent component of HDA programs, evolving as a fruit for home and marketing. The association between Florida and guavas, called "Florida's substitute peach," continues today.[86] Although guavas were commonly grown in southern Florida, one HDA declared them "a fruit that has suffered so much waste." In 1927, there was a lament that guavas were being overlooked, not just by "the northern tourist" but by Floridians themselves, who failed to see "any good in a guava."[87] HDAs and rural women sought to change that perception by creating events such as "Guava Week," which promoted guava products and culinary experiments such as ice cream, vinegar, ketchup, chutney, paste, butter, juice, jelly, mincemeat, and chili sauce. DeSoto County's HDA claimed 1925 was "a splendid guava year."[88] Eustis also celebrated a guava week, with a designated "Guava Day," when a local drug store displayed an exhibit of canned guava, and local home demonstration club women provided ten gallons of guava ice cream and other guava dishes.[89]

Guavas were profitable and women responded. When a farmer lost his trucking crop, his wife sold one hundred gallons of vinegar made from "drop guavas" at eighty cents a gallon to make up for the loss.[90] Some women sold guava products at local fairs, while others shipped homemade guava jelly to businesses, as Cora Hooten Spears of Orange County did when she sent her jelly to the Mason Hotel in Jacksonville.[91] In Lee County, one woman sold standardized guava paste and guava jelly, made from her own tree. She designed her own packaging for the guava paste she sold at the curb market and supplied hotels with the same guava products. She recreated this marketing success with roselle sauce.[92]

In selling, consuming, or promoting items made from foods that many considered unusual or unfamiliar, rural women capitalized on an American cultural fascination in the late nineteenth century and early twentieth century with the "exotic." This contributed to what historian Kristin Hoganson calls "the internationalization of the American culinary repertoire—that is, the internationalization of both recipes and ingredients." Hoganson argues that during this time, "middle-class kitchens had become places of global encounters."[93] The role of women in this process can be examined by surveying their purchases of what they believed to be "exotic" foods, as well as the popularity of gastronomic-centered travel writings.

Mangoes and avocados were noted for their tropical nature, viewed as "exquisite" (the mango) and "palatable (when one learns to like it)" and "nourishing" (the avocado).[94] The avocado, "esteemed as the choicest of delicacies," brought in "large sums at the great hotels." It was seen as a "staple" for a tropical diet, much like the "Irish potatoes in the North and cornbread in the South."[95] Mangoes were considered part of an "exotic" narrative, likely for their inclusion in Indian cooking, and "many of the varieties are most gorgeous in appearance and have a wonderful aroma."[96] "Green mango sauce and mango chutney have proved more popular than other products," asserted a Lee County report. "The Bay Shore girls and the Iona women have packed standard products for sale."[97] An early May 1929 article mentioned that the Fort Myers curb market sold "the first ripe mangoes of the season" at thirty cents per dozen.[98]

Papayas and persimmons—specifically Japanese persimmons—along with other "exotic" foods were viewed as important to keep in the garden, store in the pantry, bring to the dinner table, and add to the sale table.[99] One Miami newspaper reported in 1918 that a woman named Mrs. Wilcox, "who ha[d] lived in tropical countries and learned how to use the fruits to the best advantage, said she will have on sale . . . sauces made from green papayas and green mangoes."[100] These foods were in high demand, viewed as healthy for both one's constitution and one's wallet. Another article recounted a miniperformance, called "The Spirit of Papayas," where a costumed woman with papaya blossoms had her train carried by "semi-nude bearers from Ceylon and Hawaii," along with an "entourage" of dancing girls "all clad in gorgeous costume" representing Cuba, South America, Mexico, and Central America.[101]

DAIRYING À LA FLORIDA

While orange juice is a Florida beverage icon, milk and dairy products steadily grew as an important aspect of the Floridian diet in the 1920s. The production of milk, buttermilk, cream, cheese, and other products was emphasized in HDA programs, which was not surprising, as Florida's cattle industry was (and still is) a considerable contributor to the state's economy.[102] In 1922, an Extension report noted that because Florida was "a winter tourist state," it consumed "a much larger supply of whole milk between November and May than during the remaining months." Thus "prices paid for whole milk in tourist centers have been high, which stimulated production near these centers to supply this winter trade."[103] Dairy programs encouraged the ownership of "good home dairy cows" and advocated selling surplus for income. Florida-produced milk was promoted for health reasons—"Milk for Health" became a statewide slogan in homes and in schools, part of larger discussions concerning school lunches and national and local narratives about healthy diets and making smart choices when choosing what to drink.[104]

Women decided to benefit from this economically promising industry by creating their own businesses to take part in producing and promoting good, clean Florida milk, while also standardizing milk and dairy products. For example, Marion County's Annie McDonald Reynolds McCormick owned and operated a small dairy farm, selling milk and other dairy products for extra income.[105] An Orange County club woman in 1925 reported the "selling of milk and butter to twenty regular customers from six cows."[106] One Jefferson County girl made $173.40 from the dairy output of her cow.[107] In Davie, three women kept dairy records about the output of five cows. "Each family . . . has [sold] butter and cheese. . . . The results stimulated the interest of others."[108] Hillsborough County's Tillie Smith Snyder owned two cows in February 1926 and sold 311 quarts of whole milk for approximately $90, twelve pounds of cottage cheese, and fifteen and a half quarts of cream. A month later, she added another cow and won contests for her butter and cheese.[109] Pasco County cows produced more than women needed, so they sold extra milk, butter, and cottage cheese, with reported values of $5,514.23, $1,425.85, and $150.25.[110] In Osceola

County, one woman earned enough money from her first cow (and garden) to "screen and paint her house."[111]

Rural women tapped into home dairying for health and monetary reasons. As with other products, Florida milk and dairy products grew into a source of extra income, going beyond being part of a family's refrigerator. "Many home demonstration club members," *Rural Home Life in Florida* pointed out, "having made a success of home dairying, have entered commercial dairying with good profit."[112] Florida's dairy industry, as well as the cattle industry, was a crucial component of the Floridian economy and the economy of rural women. In other words, women saw profits from marketing their own cream of the crop.[113]

CONCLUSION

Florida's natural agricultural diversity, and the varied landscape of marketable products and gastronomic gifts it offered, allowed women and girls to become engaged as producers and merchants. Rural women capitalized on the Florida name and climate, creating businesses and utilizing their learned skills from home demonstration to create new ventures.[114] Northern Florida women sold many typical southern food staples, while expanding their use of new fruits and vegetables grown in their gardens. Women in southern Florida were able to use a more tropical climate to work with year-round fruits and vegetables, creating new ideas and expanding on what could be associated with the Florida name. Rural women saw what could be achieved with HDA involvement, personal motivation, Florida's agricultural climate, and the Florida name. Their home state helped them realize achievable fiscal gains, allowing Florida women to make their own cash-based sunshine.

CONCLUSION

REAPING THE PROFITS FROM GARDENS TO GRAPEFRUIT

Included in a 1930 report on home demonstration was a letter from Harriet Leonard, a student at Athens College (now Athens State University) in Limestone County, who wrote of her success at the Athens curb market. "Early in the summer of 1927, I left my home with two boxes. In these two boxes were cakes. . . . About nine o'clock I left with two crisp new dollar bills and a heart swelling with pride. I had some money all my own!" Leonard went back to the curb market the next summer and sold over $100 worth of cakes in over two months, which helped her pay for tuition, books, and supplies. By 1930, she was baking and selling her cakes for the Athens College YWCA store. Leonard ended her letter by stating, "I think every girl should try to earn her own money. I feel so much more independent when I have my own bank account and I am grateful for the opportunity the Athens Curb Market has given me."[1]

Harriett Leonard's letter helps encapsulate how, beginning in 1914, rural women of Alabama and Florida used home demonstration programming to create financial lifelines by selling and marketing homemade products. At the time, especially in parts of the South, homes did not have air-conditioning, and the hot, humid days were unrelenting. In addition to the other work and responsibilities they undertook throughout the day, from completing household chores to raising and caring for children, or, for farmer's wives, helping with crop or field work, women then spent time in a hot kitchen preparing the quantities needed to sell. Whether they were making jams, cakes, or even fried chicken in a can—or were painstakingly creating baskets, hats, or other handiwork—the labor was involved and time consuming. Rural women determinedly took on the work required hoping their efforts would be rewarded. These rural women saw the opportunity home demonstration programming provided and used it to their fiscal benefit.

After 1930, earning extra income for oneself or family became a matter of even greater necessity. In her 1933 book *It's Up to the Women*, Eleanor Roosevelt wrote about the hardships country women faced in their daily lives: "In the first place the farm woman has very little opportunity for earning any money which she can call exclusively her own and this makes her entirely dependent on her husband."[2] Although Roosevelt was referring to women during the Great Depression, her words also speak to the wider, enduring significance of all women who create structures for making or maintaining personal economic choices. The rural white and African American women of Alabama and Florida implemented their methods of marketing and selling, facilitated by home demonstration programming, enabling them to maintain a sustainable financial infrastructure. As historian Lu Ann Jones writes, "Farm women were crucial players in their household and local economies; perhaps unbeknownst to them, their goods entered regional and national economic channels."[3]

Usually, this included creating, crafting, and cooking for monetary gains. As Rebecca Sharpless writes, "In raising food for the market, women provided nutrition both for their families and their customers, as well as cash to use at home." The use of food to earn extra income was unsurprising. Food is a symbolic and physical gesture of care, of concern, and, for these purposes, of cash. To quote Lu Ann Jones again, "Just as food has shaped Southern cultures, so has it played a central role in the female economy of the South.... Food could satisfy hunger *and* generate income."[4] The process of preparing, marketing, and selling food-based products can be viewed as an act of independent choice, which intersected with gender expectations, as well.

Curb markets opened new financial possibilities to women, enhancing their growth as producers and consumers. Elizabeth S. D. Engelhardt's observation about curb markets in North Carolina can apply to Alabama and Florida too: "Most of the buyers (who made purchases and ran the kitchens of boarding houses and homes in town) and most of the sellers (who did the daily work of staffing the curb markets tables every time it convened) were women, and the curb market could not exist without them."[5] Sometimes, a curb market stall led to women creating their own small businesses or cottage industries. Curb markets were also a physical representation of reliable money, as one could sell a variety of products and feel confident they would have buyers for either their edible or nonedible items.

State-specific branding is not a new idea but is an enduring one. Alabama's current "Sweet Grown Alabama" program brings together agritourism, marketing, and producers and consumers.[6] "Florida" is a modifier commonplace in food-based advertising and grocery stores.[7] For many, thinking of the state brings to mind, besides beaches, the images of orange groves, grapefruit trees, and key lime pies.[8] Throughout the twentieth century, the word "citrus" became associated with various sports teams and events. For example, the "Grapefruit League," a term with mixed origins coined in the 1910s, describes the Major League baseball teams that conduct their spring training in Florida.[9] The Orange Bowl, started in 1935 and played in Miami, remains a firm presence in the college football postseason. The Citrus Bowl, formerly known as the Tangerine Bowl, began in 1947 and is held in Orlando, while the Orange Blossom Classic, started in 1933, is played with teams from historically Black colleges and universities (HBCUs), with frequent appearances by Florida A&M.[10]

The Florida Orange Bird is a character created by the Walt Disney Company in the 1970s for the Florida Citrus Commission. Orange Bird, as he is most commonly referred to, was used in advertising in exchange for the Citrus Commission's sponsorship of Walt Disney World's Tropical Serenade attraction—later the Enchanted Tiki Room—and its quick-service food location the Sunshine Tree Terrace. Although the business relationship between Disney and the commission ended in the 1980s, Orange Bird is still used at the park and is viewed as a fan favorite among the theme park's visitors. Meanwhile, at the Disney Springs entertainment district, the Flavors of Florida is an annual food event, highlighting Florida-inspired dishes and drinks.[11] Using Florida food in events such as these hark back to women like Ruby Geddie Richardson, whose "Florida Goodies" gift packages supplemented her income a century ago (see chapter 5).

While the home demonstration records from Alabama and Florida reveal the stories of rural women whose creativity and initiative allowed them to turn home demonstration programming knowledge into much-needed cash, the legal and social reality of life at the time meant that not everyone benefited equally. The permeation of racism, discrimination, and systematic disenfranchisement that African American women faced on an everyday basis did not disappear with their involvement in home demonstration. African American HDAs and rural women navigated a difficult and sometimes dangerous environment, not just in Alabama and Florida but throughout the southern states. In her study of African American women involved in home demonstration in Tennessee, Melissa Walker notes that these women may have been viewed as less successful in earning money from a poultry project when compared with their white counterparts. But, as Walker points out, any lower numbers did not necessarily indicate African American women "reap[ed] lower benefits; they may have been using a higher proportion of their flocks to feed their families. . . . Likely [they] underreported their incomes for fear that they might be penalized by the white bureaucracy for making too much money."[12] Despite the obstacles they faced, rural African American women nevertheless found ways to navigate and construct their own economic pathways by using home demonstration programming. Although they had fewer resources and materials, African American women in both Alabama and Florida utilized and worked with the opportunities available to them.

A U.S. Department of Agriculture pamphlet published in 1933 described the importance of HDAs in helping their members earn extra money: "As a means of increasing the family income, rural women and girls are helped to produce and to market products of their homes and gardens. . . . Much of the money earned by these means has been used for such purposes as additional education for boys and girls, labor-saving equipment, and improved furnishings for the home."[13]

The rural white and African American women involved with home demonstration after 1930 could look to their predecessors for models on how to earn disposable income, which offered hope in poor economic circumstances. They also had examples of rural women who learned to adapt their ideas and products, not only to meet the needs of themselves and their families, but as reliable paths of revenue, allowing subsequent generations to attain a degree of economic self-sufficiency.

Home demonstration agents and the programming they offered produced immeasurable influence in the South. While their role initially was to help modernize rural life, this impact grew exponentially as rural women used the programming to their economic benefit. Rural women could keep a family home from being lost due to unpaid taxes or rent, or buy a car and not have to consistently ask for ride, or see a daughter finish her education. There were also the intangible benefits that came with confidence gained and relief felt.

The act of selling and marketing canned tomatoes, crystallized grapefruit, or a woven basket literally transformed lives—not just of individuals, but of entire families. Whether rural women sold their goods at a curb market or through a home demonstration shop, at a Birmingham department store or simply from their front porch, the financial and psychological impact was often long-lasting. These women who chose to participate by using their home demonstration education did so on their own terms and, as a result, reaped the profits.

SELECTED RECIPES

All recipes are in their original format and context, given for their historical value, and have not been modified or updated.

BAKED GOODS

Recipe for Biscuits

Source: Elizabeth Striplin, "Home Demonstration Agent Report, Cullman County, Alabama, November 1, 1924–November 1, 1925," 34, Alabama Cooperative Extension System Records, RG no. 71, Ralph B. Draughon Library, Auburn University (hereafter cited as ACES Records)

2 cups of flour	½ teaspoon soda
1 teaspoon salt	2 tablespoons lard
1 teaspoon baking powder	1 cup buttermilk

Method of mixing—mix and sift together the flour, salt, baking powder, and soda. Work in the lard with the finger tips or a mixing spoon. Add the milk gradually, mixing with a spoon, to make a soft dough. Knead until a smooth dough. Roll to one-half inch thickness, and cut with a biscuit cutter. Place close together on a greased pan and bake until a pretty brown in a hot oven.

Recipe for Corn Bread

Source: Elizabeth Striplin, "Home Demonstration Agent Report, Cullman County, Alabama, November 1, 1924–November 1, 1925," 34, ACES Records

2 cups meal (measure before sifting)	3–4 teaspoon salt
	1 tablespoon melted butter
3–4 teaspoon baking soda	1½ to 2 cups of sour milk

Method of mixing—Beat the eggs until light, add to the meal the dry ingredients and sift together. Add the liquid and mix well. Bake in bread sticks or in a shallow pan that has been greased and heated. Bake until a pretty brown color, always in a hot oven.

Light Roll Recipe

As baked by Mrs. H. C. Taylor, Dothan, Alabama. *Source*: Wyche G. Pruett, "Narrative Report, Houston County, Alabama, November 1, 1928–November 1, 1929," 8, ACES Records

2 cups scalded milk	2 teaspoonfuls sugar
1 Fleischman's yeast cake	2 teaspoonfuls fat
1 teaspoonful salt	6 to 7 cups of flour

Scald milk, add sugar, fat, salt, and when milk has cooled until luke warm stir well in above. Dissolve yeast cake in other cup of milk and stir well in mixture.

Add enough flour to make a stiff batter and turn into bread pan and knead well. Set away to rise for 1½ to 2 hours. Then knead again. Shape and put in greased pans to rise the same length of time as before. Cook in an oven about the same temperature as biscuit unless it is in large loaves. The larger loaves require a lower temperature.

Spider Corn Bread

Source: "Women's Club" folder, Alabama, 1921, 3, ACES Records

1½ cups corn meal	1 teaspoon salt
2 cups sour milk	2 eggs
1 teaspoon soda	2 tablespoons butter

Mix the dry ingredients. Add the eggs well beaten, and the milk. Place the butter in a frying pan, melt it, and grease the pan well. Heat the pan and turn in the mixture. Place in a hot oven and cook 20 minutes. This serves six people.

Lemon Cheese Cake or Layer Cake

As baked by Mrs. H. C. Taylor, Dothan, Alabama. *Source*: Wyche G. Pruett, "Narrative Report, Houston County, Alabama, November 1, 1928–November 1, 1929," 8, ACES Records

Recipe for layer cake:

¾ cupful of butter	2 teaspoons baking powder
2 cupful sugar	1 cupful milk
3 eggs	2½ cupfuls flour
1 teaspoon lemon flavoring	

Cream the butter, add the sugar gradually and cream together. Add unbeaten eggs, one at a time and beat well. Measure 2½ cupfuls shifted flour and sift with baking powder. Add milk alternately. Bake in three layers in a moderate oven and fill with lemon cheese filling made as follows:

1 cup sugar	1 egg
2½ teaspoonfuls flour	1 teaspoonful butter
¼ cup lemon juice	grated rind of 2 lemons

Mix the dry ingredients, add egg slightly beaten and butter. Add lemon juice gradually stirring constantly. Cook in a double boiler until thick continue stirring. Cool and spread between layers and on top.

Guava Duff

Source: Mrs. Delaware Kraemer, Eustis, Florida, in Isabelle S. Thursby, *The Goodly Guava*, Bulletin 70 (Agricultural Extension Service, University of Florida, et. al) October 1932), 21.

Peel and remove seeds from enough guavas to cover bottom of 8 inch pudding pan 1 inch deep. Add sufficient water to nearly cover. Sprinkle with: 1 cup sugar, dot with 2 tablespoonfuls butter and 1 tablespoonful lemon juice. Dust lightly with nutmeg or cinnamon. Place in oven and allow to cook while the batter is being mixed.

Put in mixing bowl:

1 cup flour	2 tbsp. butter
1 tsp. sugar	2 tsp. baking powder
½ to ¾ cup milk or water— enough to make thick batter	

Mix and sift dry ingredients. Add shortening and liquid; beat and pour over guavas. Bake in moderate oven 40 minutes. Serve with cream or lemon sauce.

Papaya Whip

Source: "Keep These Recipes for Your Files," *Miami News*, June 23, 1933, 11

To one and one-half cups papaya pulp add juice one lemon, half cup sugar, and beat into two stiffly whipped whites of eggs. Bake. Serve with whipped cream.

Guava Gingerbread

Source: Isabelle S. Thursby, *The Goodly Guava*, Bulletin 70 (Agricultural Extension Service, University of Florida, et. al, October 1932), 22–23

Pare, remove seed and slice guavas, sufficient to make a pint, into a buttered baking dish and mix with ½ cupful of sugar and 1 tablespoonful of lemon juice. Cook 20 minutes in a moderate oven while the following batter is mixed:

1 egg	1 tsp. ginger
½ cup sugar	¼ tsp. cinnamon
½ cup sour milk	¼ tsp. nutmeg
¾ tsp. soda	1 tsp. baking powder
1 cup flour	¾ cup molasses
¼ tsp. salt	

Beat egg, add sugar, sour milk, molasses, and the dry ingredients sifted together; add the melted butter. Mix well and pour batter over guavas. Bake in moderate oven (350 degrees F.) until the gingerbread is done. Serve with cream, lemon or orange sauce, or a honey topping.

Lemon Sauce

Source: Isabelle S. Thursby, *The Goodly Guava*, Bulletin 70 (Agricultural Extension Service, University of Florida, et. al, October 1932), 23

1 cup sugar	3 tbsp. lemon juice
1¾ cup boiling water	¼ tsp. grated lemon rind
2 tbsp. butter	Pinch salt
2 tbsp. flour	

Mix dry ingredients thoroughly; add boiling water; cook 3 minutes. Add lemon juice and butter and remove from stove. Substitute ½ cupful orange juice for

½ cupful water in the foundation recipe and grated orange rind for lemon rind for an orange sauce.

Honey Topping

Source: Isabelle S. Thursby, *The Goodly Guava*, Bulletin 70 (Agricultural Extension Service, University of Florida, et. al, October 1932), 23

1 egg white	1 cup honey
4 tbsp. water	¼ tsp. cream of tartar
Pinch of salt	

Combine all ingredients and cook very slowly over low heat on an electrical range or in a double boiler, beating constantly with a rotary beater until mixture stands up in peaks. It may be beaten until creamy when removed from heat. This is a delicious meringue topping. It does not set on the outside, but is creamy and fluffy.

Orange Dessert Cake

Source: Isabelle S. Thursby, "Baking with Florida Citrus Fruits," reprinted in the *Orlando Sentinel*, March 20, 1939, 5.

1½ cups sugar	½ cup butter
1 cup sour milk	1 teaspoon soda dissolved in
2 eggs, beaten light	the milk
¼ teaspoon salt	2 cups flour
1 orange, medium size	1 cup raisins

Select a choice, tree-ripened orange in order to have fine flavored peel. Grate the fruit slightly. Cut and squeeze out juice. Do not take out all the juice, as it might make the cake too moist. Add one-half cup of the sugar to juice and let stand. Cut out and discard the central core with seeds and grind the balance, rind, and pulp, with the raisins, using the medium blade of the food chopper. Cream shortening and sugar together. Add the beaten eggs and the well sifted flour with the other dry ingredients alternately with the liquid. Add the orange and raisin mixture last.

Pour into an 8×8×2-inch pan and bake until well done, or about 45 minutes. After baking and while still hot, cover with orange juice and sugar mixture and let stand in the pan until juice is absorbed. Do not dissolve sugar entirely as it should glaze top of the cake. Artificially colored fruit should not be used.

Strawberry Pie

Source: Eunice Grady, Home Demonstration Agent, Dade County, seen in "Approved Recipes Listed by Home Economic Expert," *Miami News*, January 7, 1938, 17

Wash berries carefully, remove caps. Place in container and add about pound of sugar for each two quarts of berries, depending, of course, on sweetness. Let stand overnight. The next day drain off juice and bring to boil. Thicken with cornstarch, tapioca, or flour by blending with small amount of the juice. Pour into boiling mixture and stir constantly until of proper consistency. Remove from fire, stir in berries and allow to cool. Add mixture to the previously baked pastry shell, cover with meringue and bake only long enough to lightly color and set meringue. Or, freshly sweetened berries may be added to individual tart shells and covered with whipped cream. Serve at once. This makes a dessert of rare fruitiness and flavor.

Angel Food Cake

Source: *Recipes*, compiled by Hester Foster Benner, Alabama Polytechnic Institute Extension Service Circular 74, July 1924, 56

- 1 c. egg whites (8–10 eggs)
- 1 tsp. cream of tartar
- 1½ c. granulated sugar
- 1 c. flour sifted once, measured and then sifted four times
- ¼ tsp. salt
- ¾ tsp. vanilla

Beat egg whites with salt until foamy, add cream of tartar and continue beating until eggs are stiff enough to hold their shape. Fold in sugar, a little at a time, and fold in flour in the same manner, adding vanilla. Pour in an ungreased angel cake pan and bake in a slow oven 1 hour. Remove cake from oven and invert pan for an hour or until cake is cold.

SIDES AND ENTRÉES

Tomato Soup

Source: *Recipes*, compiled by Hester Foster Benner, Alabama Polytechnic Institute Extension Service Circular 74, July 1924 (reprinted August 1925, September 1927), 13

- 1 qt. tomatoes
- 2 c. water
- 12 peppercorns
- bit of bay leaf
- 4 cloves
- 1 tbsp. onion
- 1 tbsp. sugar
- ⅛ tsp. soda
- 4 tbsp. butter
- 4 tbsp. flour
- 1 tsp. salt
- ¼ tsp. pepper

Cook slowly the first seven ingredients for 30 minutes. Strain and add soda. Combine last four ingredients as for white sauce, add tomatoes and when mixture reaches boiling point, serve.

Stuffed Tomato Salad

Source: Elizabeth Striplin, "Home Demonstration Agent Report, Cullman County, Alabama, November 1st, 1924—November 1st, 1925," 33, ACES Records

Peel medium sized tomatoes, remove a slice from the top of the tomato, take out the seeds and some of the pulp, sprinkle the inside with salt, invert and let stand one-half hour. Fill the tomato with one of the following mixed with mayonnaise. Arrange on lettuce leaves and garnish top with mayonnaise.

Fillings—
1. Diced pineapple and nut meats
2. Celery, apples, and nuts
3. Diced cucumber
4. Chicken salad
5. Vegetable salad

Spiced Green Tomatoes

Source: "Home Demonstration Department" (conducted by Isadora Williams, assistant county home demonstration agent and market master), *Tuscaloosa News & Times Gazette*, August 17, 1925, 4

6 lbs. small whole green tomatoes	1–2 tablespoonful cloves
4 lbs. sugar	1–2 tablespoonful all-spice
1 pt. vinegar	1–2 tablespoonful mace
1 tablespoonful cinnamon	

Small green fig or plum tomatoes are suitable for this pickle. Scald and peel. Make a syrup of the sugar, vinegar, and spices. Drop in the whole fruit and boil until the tomatoes become clear, pour all into trays, cool quickly, pack into jars, strain syrup over them, seal and process.

Eggplant Creole

Source: "Helping Florida Feed Herself," Garden Series No. 15, April 8, 1929, 6, University of Florida Institute for Food and Agricultural Sciences (IFAS) Extension Records, University Special Collections and Archives, George A. Smathers Library, University of Florida, Gainesville, Florida (hereafter cited as UF Archives)

2 small eggplants	1½ cup soft bread crumbs
2 onions	½ teaspoon salt
1 green pepper	½ teaspoon paprika

Pare eggplant; cut in ½ inch cubes. Cook in boiling salted water under tender. Melt 2 tablespoons butter or bacon fat and sauté in it chopped pepper and onion until onions become slightly yellow. Add drained eggplant and other ingredients to onions. Bake in buttered baking dish. Cover top with bread crumbs. May be served in bell peppers or ramekins.

Greens Cooked "Spanish"

Source: Isabelle S. Thursby, "Helping Florida Feed Herself," Garden Series No. 17, July–August, 4–5, IFAS Extension Records, UF Archives

Thoroughly wash mustard or turnip greens or rutabaga tops, or a mixture of these. Lay on a meat or vegetable board and cut fine like cabbage. In a sauce pan, fry large, chopped onion in a tablespoonful of bacon fat or beef drippings until it begins to lightly brown, (covering skillet prevents burning). Cut fine [1] or 2 green peppers and cook with the onion for two minutes. Then add the greens with a little hot water, a pinch of dried powdered celery leaves, a small bay leaf and cover tightly to steam slowly. These last three ingredients may be omitted if the family objects to them. Season with salt, cayenne pepper and paprika. Stir often and add water as needed to prevent scorching. Raw potatoes, cut in small cubes may be added at the same time as the greens to give variety and richness to the dish. Then it will be almost a meal cooked in one pot, especially if rich milk is added just before serving.

Canned Pork Salad

Source: Isabelle S. Thursby, *Meat Canning*, Bulletin 87 (Agricultural Extension Service, University of Florida, et. al, December 1936), 36

2 cups diced, canned pork	2 hard cooked eggs
1 medium sized onion chopped fine	1 cup chopped celery
	Mayonnaise
1 cup canned peas	

Heat canned pork thoroughly in the can in the oven or in boiling water. Cool, remove bone if any and cut into neat half-inch dice. Combine the ingredients and moisten thoroughly with mayonnaise. Served as the meat course with fresh fried potatoes, this is a satisfying dish. Chopped head lettuce, cabbage, chayote or radishes and celery seed may be used in place of the chopped celery.

Avocado and Scrambled Eggs

Source: "Keep These Recipes for Your Files," *Miami Daily News*, June 23, 1933, 11

Scramble eggs in the usual way with butter and a little milk, adding cubed or diced avocado (thinly sliced) before eggs are set. Serve on toast.

Baked Eggplant

Source: "Helping Florida Feed Herself," Garden Series No. 15, April 8, 1929, 6, IFAS Extension Records, UF Archives

Slice ¾ inches thick, place in thickly buttered pan, dust with salt and pepper, dot with butter and bake in hot oven until brown. Turn over while baking. Or, dust slice with salt and pepper, dip in flour then in an egg slightly beaten with 1 tablespoon milk. Roll in fine, dry bread crumbs or corn flakes and fry. Drain on oil paper.

Casserole Rabbit

Source: "Rabbit Cooked Many New Ways," *St. Petersburg Times*, April 23, 1921, 9 (via Isabelle S. Thursby)

Eight slices of bacon	2 cups hot water
One rabbit cut into pieces	1 teaspoon salt
Two medium sized potatoes	1–3 teaspoon pepper
Two small onions	

Fry bacon until light brown and remove fat. Dredge rabbit with flour and brown in bacon fat. Arrange rabbit, sliced onions, potatoes, strips of bacon in casserole. Dredge lightly with flour. Pour water over all. Cover and cook slowly two hours.

Florida Fruit Cup

Source: Isabelle S. Thursby, *The Goodly Guava*, Bulletin 70 (Agricultural Extension Service, University of Florida, et. al, October 1932), 27

1 cup each guavas (fresh or canned)	Pineapple
Grapefruit or tangelo hearts	¾ cup rose-apple or carissa

Slice guavas, cut up pineapple and grapefruit in medium pieces, slice rose-apple or carissa thinly. Cover with guava juice. Add juice of one lemon or lime and sugar lightly. Let stand in refrigerator two hours before serving. (This is a good fruit cocktail.)

Pine Bark Stew—4-H Brand

Source: Isabelle S. Thursby, *Home Canning of Meat*, Bulletin 51 (Agricultural Extension Division, University of Florida, et. al, May 1929), 17–18

5 lbs. cleaned fish (catfish, bream, seabass, trout, red snapper or similar fish)	6 medium sized onions, minced
	1 bunch celery cut fine
1 quart of tomatoes or equivalent amount of fresh tomatoes	1 pint pimientoes [*sic*] or equivalent in fresh pimientoes, peeled (other sweet peppers may be used)
2 cups olive, peanut or other cooking oils	
1 bay leaf (may be omitted)	1 quart okra (finely cut crosswise)
1 lb. finely diced carrots (may be added)	12 whole pepper corns
	Salt and pepper to taste
1 clove of garlic, finely minced (may be omitted)	

The oil is heated in an enamel kettle, the minced onions (and garlic) are added and cooked until tender. Then add the finely cut celery and okra and cook for ten minutes. The tomatoes, pimientoes, whole pepper (bay leaf) salt and pepper are next added, the whole is allowed to simmer for 20 minutes. The cleaned fish is next added, cut in suitable pieces. (If large fish is used, remove the backbone and large ribs.) Cover the fish pretty well with the vegetable mixture and simmer until tender. If too thick, a little water may be added. Pack boiling hot into inside lacquered tin cans. Seal at once and process. Serve hot, poured over rice, boiled "Southern Style."

NOTE: The name is due to the custom of serving this fish stew at public gathering on a piece of clean pine bark, used as a plate.

Goulash

Source: Isabelle S. Thursby, *Home Canning of Meat*, Bulletin 51 (Agricultural Extension Division, University of Florida, et. al, May 1929), 10

2 lbs. meat—beef, veal, pork, or a mixture of the three	1 chopped green pepper
	4 to 5 cloves
2 medium onions, chopped fine	2 medium sized carrots, shredded
2 cups tomatoes, fresh or canned	2 finely chopped parsley
2 stalks celery including leaves chopped fine	Salt to taste
	Fat

Wipe meat, cut in small pieces and sprinkle with flour mixed with salt and pepper. Try out fat in frying pan, add meat and cook until well seared. Add onions, carrots, and celery and brown lightly, stirring to prevent sticking and burning. When nicely browned add tomatoes and other seasonings, and simmer, covered for 45 minutes. Soy or Worcester sauce may also be added if desired. Add parsley. Fill hot into cans and process immediately.

Heat thoroughly before serving. Noodles, macaroni, spaghetti, or potatoes may be cooked with goulash when it is reheated for serving.

PICKLES AND SAUCES

Olive Oil Pickles

Source: "Home Demonstration Department" (conducted by Isadora Williams, assistant county home demonstration agent and market master), *Tuscaloosa News & Times Gazette*, August 17, 1925, 4

Wash cucumbers thoroughly, slice them very thin, 1 lb. cucumber, salt, one-half lb. onion, salt. Place layer cucumbers and layer of salt in 1 ve[s]sel, let stand over night. Put layer of onion and layer salt and let stand over night. Put in a little more salt than necessary to season. Next morning wash thoroughly, then soak in clear water for several hours or over night. 1 pt. vinegar, three fourths pt. sugar, one eighth C. olive oil, one-half tb. each of white mustard seed, celery seed and turmeric. Bring sugar, vinegar, and spices to boil, cook onions in this syrup 5 min., then add cucumbers and cook until transparent. Remove from the fire and let cool, add one eighth C. olive oil. Fill sterilized jars, garnish with strips of pemientoes [*sic*], process 10 min. Store in dark, cool place.

Sweet Peach Pickle

Source: "Home Demonstration Department" (conducted by Isadora Williams, assistant county home demonstration agent and market master), *Tuscaloosa News & Times Gazette*, August 17, 1925, 4

Use 7 pounds peaches, 4 pounds sugar, 1 qt. vinegar, 2 oz. stick cinnamon. Peel or scald and rub, clingstone peaches. Stick four cloves into each peach. Cook sugar, vinegar, and cinnamon for twenty minutes, add the peaches, and cook gently until tender. Pack in jars and cover with the syrup. Seal while hot. Pickles, owing to the condiments used, are more difficult to digest than preserves.

Pears may be pickled in the same way. Whole small apples are delicious prepared in this way.

Chile Sauce

Source: "Home Demonstration Department" (conducted by Isadora Williams, assistant county home demonstration agent and market master), *Tuscaloosa News & Times Gazette*, August 17, 1925, 4

1 gal. of chopped ripe tomatoes	1 tablespoonful of cinnamon
One-half cupful of chopped white onions	1 tablespoonful of mustard
	1 nutmeg (grated)
One-half cupful of chopped sweet green peppers	1 qt. of vinegar
	5 tablespoonfuls of salt
One-half cupful of brown sugar	One-half teaspoonful of cayenne pepper
2 tablespoonfuls of ginger	

Peel the tomatoes and onions. Chop the onions and peppers fine. Boil all the ingredients except the vinegar together for 2 hrs. or until soft and broken. Add vinegar and simmer for one hour. Stir frequently. Bottle and seal while hot.

Barbeque Sauce No. 1

Source: Isabelle S. Thursby, *Meat Canning*, Bulletin 87 (Agricultural Extension Service, University of Florida, et. al, December 1936), 35

½ pound butter	¼ teaspoon red pepper
2½ cups water	½ tablespoon Worcestershire sauce
¼ cup vinegar	
1 teaspoon mustard	½ teaspoon tabasco sauce
1 tablespoon sugar	¼ onion, chopped fine
2½ teaspoons salt	½ teaspoon black pepper
2 teaspoons chili powder	¼ garlic, chopped fine

Put ingredients in saucepan, mix thoroughly and simmer ten minutes. Use to baste roast and also to season barbeque sandwich.

SANDWICHES

4-H Garden Club Sandwich

Source: "Cultivate the Garden Sandwiches" (possibly 1929), IFAS Extension Records, UF Archives

1 cupful shredded cabbage	¼ cupful chopped green sweet pepper
1 tbsp. chopped onion	
12 large slices of tomatoes	6 eggs—hard cooked

Mix cabbage, green pepper and onion and moisten with salad dressing. Spread this mixture between slices of buttered peanut bread. Use the ½ egg and 1 large slice of tomato between the top slices of bread. Serve with a lettuce leaf, endive, or other green leaf.

Marglobe Special

Source: "Cultivate the Garden Sandwiches" (possibly 1929), IFAS Extension Records, UF Archives

Slice firm cold Marglobe tomatoes. Dip in heavy salad dressing; then in chopped salted peanuts and place between slices of buttered bread whole wheat bread. Serve with a lettuce leaf or other green.

4-H Health Sandwich

Source: "Cultivate the Garden Sandwiches" (possibly 1929), IFAS Extension Records, UF Archives

- 1 cupful grated carrot
- 1/2 cup of chopped celery or chayote
- 1 cupful cabbage or cauliflower
- 1/2 cup chopped cucumber
- 1/4 cup peanuts or pecans, broken in small pieces

Mix all together and bind with mayonnaise or Chili sauce. Spread on slices of buttered whole wheat bread. Serve with lettuce leaf.

Palm Beach Sandwich

Source: "Cultivate the Garden Sandwiches" (possibly 1929), IFAS Extension Records, UF Archives

- 1/2 cup peanut butter
- 2 1/2 cups crushed pineapple
- 1/2 cup cream cheese

Mix crushed pineapple and peanut butter. Spread slices of whole wheat bread with cream or cottage cheese. Spread the mixture and garnish parsley or lettuce.

Florida Sandwich

Source: "Cultivate the Garden Sandwiches" (possibly 1929), IFAS Extension Records, UF Archives

Spread buttered whole wheat bread with orange marmalade or fruit butter, such as plum, fig, guava, etc. Sprinkle with chopped nuts. Nut bread may be used in place of the whole wheat bread and chopped nuts omitted from the mixture. Serve with crisp lettuce leaf.

Avocado Sandwich

Source: "New Avocado Recipes Furnished by Experts," *Miami Herald*, September 29, 1928, 21

Substantial and delicious sandwiches may be made by slicing the avocado very thin, sprinkling with salt and pepper, grated onion and lemon or lime juice and placing between slices of buttered whole-wheat bread.

FROZEN TREATS AND JUICES

Grape Sherbet No. 1

Source: Isabelle S. Thursby, "Grape and Grape Products," Circular 23, 1930, 4

2 cups grape juice	1 cup sugar
1/4 cup lemon juice	3 cups rich, cold milk

Scald the grape juice, add sugar and stir until sugar is dissolved. Cool, add lemon juice and set aside until cold. Stir into milk and freeze at once.

Frozen Honey Custard

Source: "Use of Florida Products by Florida People," Eunice F. Gay, home demonstration agent, Brevard County, *Cocoa Tribune*, August 8, 1935, 3 (this touted the use of Brevard County honey, which is assumed to be the honey used in the recipe)

4 egg yolks	2 c. rich milk
2 c. water	1 c. honey
Pinch of salt	

Cook the egg yolks and water over hot water for a few minutes. When cool add the milk and honey and freeze. Stir a few times. Makes two trays. Serve with crisp butter wafers that are a little salty. You may want to use less honey if you don't care for a sweet cream.

Avocado Punch

Source: "Keep These Recipes for Your Files," *Miami Daily News*, June 23, 1933, 11

Mash the pulp of six avocados finely through a sieve, add this to one cup of lime juice which has been diluted with water to suit taste. Add sugar to suit taste. To garnish add mint leaves.

Guava Ice Cream

Source: Isabelle S. Thursby, *The Goodly Guava*, Bulletin 70 (Agricultural Extension Service, University of Florida, et. al October 1932), 29–30

Use any foundation cream recipe. Add pulp of guavas—with seeds removed—as you would peach, strawberry or other fruit pulp. One method follows:

3 cups guava pulp	2 cups sugar
1 pt. cream	2 tbsp. lemon juice
1 pt. milk	

To the guava pulp, add the sugar and lemon juice. Scald the milk and combine carefully with the fruit mixture. Add cream and freeze in the usual way. After freezing, pack and allow to stand an hour more to ripen.

Hollywood Highball

Source: Isabelle S. Thursby, *The Goodly Guava*, Bulletin 70 (Agricultural Extension Service, University of Florida, et. al, October 1932), 32

Juice of 12 limes	3 qts. of water
Juice of 12 oranges	2 pts. Ginger ale

1 pt. tamarind juice
1 qt. guava juice
1 pt. crushed pineapple
Honey to sweeten

Warm honey and add to water. Blend and add fruit juices and crushed pineapple and chill. When ready to serve, add ginger ale. Garnish with thin slices of lemon and orange and pour over ice.

CANDIES AND JELLIES

Crystallized Whole Grapefruit

Source: Isabelle S. Thursby, *Preserving Florida Citrus Fruits*, Bulletin 75 (Agricultural Extension Service, University of Florida, et. al, April 1933), 21

Select bright, smooth fruit with thick peel. Wash and grate lightly with medium fine grater, removing all yellow oil cells. Cut circles three inches in diameter from stem end of fruit and remove meat and connective tissue, being careful to leave all of the thick part of the peel. Boil until tender and if it is desired to remove the bitter, change the water during cooking, each time putting the fruit into cold water and bringing it slowly to the boiling point.

Several changes of water often are necessary to accomplish this. If too much of the bitter flavor is removed, an undesirable, insipid, characterless product results.

Cool fruit and put into a syrup made of equal parts of sugar and water. Sufficient syrup must be made to float the fruit. Cook to 220° F. and let fruit stand in syrup 24 hours, then cook to 228° F. Take immediately out and put in sun to cool. If fruit is very large and will not hold its shape, turn over a glass or olive bottle to dry (for 24 hours).

Fill the fruit with small pieces of crystallized fruits, nuts or other confections. French fondant with nuts may be used as a filling. When this is done then cut as one cuts a cake. It may be used for a garnish when prepared this way.

If it is desired to keep the fruit any length of time it is necessary to leave the fruit in the heavy syrup for at least three weeks.

Sweet Fig Paste

Source: Isabelle S. Thursby, "The Fig: A Prize Package of Food and Medicine," Circular 24 (possibly 1930), 4

Wash ripe figs, drain and put through a food chopper or a colander. Measure. Allow one pound of sugar for each quart of pulp. Mix and cook until it is a rather solid mass. Spread with an oiled spatula on the oiled surface of a flat dish, marble, or glass slab, and finish drying in the sun. Three or four days will be required for drying. The trays should be brought into the house each night, and they should be protected from both flying and crawling insects. It can be dried in a cool oven or in a home fruit and vegetable evaporator but the color is brighter if the product is dried in the sun. When perfectly dry sprinkle with sugar. Cut into two-inch squares and make into little finger-shaped hollow rolls. To roll the paste use a small, smooth, oiled stick about the size of a pencil.

These little fruit rolls, or lady fingers, as they are sometimes called, add variety of shapes to the sweets used in packing boxes of mixed candied fruits. They also make a most delicious single product and a very attractive box when packed alone in layers between sheets of oiled paper.

Nut Molasses Candy

Source: "Hints to Housewives: Weekly from the Home Demonstration Specialist, Tallahassee," *Vero Press*, December 13, 1923, 8

When making molasses candy, add roasted Florida peanuts, pecans, walnuts or any other nuts which you have. Put them in after the syrup has thickened and is ready to take from the fire. Pour the cooked, hot candy on buttered tins. Mark off in squares before it gets too cooled.

Mint Jelly

Source: Elizabeth Striplin, "Home Demonstration Agent Report, Cullman County, Alabama, November 1st, 1924–November 1st, 1925," 33, ACES Records

- 1 pint of orange or apple juice
- 1 pint sugar
- 2 drops oil of peppermint
- 2 drops green vegetable food coloring

Heat the juice to boiling, add the sugar gradually, continue boiling until the jelly will flake from the side of a spoon, at this point drop in two drops of oil of peppermint together with two drops of food coloring. . . Stir gently and pour while hot into clean glasses. When cold, pour hot paraffin wax over it.

Cocoanut Candy

Source: "Hints to Housewives: Weekly from the Home Demonstration Specialist, Tallahassee," *Vero Press*, December 13, 1923, 8

One Florida cocoanut and three cups of granulated sugar will make a delicious candy. Mix sugar and milk of cocoanut, beat slowly until the sugar is melted, then boil five minutes. Add cocoanut (finely grated), boil 10 minutes longer, stirring constantly to keep from burning. Pour on buttered tins and cut into squares. It will take about two days to harden.

A Roselle Gelatine Salad [not its official name, but as described]

Source: "Florida Cranberries," Isabelle S. Thursby, *Palm Beach Post*, December 23, 1934, 26

- 1 pt. raw roselle—with seed pods removed
- 1 cup sugar
- 1 cup nuts (pecans)
- ½ orange (peel and pulp)
- 1—10c can crushed pineapple
- 1 box lemon jello
- 1 cup hot water

Grind the raw roselle calyxes, orange, and nuts, add pineapple, sugar, and jello (dissolve jello first in the cup of hot water, then add to other mixture). Chill and serve with salad dressing or whip cream.

Guava Gumdrops

Source: Isabelle S. Thursby, *The Goodly Guava*, Bulletin 70 (Agricultural Extension Service, University of Florida, et. al, October 1932), 15

2 cups guava pulp	2 tbsp. gelatin
2 cups sugar	8 tbsp. cold water
1 to 1½ cups chopped pecans	1 tbsp. lemon juice

Put guavas through fruit press. Soak gelatin in cold water. Add sugar to guava pulp and cook until thick, stirring constantly. Remove from the heat, add the gelatin and stir until thoroughly dissolved. Add the nuts and lemon juice and pour into shallow pans to cool. When set, cut into rectangular pieces and roll in powdered sugar.

NOTES

INTRODUCTION. WOMEN AND DEVELOPING RURAL REFORM IN THE TWENTIETH-CENTURY SOUTH

1. Mary Bailey, "Annual Report of Extension Work in Lee County, Alabama, 1927," 7, Alabama Cooperative Extension System Records, RG no. 71, Ralph B. Draughon Library, Auburn University (hereafter cited as ACES Records); Florence Ellington Robertson information: *1920 U.S. Census*, Chambers County, Alabama, census place, Oak Bowery, Enumeration District (ED) 32, p. 10A (penned), https://www.ancestry.com; *1930 U.S. Census*, Chambers County, Alabama, census place, Oak Bowery, ED 0026, p. 1B (penned), https://www.ancestry.com; "Florence Ellington Robertson," Find a Grave, accessed March 14, 2020, https://www.findagrave.com/memorial/27676783.

2. According to the IRS's *Statistics of Income for 1927*, the "average" net income for 1927 in Alabama was $4,759.38, which, adjusted to 2018 dollars, is $70,993.67. *Statistics of Income for 1927: Compiled from Income-Tax Returns and Including Statistics from Estate-Tax Returns* (Government Printing Office, 1929), 163; MeasuringWorth, https://www.measuringworth.com.

3. Some monographs on the New South since 1990 include Edward L. Ayers, *The Promise of the New South: Life after Reconstruction* (Oxford University Press, 1992); James S. Humphreys, ed., *Interpreting American History: The New South*, (Kent State University Press, 2017); John B. Boles and Bethany L. Johnson-Dylewski, eds., *"Origins of the New South" Fifty Years Later: The Continuing Influence of a Historical Classic* (Louisiana State University Press, 2003); Virginia Bernhard, Betty Brandon, Elizabeth Fox-Genovese, Theda Perdue, and Elizabeth H. Turner, eds., *Hidden Histories of Women in the New South* (University of Missouri Press, 1994).

4. See the charts on pages 5–6.

5. For more, see Marcia Chatelain, *South Side Girls: Growing Up in the Great Migration* (Duke University Press, 2015); Peter M. Rutkoff and William B. Scott, *Fly Away: The Great African American Cultural Migrations* (Johns Hopkins University Press, 2010); Isabel Wilkerson, *The Warmth of Other Suns: The Epic Story of America's Great Migration* (Random House, 2010); James N. Gregory, *The Southern Diaspora: How the Great Migrations of Black and White Southerners Transformed America* (University of North Carolina Press, 2007); Kimberley Louise Phillips, *AlabamaNorth: African-American Migrants, Community, and Working-Class Activism in Cleveland, 1915–45* (University of Illinois Press, 1999); Alferdteen Harrison, ed., *Black Exodus: The Great Migration from the American South* (University Press of Mississippi, 1992); James R. Grossman, *Land of Hope: Chicago, Black Southerners, and the Great Migration* (University of Chicago Press, 1991).

6. The statistical breakdown for those living on rural farms versus rural nonfarms was not given or calculated in 1910. Percentage totals are rounded up. *Fifteenth Census of the United States: 1930; Population Volume III, Part I; Reports by States, Showing the Composition and Characteristics of the Population for Counties, Cities, and Townships or Other Minor Civil Divisions* (Government Printing Office, 1932), 83, 395.

7. "Conecuh County, Alabama," *Modern Farmer* 1, no. 8, October 15, 1929, 1, 6.

8. For some literature on this topic, see Barbara Welter, "The Cult of True Womanhood, 1820–1860," *American Quarterly* 18, no. 2 (Summer 1966): 151–175; Jeanne Boydston, *Home and Work: Housework, Wages, and the Ideology of Labor in the Early Republic* (Oxford University Press, 1990); Jeanne Boydston, "The Woman Who Wasn't There: Women's Market Labor and the Transition to Capitalism in the United States," *Journal of the Early Republic* 16, no. 2 (Summer 1996): 183–206; Nancy F. Cott, *The Bonds of Womanhood: "Woman's Sphere" in New England, 1780–1835* (Yale University Press, 1977); Nancy Grey Osterud, *Putting the Barn before the House: Women and Family Farming in Early Twentieth-Century New York* (Cornell University Press, 2012); Nancy Grey Osterud, *Bonds of Community: The Lives of Farm Women in Nineteenth-Century New York* (Cornell University Press, 1991); Glenna Matthews, *"Just a Housewife": The Rise and Fall of Domesticity in America* (Oxford University Press, 1989); Joan M. Jensen, *Loosening the Bonds: Mid-Atlantic Farm Women, 1750–1850* (Yale University Press, 1986).

9. Kathleen R. Babbitt, "The Productive Farm Woman and the Extension Home Economist in New York State, 1920–1940," *Agricultural History* 67, no. 2 (Spring 1993): 86. See also Ariel Ron, "Farmers, Capitalism, and Government in the Late Nineteenth Century," *Journal of the Gilded Age and Progressive Era* 15, no. 3 (July 2016): 294–309.

10. Lu Ann Jones, *Mama Learned Us to Work: Farm Women in the New South* (University of North Carolina Press, 2002), 52.

11. Ibid. Jones's other work also focuses on rural women and economy: "Gender, Race, and Itinerant Commerce in the Rural New South," *Journal of Southern History* 66, no. 2 (May 2000): 297–320; "Taking What She Had and Turning It into Money: The Female Farm Economy," in *Cornbread Nation 1: The Best of Southern Food Writing*, ed. John Edgerton (University of North Carolina Press, 2002), 223–234; "Women's Roles in Foods and Markets," in *Agriculture and Industry: The New Encyclopedia of Southern Culture*, vol. 11, ed. Melissa Walker and James C. Cobb (University of North Carolina Press, 2008), 72–75.

12. Minoa D. Uffelman, "Tomato Clubs as Salvation: Canning Clubs for Girls and the Uplift of Southern Rural Society," in *Tennessee Women in the Progressive Era: Toward the Public Sphere in the New South*, ed. Mary A. Evins (University of Tennessee Press, 2013), 84.

13. Elizabeth S. D. Engelhardt, *A Mess of Greens* (University of Georgia Press, 2011), 99.

14. Melissa Walker's other publications include "Home Extension Work among African American Farm Women in East Tennessee, 1920–1939," *Agricultural History* 70, no. 3 (Summer 1996): 487–502; *All We Knew Was to Farm: Rural Women in the Upcountry South, 1919–1941* (Johns Hopkins University Press, 2002); "Farm Wives and Commercial Farming: The Case of Loudon County, Tennessee," *Tennessee Historical Quarterly* 57, no. 1 (Spring/Summer 1998): 42–61; "Making Do and Doing Without: East Tennessee Farm Women Cope with Economic Crisis; 1920–1941," *Journal of East Tennessee History* 68 (1996): 8–30; and *Country Women Cope with Hard Times: A Collection of Oral Histories* (University of South Carolina Press, 2004).

15. Rebecca Sharpless, *Fertile Ground, Narrow Choices: Women on Texas Cotton Farms, 1900–1940* (University of North Carolina Press, 2005); Rebecca Sharpless, "'She Ought to Have Taken Those Cakes': Southern Women and Rural Food Supplies," *Southern Cultures*

18, no. 2 (Summer 2012): 45–58; Rebecca Sharpless, *Grain and Fire: A History of Baking in the American South* (University of North Carolina Press, 2022).

16. Lynne A. Rieff, "'Rousing the People of the Land': Home Demonstration Work in the Deep South, 1914–1950" (PhD diss., Auburn University, 1995); Lynne A. Rieff, "'Go Ahead and Do All You Can': Southern Progressives and Alabama Home Demonstration Clubs, 1914–1940," in Bernhard et al., *Hidden Histories of Women*, 134–149; Lynne Rieff, "Revitalizing Southern Homes: Rural Women, the Professionalism of Home Demonstration Work, and the Limits of Reform, 1917–1945," in *Work, Family, and Faith: Rural Women in the Twentieth Century*, ed. Melissa Walker and Rebecca Sharpless (University of Missouri Press, 2006), 135–165; Lynne A. Rieff, "Improving Rural Life in Florida: Home Demonstration Work and Rural Reform, 1912–1940," in *Making Waves: Female Activists in Twentieth-Century Florida*, ed. Jack E. Davis and Kari Frederickson (University Press of Florida, 2003), 105–127.

17. Grey Osterud, "Farm Crisis and Rural Revitalization in South-Central New York during the Early Twentieth Century," *Agricultural History* 84, no. 2 (Spring 2010): 141–165; Katherine Jellison, *Entitled to Power: Farm Women and Technology, 1913–1963* (University of North Carolina Press, 1993); Mary Neth, *Preserving the Family Farm: Women, Community and the Foundations of Agribusiness in the Midwest, 1900–1940* (Johns Hopkins University, 1995); Deborah Fink, *Agrarian Women: Wives and Mothers in Rural Nebraska, 1880–1940* (University of North Carolina Press, 1992).

18. Dorothy Schwieder, *75 Years of Service: Cooperative Extension in Iowa* (Iowa State University Press, 1993); Joan M. Jensen, "Crossing Ethnic Barriers in the Southwest: Women's Agricultural Extension Education, 1914–1940," *Agricultural History* 60, no. 2 (Spring 1986): 169–181; Joan M. Jensen, "Canning Comes to New Mexico: Women and the Agricultural Extension Service, 1914–1919," *New Mexico Historical Review* 57 (1982): 361–386.

19. Ann E. McCleary, "'Seizing the Opportunity': Home Demonstration Curb Markets in Virginia," in Walker and Sharpless, *Work, Family, and Faith*, 99. See also by McCleary, "Negotiating the Urban Marketplace: Farm Women's Curb Markets in the 1930s," *Perspectives in Vernacular Architecture* 13, no. 1 (2006): 87.

20. McCleary, "Negotiating the Urban Marketplace," 87.

21. See also Sharpless, "She Ought to Have Taken"; Jones, "Taking What She Had"; Jones, "Women's Roles in Foods"; Lu Ann Jones, "Food and Markets," in *The New Encyclopedia of Southern Culture*, vol. 13: *Gender*, ed. Nancy Bercaw and Ted Ownby (University of North Carolina Press, 2014), 118–122; Rieff, "'Rousing the People,'" 134–136, 249.

22. Jones, *Mama Learned Us to Work*, 69–70. See also Engelhardt, *Mess of Greens*, 165–190.

23. According to a terminology tracker, "curb markets" was the most commonly used name until the 1950s and 1960s, with a brief comeback in the early 1990s. The term "farmers' market" began to gain more traction in the 1940s and increased in the 1980s. John Truman Horner, *Agricultural Marketing* (John Wiley & Sons, 1925); Henry E. Erdman, *American Produce Markets* (D. C. Heath and Company, 1928). See also Ronald R. Kline, *Consumers in the Country: Technology and Social Change in Rural America* (Johns Hopkins University Press, 2000).

24. Barbara R. Cotton, *The Lamplighters: Black Farm and Home Demonstration Agents in Florida, 1915–1965* (Tallahassee, Florida: The United States Department of Agriculture and Florida A&M University, 1982), 112.

25. See also Mary Kyes Stevens, "'By Our Surroundings Ye Shall Know Us': Alabama Black Home Demonstration Agents and the Complexities of Moral and Social Uplift, 1928–1936" (master's thesis, Sarah Lawrence College, 1999); Mary Amanda Waalkes, "Working in the Shadow of Racism and Poverty: Alabama's Black Home Demonstration Agents, 1915–1939" (PhD diss., University of Colorado, 1999).

26. Carmen V. Harris, "'A Ray Hope of Liberation': Blacks in the South Carolina Extension Service, 1915–1970" (PhD diss., Michigan State University, 2002), iii; Carmen V. Harris, "Grace under Pressure: The Black Home Extension Service in South Carolina, 1919–1966," in *Rethinking Home Economics: Women and the History of a Profession*, ed. Sarah Stage and Virginia B. Vincenti (Cornell University Press, 1997), 209. See also by Harris: "'Well I Just Generally Bes the President of Everything': Rural Black Women's Empowerment through South Carolina Home Demonstration Activities," *Black Women, Gender + Families* 3, no. 1 (Spring 2009): 91–112; "'The Extension Service Is Not an Integration Agency': The Idea of Race in the Cooperative Extension Service," *Agricultural History* 82, no. 2 (Spring 2008): 193–219; "The South Carolina Home in Black and White: Race, Gender, and Power in Home Demonstration Work," *Agricultural History* 93, no. 3 (Summer 2019): 477–501.

27. Cherisse Jones-Branch, "African American Home Demonstration Agents in the Field and Rural Reform in Arkansas, 1914–1965," in *Women in Agriculture: Professionalizing Rural Life in North America and Europe, 1880–1965*, ed. Linda M. Ambrose and Joan M. Jensen (University of Iowa Press, 2017), 162.

28. Debra A. Reid, *Reaping a Greater Harvest: African Americans, the Extension Service, and Rural Reform in Jim Crow Texas* (Texas A&M University Press, 2007); Debra A. Reid and Evan P. Bennett, eds., *Beyond Forty Acres and a Mule: African American Landowning Families since Reconstruction* (University of Florida Press, 2012); Debra A. Reid, "African Americans and Land Loss in Texas: Government Duplicity and Discrimination Based on Race and Class," *Agricultural History* 77, no. 2, (Spring 2003): 258–292; Pete Daniel, *Dispossession: Discrimination against African American Farmers in the Age of Civil Rights* (University of North Carolina Press, 2013).

29. See also Kathleen C. Hilton, who wrote about the U.S. Department of Agriculture: "Both in the Field, Each with a Plow: Race and Gender in USDA Policy, 1907–1929," in Bernhard et al., *Hidden Histories of Women*, 114–132; Kelly Anne Minor, "'Consumed with a Ghastly Wasting': Home Demonstration Confronts Disease in Rural Florida, 1920–1945," in *Entering the Fray: Gender, Politics, and Culture in the New South*, ed. Jonathan Daniel Wells and Shelia R. Phipps (University of Missouri Press, 2010), 68–95.

30. Jones, *Mama Learned Us to Work*, 79.

CHAPTER ONE. SOWING A PROGRESSIVE BUCOLIC HAVEN

1. Article 13, Section 11, *Constitution of Michigan of 1850*, https://www.legislature.mi.gov/documents/historical/miconstitution1850.htm.

2. "History," Michigan State University, accessed August 26, 2020, https://msu.edu/about/history.

3. Edmund J. James, *The Origin of the Land Grant Act of 1862 (The So-Called Morrill Act) and Some Account of Its Author, Jonathan B. Turner* (University of Illinois, 1910), 14–15; *Annual Report of the Illinois Farmers' Institute* 16, 1911, 126; Mary Turner Carriel, *The Life of Jonathan Baldwin Turner* (1911), 127–129, 138, 152.

4. James, *Origin of the Land Grant Act*, 20–21, 25.

5. Carriel, *Life of Jonathan Baldwin Turner*, 159.

6. Ibid., 157–159; Donald R. Brow, "Jonathan Baldwin Turner and the Land-Grant Idea," *Journal of the Illinois State Historical Society* 55, no. 4 (Winter 1962): 375.

7. Heather Cox Richardson and Joanne Freeman, "Higher Ed in Peril," *Now & Then* podcast, episode 75, October 19, 2022.

8. Ibid.; Morrill Act (1862), Milestone Documents, U.S. National Archives, https://www.archives.gov/milestone-documents/morrill-act. See also Margaret A. Nash, "The Dark History of Land-Grant Universities," *Washington Post*, November 8, 2019, https://www.washingtonpost.com/outlook/2019/11/08/dark-history-land-grant-universities/; Tristan Ahtone and Robert Lee, "Ask Who Paid for America's Universities," *New York Times*, May 7, 2020, https://www.nytimes.com/2020/05/07/opinion/land-grant-universities-native-america.

9. The land-grant colleges and universities in the territories include American Samoa Community College, University of the District of Columbia, University of Guam, Northern Marianas College, College of Micronesia, University of Puerto Rico at Mayagüez, and the University of the Virgin Islands.

10. Act of July 2, 1862 (Morrill Act), Pub. L. 37–108, 12 Stat. 503 (1862). The Improving America's Schools Act of 1994, which reauthorized the Elementary and Secondary Education Act of 1965, conveyed retroactive land-grant status to twenty-nine tribal colleges and universities, a number that has now expanded to thirty-five. These colleges and universities include Sitting Bull College (North Dakota), College of the Muscogee Nation (Oklahoma), Haskell Indian Nations University (Kansas), Chief Dull Knife Community College (Montana), Ilisagvik College (Alaska), and Saginaw Chippewa Tribal College (Michigan). "College Partners Directory," USDA National Institute of Food and Agriculture (NIFA), https://nifa.usda.gov/land-grant-colleges-and-universities-partner-website-directory; "NIFA Tribal Programs," https://nifa.usda.gov/programs/nifa-tribal-programs. For a complete list of land-grant colleges and universities, see "Land-Grant University Website Directory," https://nifa.usda.gov/land-grant-colleges-and-universities-partner-website-directory.

11. Frederick S. Humphries, "1890 Land-Grant Institutions: Their Struggle for Survival and Equality," in "The 1890 Land-Grant Colleges: A Centennial View," special issue, *Agricultural History* 65, no. 2 (Spring 1991): 4.

12. "Morrill Act of 1890," Alabama A&M University, https://www.aamu.edu/about/our-history/morrill-act-1890.html. See also Coy Cross, *Justin Smith Morrill: Father of the Land-Grant Colleges* (Michigan State University Press, 1999).

13. Agricultural College Act of 1890 Second Morrill Act of 1890, 7 U.S.C. § 322 (1890); Marcus M. Comer, Thasya Campbell, Kelvin Edwards, and John Hillison, "Cooperative

Extension and the 1890 Land-Grant Institution: The Real Story," *Journal of Extension* 44, no. 3 (June 2006), https://www.joe.org/joe/2006june/a4.php.

14. Thomas Aiello, associate professor of history and African American studies, Valdosta State University, email message to the author, March 3, 2019; Humphries, "1890 Land-Grant Institutions"; Carolyn B. Brooks and Alan I. Marcus, "The Morrill Mandate and a New Moral Mandate," *Agricultural History* 89, no. 2 (Spring 2015): 248–249; Wayne D. Rasmussen, "The 1890 Land-Grant Colleges and Universities: A Centennial Overview," *Agricultural History* 65, no. 2, (Spring 1991): 168–172; Leedell Neyland, *Historically Black Land-Grant Institutions and the Development of Agriculture and Home Economics, 1890–1990* (Florida A&M University Foundation, 1990), 21.

15. Wayne D. Rasmussen, *Taking the University to the People: Seventy-Five Years of Cooperative Extension* (Iowa State University Press, 1989), 26.

16. Alfred Charles True, *A History of Agricultural Education in the United States, 1785–1925*, U.S. Dept of Agriculture Miscellaneous Publication no. 36 (Government Printing Office, July 1929), 192–195, 63–65, 128–129; *From the Letter-Files of S. W. Johnson: Professor of Agricultural Chemistry in Yale University, 1856–1896, Director of the Connecticut Agricultural Experiment Station, 1877–1900,* ed. Elizabeth A. Osborne (Yale University Press, 1913), 192–203; Rasmussen, *Taking the University*, 26–28.

17. Rasmussen, *Taking the University*, 26, 28–29; Alfred Charles True, *A History of Agricultural Experimentation and Research in the United States, 1607–1925: Including a History of the United States Department of Agriculture*, U.S. Dept of Agriculture Miscellaneous Publication no. 251 (Government Printing Office, June 1937), 82–118.

18. Hatch Act of 1887, Pub. L. 49–314, 24 Stat. 440 (1887).

19. Rasmussen, *Taking the University*, 26–29; K. L. Beasley, "Sowing a Bountiful Harvest: The Methods of Cooperative Extension Service Promotion in Georgia, 1914–1924," *Journal of NACAA* 7, no. 2 (December 2014), http://www.nacaa.com/journal/index.php?jid=367; R. Grant Seals, "The Formation of Agricultural and Rural Development Policy with Emphasis on African-Americans: II. The Hatch-George and Smith-Lever Acts," *Agricultural History* 65, no. 2 (Spring 1991): 12–34.

20. *Report of the Commission on Country Life, with an Introduction by Theodore Roosevelt* (Sturgis & Walton Co., 1917), 10. The original report was published as a Senate document in 1909, becoming widely available in 1911 when it was published as a book, with subsequent reprints.

21. Clayton S. Ellsworth, "Theodore Roosevelt's Country Life Commission," *Agricultural History* 34, no. 4 (October 1960): 157. See also Horace Plunkett, "The Problems of Country Life: Round Table Discussion; Sir Horace Plunkett, Chairman," *American Economic Association Quarterly* 11, no. 1 (1910): 171–176.

22. Ellsworth, "Theodore Roosevelt's Country Life Commission," 156–159; "Liberty Hyde Bailey: A Man for All Seasons," https://rmc.library.cornell.edu/bailey/index/html; "History of the Bailey Farmhouse," Bailey Museum, *https://www.libertyhydebailey.org/*. The museum also has a Facebook page: https://www.facebook.com/libertyhydebailey/.

23. Scott J. Peters and Paul A. Morgan, "The Country Life Commission: Reconsidering a Milestone in American Agricultural History," *Agricultural History* 78, no. 3 (Summer 2004): 290.

24. Ibid., 293–294.

25. Ibid, 294.

26. U.S. Congress, Senate, *Report of the Country Life Commission,* 60th Cong., 2d sess. (1909), S. Doc. 705, https://www.fca.gov/template-fca/about/Report_of_the_Country_Life_Commission.pdf; *Report of the Commission on Country Life,* 150; Peters and Morgan, "Country Life Commission," 293–294.

27. Liberty Hyde Bailey, *The Country Life Movement in the United States* (Macmillan, 1911), 20.

28. Liberty Hyde Bailey, *The Fundamental Question in Country Life* (1910), 1–24; for a sample of scholarship, see William L. Bowers, *The Country Life Movement in America, 1900–1920* (Kennikat Press, 1974); David B. Danbom, "Rural Education Reform and the Country Life Movement, 1900–1920," *Agricultural History* 53, no. 2 (April 1979): 462–474; Mabel Carney, *Country Life and the Country School: A Study of the Agencies of Rural Progress and of the Social Relationship of the School to the Country Community* (Row, Peterson and Company, 1912); Martin T. Oliff, *Getting Out of the Mud: The Alabama Good Roads Movement and Highway Administration, 1898–1928* (University of Alabama Press, 2017); Katherine Ann Hempstead, "Agricultural Change and the Rural Problem: Farm Women and the Country Life Movement" (PhD diss., University of Pennsylvania, 1992).

29. William A. McKeever, *Farm Boys and Girls* (MacMillan, 1913), 299.

30. O. J. Stevenson, *The Country Life Reader* (Charles Scribner's Sons, 1916), vii–xii, 415.

31. Martha Foote Crow, *The American Country Girl* (Frederick A. Stokes Company, 1915), n.p.

32. Ibid., 348. Crow advocated for "the trained Country Girl," who accessed HDAs, Extension publications, and other resources.

33. U.S. Congress, Senate, *Report of the Country Life Commission,* 60th Cong., 2d sess. (1909), 8–9.

34. Joyce Mae Thierer, "The Country Life Movement and Rural Women, 1908–1931" (PhD diss., Kansas State University, 1994), 12.

35. Ibid., 232; 225.

36. Ibid., 12–13, 232.

37. South Carolina State Agricultural and Mechanical College is now South Carolina State University, Tuskegee Institute is known today as Tuskegee University, Georgia State Industrial College for Colored Youth is the predecessor institution to Savannah State University, and Massachusetts Agricultural College became the University of Massachusetts Amherst. Hubert's efforts meant creating a "model black farming community" in Georgia, which led to "a strong black rural middle class, somewhat insulated from the effects of Jim Crow laws." Mark Schultz, "Benjamin Hubert and the Association for the Advancement of Negro Country Life," in *Beyond Forty Acres and a Mule: African American Landowning Families since Reconstruction,* ed. Debra A. Reid and Evan P. Bennett (University Press of Florida, 2012), 83–105; "The Horizon," *Crisis,* November 1926, 40; Milton C. Sernett, *Bound for the Promised Land: African American Religion and the Great Migration* (Duke University Press, 1997), 215. See also Benjamin F. Hubert, "The Country Life Movement for Negroes," *Rural America* 7 (May 1929).

38. Peters and Morgan, "Country Life Commission," 291–292; Bowers, *Country Life Movement*, 133.

39. For some years the meeting of the American Country Life Association was known as the National Country Life Conference. Digital copies of the proceedings are available on the HathiTrust website, which were scanned and digitized from archives at the University of Wisconsin-Madison, University of Iowa, Harvard, Princeton, Indiana University, and The Ohio State University.

40. "National Civic Federation Records 1894–1949 [bulk 1900–1920]," New York Public Library Archives and Manuscripts, http://archives.nypl.org/mss/2101.

41. Owen was the daughter and sister of prominent Alabama politicians and the wife of the founder and director of the Alabama Department of Archives and History. For more on the National Civic Federation, see Christopher J. Cyphers, *The National Civic Federation and the Making of a New Liberalism, 1900–1915* (Praeger, 2002); Marie Bankhead Owen, "Rural America and the Woman's Department," *The Bulletin* 2, no. 7 (November 1914): 7–9. The Bulletin was the official publication of the Woman's Department of the National Civic Federation.

42. "Annual Report—Woman's Department," *The Bulletin* 2, no. 8 (February 1915): 2–5; Marie Bankhead Owen, "Rural America and the Women's Department," *The Bulletin* 2, no. 7 (November 1914): 7–9; "Woman's Department National Civic Federation to Hold Convention in Washington," *Tennessean*, December 5, 1915; "Training Schools for Nurses: Memorial to Mrs. Wilson," December 13, 1914, *Washington Times*. For more on the NCF's work with Ellen Axson Wilson, see Kathryn Beasley, "'I Think We Have an Angel in the White House': First Lady Ellen Axson Wilson and Her Social Activism Concerning the Washington, D.C. Slums, 1913–1914" (master's thesis, Valdosta State University, 2012).

43. Peabody College's story began in 1785 with the founding of Davidson Academy, which became Cumberland College in 1806, the University of Nashville in 1826, and Peabody Normal College in 1889. In 1979, Peabody merged into Vanderbilt University as the Peabody College of Education and Human Development. Paul K. Conkin, *Peabody College: From a Frontier Academy to the Frontiers of Teaching and Learning* (Vanderbilt University Press, 2002), 207.

44. Samuel C. Mitchell, "Industrial Education in the South," *Southern Workman* 39, no. 6 (June 1910): 331.

45. Conkin, *Peabody College*, 207–208; Mary S. Hoffschwelle, "The Science of Domesticity: Home Economics at George Peabody College for Teachers, 1914–1939," *Journal of Southern History* 57, no. 4 (November 1991): 663; Paul K. Conkin, "The School of Country Life," *Vanderbilt Magazine*, Spring 2010, http://www.vanderbilt.edu/magazines/vanderbilt-magazine/2010/04/the-school-of-country-life/; Helen White Gentry, "Knapp Farm," *Peabody Reflector* 26, no. 10 (November 1953): 220; Hollis B. Frissell, "Forty-Second Annual Report of the Principal," *Southern Workman* 39, no. 5 (May 1910): 302; Lu Ann Jones, "'Re-visioning the Countryside': Southern Women, Rural Reform, and the Farm Economy in the Twentieth Century" (PhD diss., University of North Carolina at Chapel Hill, 1996), 216–217. See also Oscar Baker Martin, *The Demonstration Work: Dr. Seaman A. Knapp's Contribution to Civilization* (Stratford, 1921).

46. Vanderbilt University News, "The School of Country Life," April 7, 2010, http://www.vanderbilt.edu/magazines/vanderbilt-magazine/2010/04/the-school-of-country-life/.

47. Gentry, "Knapp Farm," 219–220; "Knapp Farm Readied for Sale at $1 Million," *Peabody Reflector* 38, no. 6 (November–December 1965): 168; Vanderbilt University News, "School of Country Life"; Hoffschwelle, "Science of Domesticity," 663; Conkin, *Peabody College*, 208; "The Knapp Farm Club House," *Peabody Reflector* 32, no. 6 (November 1959): 196.

48. George Peabody College for Teachers *Bulletin* 4, no. 3 (March 1916): 44–45; Peabody College *Bulletin* 5, no. 2 (December 1916): 1–16; Peabody College *Bulletin* 7, no. 2 (November 1918): 1–16; Peabody College *Bulletin* 9, no. 5 (March 1921): 80–85; Peabody College *Bulletin* 7, no. 5 (March 1924): 88–91; Peabody College *Bulletin* 18, no. 4 (April 1929): 124–130; Hoffschwelle, "Science of Domesticity," 673. See also Joan M. Jensen, "Good Farms, Markets, and Communities: Emily Hoag and Rural Women as Producers," in *Women in Agriculture: Professionalizing Rural Life in North America and Europe, 1880–1965* (University of Iowa Press, 2017): 34–64.

49. It was named for its two sponsors, Georgia's Hoke Smith, a Democratic senator and former governor, and South Carolina's Francis Lever, a Democratic representative and leader on the Committee of Agriculture. Dewey W. Grantham, *Hoke Smith and the Politics of the New South* (Louisiana State University Press, 1967); *Smith-Lever Act of 1914: Hearings, Report, and Debate* (Virginia Agricultural Extension Service, 1959); Marvin Owings, "SC's Lever Pioneered Extension Service," blueridgenow.com, June 1, 2014, https://www.blueridgenow.com/story/news/2014/06/01/scs-lever-pioneered-extension-service/28317846007; Philip A. Grant Jr., "Senator Hoke Smith, Southern Congressman, and Agricultural Education, 1914–1917," *Agricultural History* 60, no. 2 (Spring 1986): 111–122; "An Act to Provide for Cooperative Agricultural Extension Work between the Agricultural College in the Several States Receiving the Benefits of an Act of Congress Approved July Second Eighteen Hundred and Sixty-Two, and of Acts Supplementary Thereto, and the United States Department of Agriculture," Pub. L. No. 63–95, 38 Stat. 372 (1914), Chapter 79 of the 63rd Congress.

50. "The Fifth Annual Report of the National Association for the Advancement of Colored People," *Crisis,* April 1915, 291–292. See also Carmen V. Harris, "'The Extension Service Is Not an Integration Agency': The Idea of Race in the Cooperative Extension Service," *Agricultural History* 82, no. 2 (Spring 2008): 193–219; Seals, "Formation."

51. These universities went by different names at the time. They are referred to by their current titles for clarity. Jeannie M. Whayne, "Black Farmers and the Agricultural Cooperative Extension Services: The Alabama Experiences, 1945–1965," *Agricultural History* 72, no. 3 (Summer 1998): 524.

52. These arrangements included "creating a division for this work in the extension service, or in the case of Florida and South Carolina, by securing the cooperation of the State women's colleges. . . . In Alabama [the need for access led] to the admission of women and the creation of a home-economics department of instruction in the Polytechnic Institute." True, *History of Agricultural Education*, 290; William A. Lloyd, *County Agricultural Agent Work under the Smith-Lever Act, 1914 to 1924*, United States Department of Agriculture Miscellaneous Circular 59 (May 1926), 1–60.

53. Jan Scholl, "Extension Family and Consumer Sciences: Why It Was Included in the Smith-Lever Act of 1914," *Journal of Family & Consumer Sciences* 105, no. 4 (2013): 8–16; Beasley, "Sowing a Bountiful Harvest."

54. See also Danielle Dreilinger, *The Secret History of Home Economics: How Trailblazing Women Harnessed the Power of Home and Changed the Way We Live* (Norton, 2021).

55. William L. Bowers, "Country-Life Reform, 1900–1920: A Neglected Aspect of Progressive Era History," *Agricultural History* 45, no. 3 (July 1971): 211–221. See also Florence Ward, *Home Demonstration Work under the Smith-Lever Act, 1914–1929*, U.S. Department of Agricultural Circular 43 (June 1929).

56. For clarity, these universities will be referred to by their current names, unless in a direct quote. Dwayne Cox, *The Village on the Plain: Auburn University, 1856–2006* (University of Alabama Press, 2016); "The History of Auburn University," Auburn University, accessed October 27, 2019, http://www.auburn.edu/main/welcome/aboutauburn.php.

57. "Our History," Alabama A&M University, https://www.aamu.edu/about/our-history; "Morrill Act of 1890"; "Alabama A&M University Takes a Look Back at School History," WAFF-48, Huntsville, Alabama, Feb. 9, 2023, https://www.waff.com/2023/02/09/alabama-am-university-takes-look-back-school-history; *Souvenir Program for the Formal Observance of the Seventy-Fifth Anniversary and Founder's Commemoration of the Alabama Agricultural and Mechanical College*, 1950, 5, 21, University Archives & Special Collections, the J. F. Drake Memorial Learning Resources Center, Alabama A&M University; Walter T. Gravitt obituary, printed in the program for his funeral service, September 27, 1958, University Archives & Special Collections, the J. F. Drake Memorial Learning Resources Center, Alabama A&M University.

58. "Cooperative Extension Work for Alabama," *Emancipator*, June 26, 1920, 1.

59. "History of Tuskegee University," Tuskegee University, accessed January 14, 2020, https://www.tuskegee.edu/about-us/history-and-mission; B. D. Mayberry, *The Role of Tuskegee University in the Origin, Growth, and Development of the Negro Cooperative Extension System, 1881–1990* (Brown Printing Company, 1989), xiv; Robert E. Zabawa and Sarah T. Warren, "From Company to Community: Agricultural Community Development in Macon County, Alabama, 1881 to the New Deal," *Agricultural History* 72, no. 2 (Spring 1998): 459–486; Neyland, *Historically Black Land-Grant Institutions*, 35, 44–49. See also Marcie Cohen Ferris, *The Edible South: The Power of Food and the Making of an American Region* (University of North Carolina Press, 2014), 119–123.

60. Kym Klass, "Historic ASU Discrimination Suit Changed Education in Alabama," *Montgomery Advertiser*, January 23, 2014; "Guide to the Knight v. Alabama Records," Troy University, https://www.troy.edu/about-us/dothan-campus/wiregrass-archives/inventories/036.html; James Langcuster, "Alabama Cooperative Extension System (ACES)," Encyclopedia of Alabama, last updated July 10, 2023, http://www.encyclopediaofalabama.org/article/h-3287.

61. "About Us," Alabama Cooperative Extension System, accessed January 14, 2020, *https://www.aces.edu/blog/category/about-us/*; "Cooperative Extension Program," Tuskegee University, accessed January 29, 2020, https://www.tuskegee.edu/programs-courses/colleges-schools/caens/cooperative-extension-program.

62. Campbell also worked for the USDA. Abigail Harper and Eric Walcott, "Black His-

tory Month Spotlight: T.M. Campbell—America's First Extension Agent," Michigan State University, February 15, 2019, https://www.canr.msu.edu/news/thomas-monroe-campbell-first-extension-agent-black-history-month; "Cooperative Extension Program," Tuskegee University, accessed January 29, 2020, https://www.tuskegee.edu/programs-courses/colleges-schools/caens/cooperative-extension-program; Mayberry, *Role of Tuskegee University*; Carmen V. Harris, "'Extension Service.'" The T. M. Campbell papers are located in Tuskegee University's archives.

63. N. Juanita Coleman, "Cooperative Extension Work in Agriculture and Home Economics, State of Alabama: A Supplement to the Annual Report, Agricultural Extension Service in Movable School for Women, for the Year Ending December 31, 1920," 1–2, Alabama Cooperative Extension System Records, RG no. 71, Ralph B. Draughon Library, Auburn University; T. M. Campbell, *The Movable School Goes to the Negro Farmer* (Tuskegee Institute Press, 1936), 91–96, 108–113, 116–121; B. D. Mayberry, "The Tuskegee Movable School: A Unique Contribution to National and International Agriculture and Rural Development," *Agricultural History* 65, no. 2 (Spring 1991): 85–104.

64. Mayberry, "Tuskegee Movable School," 95; Campbell, *Movable School*, 119, 107–110; Robert Zabawa, "Tuskegee Institute Movable School," Encyclopedia of Alabama, last updated March 30, 2023, http://www.encyclopediaofalabama.org/article/h-1870; "The Alabama Movable School," *Extension Service Review* 7, no. 9 (September 1936), 140. See also Clement Richardson, "Negro Farmers of Alabama: A Phase of Tuskegee's Extension Work," *Southern Workman* 46, no. 7 (July 1917): 383–390; J. A. Evans, *Extension Work among Negroes*, United States Department of Agriculture Circular 355 (September 1925), 22.

65. Darryl Palmer, "Before Extension," University of Florida blogs, May 8, 2014, https://blogs.ifas.ufl.edu/ifascomm/2014/05/08/100-years-of-extension-in-florida/; Eliot Kleinberg, "Florida History: Is UF Really Florida's Oldest State University?," *Gainesville Sun*, Sept. 5, 2019 (updated Sept. 9, 2019), https://www.gainesville.com/news/20190905/florida-history-is-uf-really-floridas-oldest-state-university; "Land Grant & Sea Grant: Acts, History & Institutions," University of Florida Institute of Food and Agricultural Sciences, accessed July 9, 2020, https://ifas.ufl.edu/land-grant-sea-grant-acts-history/; "East Florida Seminary Records," series 164, University of Florida Smathers Libraries, www.library.ufl.edu/spec/archome/Series164.htm; Benjamin F. Andrews, *The Land Grant of 1862 and the Land-Grant Colleges*, Department of the Interior, Bureau of Education, Bulletin 1918, no. 13 (Government Printing Office, 1918), 15–16; Henry Gardner Cutler, *History of Florida: Past and Present, Historical and Biographical, Issued in Three Volumes, Volume 1* (Lewis Publishing Company, 1923), 226–232; *Florida Agricultural College Grounds—Lake City, Florida* (photonegative), Florida Memory: State Library and Archives of Florida, accessed July 9, 2020, *https://www.floridamemory.com/items/show/140181*.

66. Kleinberg, "Florida History"; Sarah "Moxy" Moczygemba, "The Buckman Act and the Consolidation of Florida's Universities," U.S. Caribbean and Florida Digital Newspaper Project, June 6, 2016, www.ufndnp.domains.uflib.ufl.edu/digital-humanities/the-buckman-act-florida-universities/.

67. "About UF: History," University of Florida Faculty Handbook, accessed February 28, 2024, https://handbook.aa.ufl.edu/about_uf/; Institute of Food and Agricultural Sciences, University of Florida, accessed July 9, 2020, https://ifas.ufl.edu/about-us/; Judy

Biss, "Celebrating the 100th Anniversary of the U.S. Extension Service," University of Florida IFAS Extension, January 11, 2014, http://nwdistrict.ifas.ufl.edu/phag/2014/01/11/celebrating-the-100th-anniversary-of-the-us-extension-service/; Samuel Proctor, "The Early Years of the Florida Experiment Station, 1888–1906," *Agricultural History* 36, no. 4 (October 1962): 213–221.

68. "History of Florida A&M University," FAMU: Florida Agricultural and Mechanical University, accessed August 26, 2019, https://www.famu.edu/about-famu/history/index.php. https://www.famu.edu/about-famu/history/index.php

69. Leedell W. Neyland, *Florida Agricultural and Mechanical University: A Centennial History, 1887–1987* (Florida A&M University Foundation, 1987), 24. See also Leedell W. Neyland and John W. Riley, *The History of Florida Agricultural and Mechanical University* (University of Florida Press, 1963).

70. Neyland, *Historically Black Land-Grant Institutions*, 53–54; Charles Magee, "African-Americans' Past History in Agriculture and Why We Should Be in Agriculture Today," CAFS *Magazine* (Winter 2017): 10–13; *African American Agricultural Extension Agents in Florida* (online exhibit), University of Florida George A. Smathers Libraries, accessed July 20, 2020, www.exhibits.uflib.ufl.edu/ExtensionAgents/.

71. Barbara R. Cotton, *The Lamplighters: Black Farm and Home Demonstration Agents in Florida, 1915–1965* (U.S. Department of Agriculture and Florida A&M University, 1982), 14–17.

72. "Funeral Services Held Tuesday for A. A. Turner," *Tallahassee Democrat*, October 20, 1956, 5; "Florida's Woman Supervisor," *Modern Farmer* 1, no. 1, March 1, 1929, 1. Previously, A. A. Turner's wife, Susan, also worked within the home demonstration department but for less pay, as his requests for a counterpart female agent had been denied. Lynne A. Rieff, "Improving Rural Life in Florida: Home Demonstration Work and Rural Reform, 1912–1940," in *Making Waves: Female Activists in Twentieth-Century Florida*, ed. Jack E. Davis and Kari Frederickson (University Press of Florida, 2003), 110.

73. "Alfred Turner Taken by Death at Home Here," *Tallahassee Democrat*, October 13, 1956, 2; Neyland, *Historically Black Land-Grant Institutions*, 158–159; Darryl Palmer, "Project VI: Florida Extension in the Era of Segregation," University of Florida blogs, February 13, 2014, https://blogs.ifas.ufl.edu/ifascomm/2014/02/13/project-vi-florida-extension-in-the-era-of-segregation/; Cotton, *Lamplighters*, 18. One letter, which appears to be from A. P. Spencer to I. O. Schaub, an employee of the Southern Division of Extension Work in Washington, D.C., discussed T. M. Campbell and efforts to expand the Movable School program to Florida: "I have always felt that Campbell was a very efficient fellow. He certainly knows how to handle himself when among white people and from what I have seen among the negroes, I believe he is quite a leader so I have a good deal of confidence in the recommendations that Campbell would make." University of Florida Institute for Food and Agricultural Sciences (IFAS) Extension Records, University Special Collections and Archives, George A. Smathers Library, University of Florida, Gainesville, Florida (hereafter cited as UF Archives. (Home demonstration and Cooperative Extension Service records were merged and revised under the IFAS Extension Records, series 093, with four subseries of archival material, which includes the home demonstration records: https://findingaids.uflib.ufl.edu/repositories/2/resources/906.

74. Beluah S. Shute, "A Summary of Negro Home Demonstration Work in Florida 1915–1937 Inclusive," 2, IFAS Extension Records, UF Archives.

75. Cotton, *Lamplighters*, 43.

76. Ibid., 44. See also Shute, "Summary," 1–4.

77. Evans, *Extension Work among Negroes*, 5.

78. Alma Warren, "Home Demonstration, 1908–1960," 1, in "Histories of Home Demonstration Work by A. Harris, M. Keown, Keown & Spencer, A. Warren, L. Kiser" folder, IFAS Extension Records, UF Archives; Palmer, "Before Extension"; Agnes Ellen Harris, *Home Demonstration Work in Florida*, Extension Bulletin no. 5, (T. J. Appleyard, State Printer, February 1916), 5, IFAS Extension Records, UF Archives; Mary E. Keown, "Some Comments on Twenty-Four Years of Home Demonstration in Florida, 1912–1936," IFAS Extension Records, UF Archives; Ruby Richardson, "Counties Having Home Demonstration Work Continuously, 1912–1936," IFAS Extension Records, UF Archives.

CHAPTER TWO. RURAL ALABAMA WOMEN AND CULTIVATING COMMERCE

1. Isadora Williams, "Annual Report of County Extension Agents, Tuscaloosa County, Alabama, 1925," 5, Alabama Cooperative Extension System Records, RG no. 71, Ralph B. Draughon Library, Auburn University (hereafter cited as ACES Records). The Draughon Library also holds Extension Service records from Tuskegee University.

2. John P. Beasley, professor and former head of the Department of Crop, Soil, and Environmental Sciences at the College of Agriculture, Auburn University, interview with the author, August 6, 2019. Kiwi fruit, canola and carinata in oilseeds, and hemp as a fiber crop and medicinal oil are new additions to the agricultural economy.

3. R. H. Smith, *History of the Boll Weevil in Alabama, 1910–2007*, Bulletin 670 Alabama (Auburn Agricultural Experiment Station, July 2007), 3. See also James C. Giesen, *Boll Weevil Blues: Cotton, Myth, and Power in the American South* (University of Chicago Press, 2011). For more about rural Alabama, see Wayne Flynt, *Poor but Proud: Alabama's Poor Whites* (University of Alabama Press, 2001); Martin T. Oliff, *Getting Out of the Mud: The Alabama Good Roads Movement and Highway Administration, 1898–1928* (University of Alabama Press, 2017).

4. Zach Wilcox, "Enterprise Prepares for Boll Weevil Monument's 100th Birthday," WTVY-TV, Dothan, Alabama, December 10, 2019, https:///www.wtvy.com/content/news/Enterprise-prepares-for-Boll-Weevil-Monuments-100th-birthday-566068701.html; Chasity Maxie, "Boll Weevil Centennial Celebration," WTVY-TV, Dothan, Alabama, December 3, 2019, https://www.wtvy.com/content/news/Boll-Weevil-Centennial-Celebration-565747312.html; Emily Blewjas, *The Story of Alabama in Fourteen Foods* (University of Alabama Press, 2019), 161–163.

5. For example, Enterprise's Boll Weevil Soap Company created a special "Unbollweevible" fragrance. "Boll Weevil Soap Company," https://www.bollweevilsoapcompany.com/products/unbollweevible. Sports teams at the University of Arkansas at Monticello and Alabama's Enterprise State Community College are known as the Boll Weevils.

6. Tisby Luella Ray, "Annual Report of Home Demonstration Work for Women and Girls Calendar Year 1919, Clarke County," OEWS 753-p8, ACES Records.

7. Mary Feminear, *Report of Home Demonstration Work in Alabama in 1918*, Circular 27 (Auburn, Alabama, February 1919), 12, ACES Records.

8. There was a push to work six days a week, which also brought racial skepticism from African American farmers, despite assurances both whites and African Americans were being asked to work extra days in the name of patriotism. "How Department of Agriculture Is Helping in War Work by Promoting Production of the Nation's Food Resources Summarized in Report to President by Secretary Houston," *Official Bulletin* 1, no. 183 (Committee on Public Information, December 13, 1917), 9, 11; Angela Jill Cooley, *To Live and Dine in Dixie: The Evolution of Urban Food Culture in the Jim Crow South* (University of Georgia Press, 2015), 38–40; T. M. Campbell, "The Saturday Service League," *Southern Workman* 48, no. 3 (March 1919): 130–133. See also Glenda Gilmore, *Gender & Jim Crow: Women and the Politics of White Supremacy in North Carolina, 1896–1920* (University of North Carolina Press, 1996), 196–199.

9. *Alabama's Black Belt Counties*, University of Alabama Center for Economic Development, accessed January 14, 2020, https://www.uaced.ua.edu/uploads/1/9/0/4/19045691/about_the_black_belt.pdf; Gladys Tappan, "Annual Report of Extension Work in District III for 1924," 1, ACES Records.

10. Blewjas, *Story of Alabama*, 152.

11. Valerie Grim, "African American Rural Culture, 1900–1950," in *African American Life in the Rural South, 1900–1950*, ed. R. Douglas Hurt (University of Missouri Press, 2003), 108.

12. J. A. Evans, *Extension Work among Negroes*, United States Department of Agriculture Department Circular 355 (September 1925), 3.

13. Ibid.

14. Ibid., 7.

15. Ibid.

16. W. B. Mercier, *Extension Work among the Negroes*, 1920, United States Department of Agriculture Circular 190 (1920), 6.

17. Evans, *Extension Work among Negroes*, 7–8. See also Giesen, *Boll Weevil Blues*, 159–165.

18. "A Woman's Story at the Conference: Mrs. Calloway Urges Colored Men to Stay on Southern Farms," *Tuskegee Student*, March 3, 1917, 8.

19. Ibid., 7–8. See also Cynthia Neverdon-Morton, *Afro-American Women of the South and the Advancement of the Race, 1895–1925* (University of Tennessee Press, 1989), 126.

20. Laura R. Daly, "Annual Report of Home Demonstration Work for Women and Girls, Calendar Year 1919, Montgomery County," OEWS 753-p8, ACES Records.

21. Jeannie Whayne, "'I Have Been through the Fire': Black Agricultural Extension Agents and the Politics of Negotiation," in *African American Life in the Rural South, 1900–1950*, ed. R. Douglas Hurt (University of Missouri Press, 2003), 156–157.

22. Evans, *Extension Work among Negroes*, 15.

23. Whayne, "'I Have Been Through,'" 156. See also Carmen V. Harris, "'The Extension Service Is Not an Integration Agency': The Idea of Race in the Cooperative Extension Service," *Agricultural History* 82, no. 2 (Spring 2008): 193–219; *Beyond Forty Acres and a Mule: African American Landowning Families since Reconstruction*, ed. Debra Ann Reid

and Evan P. Bennett (University Press of Florida, 2012); Debra Reid, "Rural African Americans and Progressive Reform," *Agricultural History* 74, no. 2 (Spring 2000): 322–339.

24. Bruce J. Reynolds, "Black Farmers in America, 1865–2000: The Pursuit of Independent Farming and the Role of Cooperatives," RBS Research Report 194, United States Department of Agriculture, 2003, 8; Susan Lynn Smith, *Sick and Tired of Being Sick and Tired: Black Women's Health Activism in America, 1890–1950* (University of Pennsylvania Press, 1995), 92, 98. See also Susan M. Reverby, *Examining Tuskegee: The Infamous Syphilis Study and Its Legacy* (University of North Carolina Press, 2009); Neverdon-Morton, *Afro-American Women*; Pete Daniel, "African American Farmers and Civil Rights," *Journal of Southern History* 73, no. 1 (February 2007): 3–38; Pete Daniel, *Dispossession: Discrimination against African American Farmers in the Age of Civil Rights* (University of North Carolina Press, 2013).

25. Stephen Hudak, "Story of Ocoee Massacre Finally Being Told—100 Years after It Happened," *Orlando Sentinel*, October 29, 2020; Robert Stephens, "The Truth Laid Bare," *Pegasus: The Magazine of the University of Central Florida*, Fall 2020, https://www.ucf.edu/pegasus/the-truth-laid-bare. According to the Equal Justice Initiative, Alabama had 361 lynching victims between 1877 and 1950, while Florida had 311. Jefferson County, Alabama, was the most "active lynching county" in the state, with twenty-nine, while in Florida it was Orange County, with thirty-three. Equal Justice Initiative, *Lynching in America: Confronting the Legacy of Racial Terror*, 3rd ed., 2017, https://lynchinginamerica.eji.org/report; Valorie Lawson, "Lynching Victims Honored with Historical Marker in Lowndes County," WSFA-TV, Montgomery, Ala., https://www.wsfa.com/story/35455231/lynching-victims-honored-with-historical-marker-in-lowndes-county, May 17, 2017. See also Paul Ortiz, *Emancipation Betrayed: The Hidden History of Black Organizing and White Violence in Florida from Reconstruction to the Bloody Election of 1920* (University of California Press, 2006), 205–228.

26. Gladys Tappan, "Annual Report of Extension Work in District III, 1924," 29, ACES Records.

27. Ibid. Ida Stewart Fischer moved to Montgomery from Kentucky after 1920. *1930 U.S. Census*, Montgomery County, Alabama, census place, Precinct 9, Enumeration District (ED) 0040, p. 1B (penned), https://www.ancestry.com; "Ida Stewart Fischer," Find a Grave, accessed March 14, 2020, https://www.findagrave.com/memorial/68478074.

28. Clara Nale, "Annual Report of County Extension Workers, Henry County, Alabama, December 1, 1925, to December 1, 1926," n.p., ACES Records.

29. "Farm Demonstration Work, November 1, 1910," 7–8, ACES Records.

30. Margaret Murray Washington was also a cofounder of the National Association of Colored Women and helped form Tuskegee's Women's Club, part of the Alabama Federation of Colored Women's Clubs. Mrs. Booker T. Washington (Margaret Murray Washington), "Are We Making Good?," *Tuskegee Student*, October 16, 1915, 1–2. See Sheena Harris, *Margaret Murray Washington: The Life and Times of a Career Clubwoman* (University of Tennessee Press, 2021). For more on these federated women's clubs, see Neverdon-Morton, *Afro-American Women*); Rita B. Dandridge, ed., *The Collected Essays of Josephine J. Turpin Washington: A Black Reformer in the Post Reconstruction South* (University of Virginia Press, 2019); LaVonne Leslie, ed., *The History of the National Association*

of Colored Women's Clubs, Inc.: A Legacy of Service (Xlibris, 2012); Jacqueline Anne Rouse, "Out of the Shadow of Tuskegee: Margaret Murray Washington, Social Activism, and Race Vindication," *Journal of Negro History* 81, no. 1–4 (Winter–Autumn 1996): 31–46; "For Community Betterment," *Southern Workman* 49, no. 7 (July 1920): 296–298; Danielle Dreilinger, *The Secret History of Home Economics: How Trailblazing Women Harnessed the Power of Home and Changed the Way We Live* (Norton, 2021), 9–65.

31. Helen Johnston, "Annual Report Home Demonstration Work—Alabama 1929," 21, ACES Records; T. M. Campbell, "Annual Report of Home Demonstration Work for Women and Girls Calendar Year 1919—Summary of Negro Women Agents, Alabama," OEWS 753-6, ACES Records.

32. N. Juanita Coleman, Annual Report of Home Demonstration Work for Women and Girls: Calendar Year 1919, Macon County, Alabama," OEWS 753-p4, ACES Records.

33. Coleman, "Annual Report of Home Demonstration Work for Women and Girls: Calendar Year 1919, Macon County, Alabama," OEWS 753-p8, n.p.; N. Juanita Coleman, "Cooperative Extension Work in Agriculture and Home Economics, State of Alabama: A Supplement to the Annual Report, Agricultural Extension Service in Movable School for Women, for the Year Ending December 31, 1920," 1–3, ACES Records.

34. Coleman, "Annual Report of Home Demonstration Work for Women and Girls: Calendar Year 1919, Macon County, Alabama," OEWS 753-p8.

35. N. Juanita Coleman, "Home Demonstration Work in Alabama," *Southern Workman* 49 (January–December 1920), 412–413.

36. Ray, "Annual Report of Home Demonstration Work for Women and Girls Calendar Year 1919," OEWS 753-p4.

37. "A Supplement to the Annual Report on Agricultural Extension Service among Negroes in Alabama (Women and Girls), Movable Schools in Agriculture for The Year Ending December 31, 1921," 1, ACES Records.

38. Rosa B. Jones, originally a Virginia HDA, was appointed as the assistant HDA in Alabama in 1920. "Cooperative Extension Work for Alabama," *Emancipator*, June 26, 1920, 1; Rosa B. Jones, state agent for Negro women, "Supplement to the Annual Report of the Agricultural Extension Service as Performed by Negro Women Agents for the Year Ending December 31, 1920," 5, 7, 9, ACES Records.

39. For more about Laura Daly, see Mona Domosh, *Disturbing Development in the Jim Crow South* (University of Georgia Press, 2023); Laura Daly, "Home Demonstration Agent for Montgomery County, 1921," 1–3, ACES Records. See also Melissa Walker, "Home Extension Work among African American Farm Women in East Tennessee, 1920–1939," *Agricultural History* 70, no. 3 (Summer 1996): 487–502.

40. "Supplement to the Annual Report on Agricultural Extension Service among Negroes in Alabama (Negro Women Agents) for the Year Ending December 31, 1921," 2–3, ACES Records; T. L. Perkins, "Home Demonstration Agent for Clarke County, 1921," 1–2, ACES Records.

41. L. C. Hanna, "Annual Report of Extension Work in Alabama, 1923," 3, ACES Records.

42. T. M. Campbell, field agent, "Plan of Work in Negro Extension Work for 1926," 2, 1–6, ACES Records.

43. Evans, *Extension Work among Negroes*, 15–18.

44. Mary Amanda Waalkes, "Working in the Shadow of Racism and Poverty: Alabama's Black Home Demonstration Agents, 1915–1939" (PhD diss., University of Colorado, 1999), 47, 44.

45. Rosa B. Jones, "Annual Report of Extension Work in Alabama, 1923," 3, ACES Records.

46. Ibid. In 1923, the Movable School visited twenty-four Alabama counties, traveling more than nine thousand miles. Hanna, "Annual Report of Extension Work in Alabama, 1923," 3, ACES Records. See also Kathleen C. Hilton, "Both in the Field, Each with a Plow: Race and Gender in USDA Policy, 1907–1929," in *Hidden Histories of Women in the New South*, ed. Virginia Bernhard, Betty Brandon, Elizabeth Fox-Genovese, Theda Perdue, and Elizabeth Hayes Turner (University of Missouri Press, 1994), 114–133.

47. "Mary L. Snipes, Home Demonstration Agent, Hale and Perry Counties, 1921," 1–2, ACES Records.

48. Rosa Jones, "Supplement to the Annual Report of the Agricultural Extension Work among Negroes (in Alabama), for the Year Ending December 31, 1926," 3, ACES Records.

49. Daly, "Home Demonstration Agent for Montgomery County, 1921," 1–3. See also Walker, "Home Extension Work."

50. L. N. Duncan, "A Summary Report of the Work of the Alabama Extension Service for the Fiscal Year July 1, 1924–June 30, 1925," sheet 44, ACES Records.

51. The second movement concerned Seaman Knapp's Farmers' Improvement Society of Texas. Juanie Noland, "Jeanes Supervisors," Encyclopedia of Alabama, July 2, 2009, encyclopediaofalabama.org/article/h-2327; Mabel Carney, *Country Life and the Country School: A Study of the Agencies of Rural Progress and of the Social Relationship of the School to the Country Community* (Row, Peterson and Company, 1912), 308–309.

52. Alabama Department of Education, *The Work of the Jeans Supervising Industrial Teachers and the Homemakers' Clubs for Negro Girls, Alabama 1916*, 6, issued by the Department of Education, Montgomery, Alabama, 1917, (Brown Printing Company, Montgomery, Alabama), located at the Alabama Department of Archives and History, Montgomery, Alabama. See also "County Teaching Training Schools for Negroes, 1913," trustees of the John F. Slater Fund, Occasional Papers, no. 14, Southern Education Foundation, folder 10, box 2, Archives Research Center, Robert W. Woodruff Library, Atlanta University Center; "A Suggested Course of Study for County Training Schools for Negroes in the South, 1917," trustees of the John F. Slater Fund, Occasional Papers, no. 18, Southern Education Foundation, folder 10, box 5, Archives Research Center, Robert W. Woodruff Library, Atlanta University Center; "What Jeanes Foundation Is Doing for Negroes in the Southland," *Montgomery Advertiser*, May 4, 1913, 11; "Negro Rural Schools Have Exhibit at City Hall," *Age-Herald*, April 10, 1914, 2.

53. "Progress of the Jeanes Fund for Negroes in Alabama," *Montgomery Advertiser*, January 16, 1926, 4.

54. Jane E. McAllister and Dorothy M. McAllister, "Adult Education for Negroes in Rural Areas: The Work of the Jeanes Teachers and Home and Farm Demonstration Agents," *Journal of Negro Education* 14, no. 3 (Summer 1945): 331. See also Lily Farley Ross Dale, "The Jeanes Supervisors in Alabama 1909–1963" (PhD diss., Auburn University, 1998).

55. "Cooperative Extension Work for Alabama," *Emancipator*, June 26, 1920, 1; *An Education Study of Alabama*, Bulletin 1919, no. 41 (Government Printing Office, 1919), 330–331; "Successful Farmers' Meeting Held by Negroes," *Huntsville Times*, January 27, 1916, 6; "Tuskegee Summer School Continues," *Montgomery Advertiser*, June 28, 1915, 3; "Twenty-Sixth Annual Tuskegee Conference Is Most Largely Attended in Its History," *Montgomery Advertiser*, January 18, 1917, 9; "Workers Conference at Tuskegee Shows Growth of Education and Thrift," *Montgomery Advertiser*, January 18, 1918, 9; "Negro Training School to Be Located in This County by Vote Sale," *Dothan Eagle*, December 17, 1924, 1. See also Cherisse Jones-Branch, *Better Living by Their Own Bootstraps: Black Women's Activism in Rural Arkansas, 1914–1965* (University of Arkansas Press, 2021); Ann Short Chirhart, *Torches of Light: Georgia Teachers and the Coming of the Modern South* (University of Georgia Press, 2005).

56. Mary R. Strudwick, "Annual Report of County Extension Workers, Baldwin County, November 1, 1923 to Dec 1, 1924," 2–3, ACES Records; "Annual Report—1924, Home Demonstration Work, State Home Demonstration Agent," 43–45, ACES Records. On Martha Haupt Sanderson, see Betsy Butgerelt, "Miss Auburn of 1929 Had 'Personality Plus,'" *Auburn Plainsman*, November 8, 1979, A-10. Strudwick's report also included a newspaper clipping celebrating Haupt's win in a contest of best jars of canned vegetables. Strudwick, "Annual Report of County Extension Workers, Baldwin County, November 1, 1923 to Dec 1, 1924," 10.

57. Gladys Tappan, "Annual Report of Extension Work in District III for 1924," 1; L. N. Duncan, "A Summary Report of the Alabama Extension Service for the Year Ending December 31, 1923," 16–17, ACES Records; Mary Feminear, "Annual Report Home Demonstration Work, 1920," 3, ACES Records; McAllister and McAllister, "Adult Education for Negroes," 331–340. The first graduate in home economics at API was Gladys McCain, an HDA in Madison and Coosa Counties. Mina Willis, an assistant state home demonstration agent and home economics specialist for the state in 1920, earned a B.S. in agriculture and an M.S. in science from the University of Wisconsin before attending the University of Idaho for a B.S. degree in home economics.

58. "Annual Report by L.N. Duncan, Director, Alabama Extension Service, December 31, 1929," 30, ACES Records.

59. Mary Feminear, "Report of Home Demonstration Work in Alabama July 1, 1918 to June 30, 1919," 2, ACES Records.

60. Agnes Ellen Harris, May I. Cureton, Elizabeth Forney, Helen Johnson, and Elizabeth Mauldin, "Annual Report of Extension Work in Alabama for 1926," 31, ACES Records; Ann E. McCleary, "'Seizing the Opportunity': Home Demonstration Curb Markets in Virginia," in *Work, Family, and Faith: Rural Women in the Twentieth Century*, ed. Melissa Walker and Rebecca Sharpless (University of Missouri Press, 2006), 108. See also Pamela Tyler, "The Ideal Rural Southern Woman as Seen by Progressive Farmer in the 1930s," *Southern Studies* 2, no. 3 (1981): 315–333.

61. Mary Feminear, "Annual Report Home Demonstration Work, 1920," 6, ACES Records; Mamie C. Thorington, "Annual Report of County Extension Agents from November 15, 1924 to November 15, 1925, Montgomery County," 4, ACES Records.

62. Mamie C. Thorington, "Annual Report of County Extension Workers, Montgom-

ery County, from November 1, 1923 to November 1, 1924," 13, ACES Records; Mrs. D. B. (Diana B.) Williams, "Annual Report of Extension Work in Etowah County, Alabama, 1927," 13, ACES Records.

63. Mrs. J. E. S. Rudd, "Annual Report of County Extension Work for Clay County, Alabama, November 15, 1923 to December 1, 1924," 15, ACES Records. See also Wayne Flynt, *Alabama in the Twentieth Century* (University of Alabama Press, 2004), 277–278.

64. Mrs. D. B. (Diana B.) Williams, "Annual Report of Extension Work in Etowah County, Alabama, 1927," 13, ACES Records.

65. Ruth Dobyne, "Annual Report of County Extension Workers, Autauga County, Alabama, 1929," 11, ACES Records.

66. Elizabeth S. Delony, "Annual Report of County Extension Workers, Franklin County, Alabama, 1926," 10, ACES Records. DeLony's name is spelled as "DeLoney" in some documents and reports.

67. Ibid.

68. Mary Feminear, "Home Demonstration Work in Alabama 1919," 6, ACES Records.

69. Victoria C. Lingo, "Annual Report of County Extension Workers, Barbour County, Alabama, 1924," 1, 26, ACES Records. Maintaining "good grooming" techniques and keeping tidy appearances were frequent topics of home demonstration programming everywhere. In Virginia, for example, HDAs advised rural and farm women to "improve their dress, appearance, and posture, so that city women would respect them enough to patronize their booths." McCleary, ""Seizing the Opportunity,'" 119.

70. "Cooperative Extension Work in Agriculture and Home Economics, Annual Narrative Report of Eula Hester and Carrie B. Threaton, County Home Demonstration Agents, Pike County, 1929," n.p., ACES Records.

71. Madge J. Reese, "Annual Report—1916, Home Demonstration Work—State Home Demonstration Agent," 6–9 ACES Records; Mary Feminear, "Report of the Home Demonstration Work in Alabama 1918," 4, ACES Records. For more on canning clubs, see Minoa D. Uffelman, "Tomato Clubs as Salvation: Canning Clubs for Girls and the Uplift of Southern Rural Society," in *Tennessee Women in the Progressive Era: Toward the Public Sphere in the New South*, ed. Mary A. Evins (University of Tennessee Press, 2013), 71–94; Elizabeth S. D. Engelhardt, *A Mess of Greens* (University of Georgia Press, 2011), 83–117; Jane McKimmon, *When We're Green We Grow* (University of North Carolina Press, 1945), 27–44.

72. Madge J. Reese, "Annual Report—1915, Home Demonstration Work—State Home Demonstration Agent," 1–3, ACES Records.

73. Reese, "Annual Report—1916, Home Demonstration Work—State Home Demonstration Agent," 4.

74. Ibid., 8.

75. Ibid.

76. "Annual Report—1923, Home Demonstration Work, State Home Demonstration Agent," 13, ACES Records.

77. Mary Feminear, *Report of Home Demonstration Work in Alabama 1919*, Circular 41 (Auburn, Alabama, March 1920), 48, ACES Records.

78. Ruth Whorton, "Annual Report of County Extension Workers, 1925, Lee County, Alabama, 15/16"; Flossie Ozella Bonner Malloy information: *1920 U.S. Census*, Lee

County, Alabama, census place, Smith's Station, ED 182, p. 11A (penned), https://www.ancestry.com; *1930 U.S. Census,* Lee County, Alabama, census place, Smith's Stations, ED 0027, p. 12A (penned), https://www.ancestry.com; "Flossie B. Malloy," Find a Grave, accessed June 4, 2020, https://www.findagrave.com/memorial/84541929.

79. Ida Brunson, "Annual Report of County Extension Workers, Crenshaw County, November 1, 1923 to October 31, 1924," 2, ACES Records.

80. Elizabeth Collings, "Annual Report of Extension Work in Tuscaloosa County, Alabama for 1927"; "Local Women Aid in Sale" (undated clipping from unknown newspaper), n.p., ACES Records.

81. "Annual Report by L.N. Duncan, Director, Alabama Extension Service, December 31, 1929," 75. For an example of poultry sales, see "Poultry Raisers Realize $18,000 from Sales Here," *Dothan Eagle,* 1, April 4, 1929.

82. "Annual Report—1922, Home Demonstration Work," 17, ACES Records; Feminear, *Report of Home Demonstration Work in Alabama 1919,* 51.

83. Females and males participated in beekeeping. Mary W. Segers, "Annual Report of Extension Work in Escambia County, Alabama, 1928," 4–5, ACES Records.

84. Thorington, "Annual Report of County Extension Workers, Montgomery County, from November 1, 1923 to November 1, 1924," 5.

85. Agnes Ellen Harris et al., , "Annual Report of Extension Work in Alabama for 1926," 19, ACES Records; Mabel Feagin, "Annual Report of County Extension Workers, Bullock County, Alabama, December 1, 1924 to December 1, 1925," 5, ACES Records.

86. Pearl Jones, "Annual Report of Extension Work in Food Preservation for 1926," 10–11, ACES Records.

87. Cindy Lester, "Annual Report of Extension Work, Conecuh County, 1928," 10, ACES Records.

88. "Muscadine Grape Industry Boost in this Section," *Montgomery Advertiser,* February 8, 1920, 27.

89. "Muscadine Grape in Favor," *Marion County News,* May 5, 1920, 2.

90. Lingo, "Annual Report of County Extension Workers, Barbour County, Alabama, 1924," 34.

91. "Busy Farm Women Make the Farm Pay," *Geneva County Reaper,* January 15, 1926, 4; *Ashland Progress,* July 12, 1928, 5; *Alexander City Outlook,* December 20, 1928, 4; "Annual Report of Pearl Jones, State Food Preservation Specialist, Auburn, Alabama, 1926," n.p., ACES Records; Victoria Lingo, "Narrative Report of County Home Demonstration Agent, Barbour County, October 31, 1929," 13–15, ACES Records; Rosebud Baker Davis information: *1920 U.S. Census,* Barbour County, Alabama, census place, Eufaula, ED 7, p. 1B (penned), https://www.ancestry.com; *1930 U.S. Census,* Barbour County, Alabama, census place, Eufaula, ED 0010, p. 27A (penned), https://www.ancestry.com; "Rosebud B. Davis," Find a Grave, accessed October 17, 2022, https://www.findagrave.com/memorial/27560942/rosebud-b-davis.

92. "Annual Report of Pearl Jones, Specialist in Food Preservation from June 1–25 to November 30–25," 12, ACES Records.

93. "Calendar of Work 1922–1923, Helen Johnston Assistant State Home Demonstration Agent in charge [of] District 4," 2, ACES Records.

94. Mrs. J. E. S. Rudd, "Annual Report of County Extension Agents, Clay County, Alabama, November 1, 1927–November 1, 1928," 40–41, ACES Records.

95. "Annual Report Home Demonstration Work, 1916, Home Demonstration Agent," 5, ACES Records.

96. Olga Acree, "Annual Report of County Extension Workers, Tallapoosa County, Jan 16, 1924 to Sept 30, 1924," 6, ACES Records; Martha McCall, "Annual Report of County Extension Workers, Henry County, Alabama, 1924," 13, ACES Records.

97. Ola Overby, "Annual Report of County Extension Workers, Pickens County, Alabama, November 1, 1926 to November 1927," 10, ACES Records.

98. "State Report, All Agents, December 1924–December 1925," 81, ACES Records. See also Erin Kellen, "Extension Service Promoted Women's Home Industry through Craft Activity," Alabama Folkways Articles, Alabama State Council on the Arts, February 1994, http://www.arts.alabama.gov/traditional_culture/folkwaysarticles/EXTENSIONSERVICE.aspx.

99. Mary Strudwick, "Annual Report of County Extension Workers, Baldwin County, Alabama, December 1924–December 1925," 6, 10, ACES Records.

100. Ruth Dobyne, "Annual Report of County Extension Workers, Autauga County, Alabama, November 1, 1926 to November 1, 1927," 11, ACES Records; Ruth Dobyne, "Annual Report of Extension Work in Autauga County, Alabama for 1928," n.p., ACES Records.

101. Mary Strudwick, "Annual Report of Extension Work in Baldwin County, 1927," 6, ACES Records.

102. Regina Matlock, "Annual Report of County Extension Workers, Perry County, Alabama, 1928," 15, 30, ACES Records; Annelu Hairston Mason information: *1930 U.S. Census*, Perry County, Alabama, census place, Oak Grove, ED 0015, p. 2B (penned), https://www.ancestry.com; "Annelu Hairston Mason," Find a Grave, accessed March 3, 2020, https://www.findagrave.com/memorial/69373647.

103. Wyche G. Pruett, "Annual Report of County Extension Workers, Houston County, Alabama, November 1, 1926 to November 1, 1927," 25, ACES Records.

104. Mrs. D. B. (Diana B.) Williams, "Annual Report of Extension Work in Etowah County, Alabama, 1927," 13.

105. "State Report, All Agents, December 1924–December 1925," 81; Mary Lessie Beaty Bedsole information: *1930 U.S. Census*, Barbour County, Alabama, census place, Coxs Mill, ED 0017, p. 5A (penned), https://www.ancestry.com; "Mary Lessie Beaty Bedsole," Find a Grave, https://www.findagrave.com/memorial/59529079.

106. "Annual Report—1927 Home Demonstration Work, State Home Demonstration Agent," 61, ACES Records; "Pine Needle Basketry in Clay County" (undated clipping from unknown newspaper), in J. E. S. Rudd, "Annual Report of County Extension Workers, Clay County, Alabama, December 1, 1926 to November 1, 1927," n.p., ACES Records; Anna Lee Goza Kelley information: *1930 U.S. Census*, Clay County, Alabama, census place, Ashland, ED 0006, p. 8A (penned), https://www.ancestry.com; "Anna Lee Goza Kelley," Find a Grave, https://www.findagrave.com/memorial/45344361.

107. Mrs. J. E. S. Rudd, "Annual Report of County Extension Workers, Clay County, Alabama, December 1, 1925 to December 1, 1926," 23.

108. Mrs. W. L. Murdoch, "Pine Needle Industry Aiding Farm Women in Bringing Amenities into Home Life" (undated clipping from unknown newspaper), in Rudd, "Annual Report of County Extension Agents, Clay County, November 1, 1927–November 1, 1928," n.p.; "Pine Needle Basketry in Clay County" (undated clipping from unknown newspaper), in Rudd, "Annual Report of County Extension Workers, Clay County, Alabama, December 1, 1926 to November 1, 1927, n.p. For one history on 4-H, see Gabriel Rosenberg, *The 4-H Harvest: Sexuality and the State in Rural America* (University of Pennsylvania Press, 2015).

109. "Annual Report—1927 Home Demonstration Work," 61–64.

110. Rudd, "Annual Report of County Extension Workers, Clay County, Alabama, December 1, 1926 to November 1, 1927," 3–4.

111. "Annual Report—1927 Home Demonstration Work, State Home Demonstration Agent," 62–63.

112. Rudd, "Annual Report of County Extension Workers, Clay County, Alabama, December 1, 1926 to November 1, 1927," 3.

113. Johnston, "Annual Report Home Demonstration Work—Alabama 1929," 59.

114. "Annual Report—1927 Home Demonstration Work," 62.

115. Rudd, "Annual Report of County Extension Workers, Clay County, Alabama 1926," 22.

116. The photo of Clara Bow appears in Rudd, "Annual Report of County Extension Agents, Clay County, November 1, 1927–November 1, 1928," n.p.

117. Ibid., 11, 18.

118. Ibid., 17.

119. Ibid., 19.

120. Ibid., 18, "Foreword."

121. Ibid., 29. This might be Martha Lou Sims Harris, wife of Charles D. Harris, *1930 U.S. Census*, Clay County, Alabama, census place, Ashland, ED 0007, p. 1B (penned), https://www.ancestry.com; "Martha L. Sims Harris," Find a Grave, https://www.findagrave.com/memorial/13495991.

122. Rudd, "Annual Report of County Extension Agents, Clay County, November 1, 1927–November 1, 1928," 34. Emma Gerda/Gorda Mitchell Green information: *1920 U.S. Census*, Clay County, Alabama, census place, Ashland, ED 42, p. 7A (penned), https://www.ancestry.com; *1930 U.S. Census*, Clay County, Alabama, census place, Ashland, ED 0006, p. 7B (penned), https://www.ancestry.com; "Emma Gorda Green," Find a Grave, https://www.findagrave.com/memorial/7074449.

123. Rudd, "Annual Report of County Extension Agents, Clay County, November 1, 1927–November 1, 1928," 30.

124. Johnston, "Annual Report Home Demonstration Work—Alabama 1929," 72–74; J. E. S. Rudd, "Annual Report of County Extension Workers, Clay County, Alabama, 1929, 41–43, ACES Records.

125. Rudd, "Annual Report of County Extension Workers, Clay County, Alabama, 1929," 46–50.

126. Ibid., 50.

127. Evelyn Peyton, "Annual Report of County Extension Workers, Madison County, Alabama, November 1923–November 1924," 31, ACES Records.

128. Blanche Heard, "Annual Report of Extension Work for 1927 in Limestone County, Alabama," n.p., ACES Records; Bertha Cox Hull information: *1930 U.S. Census*, Limestone County, Alabama, census place, Quid Nune, ED 0025, p. 18B (penned), https://www.ancestry.com; "Bertha B. Cox Hull," Find a Grave, accessed August 31, 2020, https://www.findagrave.com/memorial/35631884.

129. Heard, "Annual Report of Extension Work for 1927 in Limestone County, Alabama," n.p. Inez Mae McGraw Stewart information: *1930 U.S. Census*, Limestone County, Alabama, census place, Mooresville, ED 0022, p. 16B (penned), https://www.ancestry.com; "Inez Mae McGraw Stewart," Find a Grave, accessed February 21, 2020, https://www.findagrave.com/memorial/30150640.

130. "Annual Report of Josephine P. Eddy, State Clothing Specialist, Auburn, Alabama, 1926," 14, ACES Records.

131. May I. Cureton, "Annual Report of Extension Work in Dist. 1 for 1926," n.p. ACES Records.

132. Elizabeth Collings, "Annual Report of County Extension Workers, Tuscaloosa County, Alabama, 1928," 20; ACES Records; Dorothy Dean, "Annual Report of Extension Work in Clothing and Handicraft, 1929," 113, ACES Records; "Leather Lesson Given Saturday," *Tuscaloosa News & Times Gazette*, November 21, 1926, 1; "Women Working in Leather Are to Get Lesson," *Tuscaloosa News & Times Gazette*, December 1, 1926, 5.

133. "Annual Report of Pearl Jones, Specialist in Food Preservation from June 1–25 to November 30–25," 12.

134. *Digest* 7, no. 7 (April 1930): 22, ACES Records. Tallapoosa County's HDA reported that "one lady is assisting her husband in selling cedar mixing paddles," and "seven ladies have established a sale on fancy work." Nonnie Wood, "Annual Report of County Extension Workers, Tallapoosa County, Alabama, November 1, 1926 to November 1, 1927," n.p., ACES Records.

135. Loveman, Joseph, and Loeb Department Store sold products made by rural women and allowed women to visit the store for demonstrations. "Local Women Aid in Sale" (undated clipping from unknown newspaper), in Collings, "Annual Report of Extension Work in Tuscaloosa County, Alabama for 1927," n.p. See also "Alabama Handiwork Placed on Display," *Birmingham News*, October 27, 1927, 25.

136. "Making Good with Fans in Alabama," *Southern Ruralist*, September, no year given, clipping in Lida Jones, "Annual Report of County Extension Workers, Macon County, Alabama, November 1, 1923 to November 1, 1924," 22, ACES Records; "Mrs. R. N. Lightfoot of Shorter Makes Beautiful Fans" (undated clipping from unknown newspaper), in Jones, "Annual Report of County Extension Workers, Macon County, Alabama, November 1, 1923 to November 1, 1924," 22 (the same clippings are also in May Cureton, "Report of Northwest Alabama District No. 1, 1924," 41, ACES Records); "Sixty-Six Year Old Woman Creates Unique Industry," *Montgomery Advertiser*, November 22, 1923, 12; Martha/Mattie Visscher Lightfoot information: *1920 U.S. Census*, Macon County, Alabama, census place, La Place, ED 138, p. 3A (penned), https://www

.ancestry.com; *1930 U.S. Census*, Montgomery County, Alabama, census place, Montgomery, ED 0034, p. 5A (penned), https://www.ancestry.com; obituary of Mrs. Martha V. Lightfoot, *Montgomery Advertiser*, April 7, 1949, 2; "Miss Mattie Visscher," *Montgomery, Alabama Directories, 1880–1895*, 1891; "Martha Gazena Lightfoot," in *Alabama, U.S., Deaths and Burials Index, 1881–1974*, FHL film number 1908838, https://www.ancestry.com.

137. Mabel Feagin, "Annual Report of County Extension Workers, Bullock County, Alabama, November 1, 1927 to November 1, 1928," 3, ACES Records; "Death Claims Mrs. Tompkins," *Union Springs Herald*, April 7, 1977, 10; Eva Ingram Tompkins information: *1920 U.S. Census*, Bullock County, Alabama, census place, Union Church, ED 44, p. 3A (penned), https://www.ancestry.com; *1930 U.S. Census*, Bullock County, Alabama, census place, Union Church, ED 0023, p. 1B (penned), https://www.ancestry.com; "Eva Tompkins," Find a Grave, accessed October 31, 2022, https://www.findagrave.com/memorial/160346378/eva-tompkins.

138. Stella Harms, "Annual Report of County Extension Workers, Calhoun County, Alabama, 1924," 7, ACES Records.

139. Mary Strudwick, "Annual Report of County Extension Workers, Baldwin County, Alabama, 1923," 3, 15, ACES Records.

140. Zelma Jackson, "Annual Report of County Extension Workers, Chambers County, Alabama, November 5, 1923 to December 1, 1924," 3, ACES Records.

141. Thorington, "Annual Report of County Extension Workers 1924, Montgomery County," 8.

142. Ruth Kernodle, "Annual Report of County Extension Workers, 1925, Hale County, Alabama," 3, ACES Records.

143. Harms, "Annual Report of County Extension Workers, Calhoun County, Alabama, 1924," 13–14.

144. Josephine Eddy, "Annual Report of Extension Work in Clothing for 1926, State Clothing Specialist," 50, ACES Records.

145. "Annual Report of Josephine P. Eddy, State Clothing Specialist, Auburn, Alabama, 1926," 14.

146. Agnes Ellen Harris et al., "Annual Report of Extension Work in Alabama for 1926," 35–36; Lula Brown Keller information: *1930 U.S. Census*, Escambia County, Alabama, census place, Jack Springs, ED 0011, p. 14B (penned), https://www.ancestry.com; "Lula Virginia Brown Keller," Find a Grave, accessed January 17, 2020, https://www.findagrave.com/memorial/39693400.

147. Mabel Feagin, "Annual Report of Extension Work in Bullock County, Alabama, 1927," 5, ACES Records; Elizabeth DeLoney, "Annual Report of Extension Work in Franklin County, Alabama, 1927," 16, ACES Records; "Fingers Flew All over All Alabama," *Birmingham News*, October 31, 1927, 20; "Home Products Are Being Sold," *Birmingham Post-Herald*, November 13, 1927, 89.

148. Annual Report of Josephine P. Eddy, State Clothing Specialist, Auburn, Alabama, 1926," 14.

CHAPTER THREE. GROWING DISPOSABLE INCOME THROUGH FLORIDA'S
HOME DEMONSTRATION PROGRAMS

1. During her career Harris was also the state home demonstration agent in Alabama, as well as dean of women at Auburn University and at the University of Alabama in the 1920s. Minoa D. Uffelman, "Tomato Clubs as Salvation: Canning Clubs for Girls and the Uplift of Southern Rural Society," in *Tennessee Women in the Progressive Era: Toward the Public Sphere in the New South*, ed. Mary A. Evins (University of Tennessee Press, 2013), 71–93; "Agnes Ellen Harris," Find a Grave, accessed September 6, 2020, https://www.findagrave.com/memorial/93913969/agnes-ellen-harris.

2. Darryl Palmer, "Extension Can-Do," University of Florida blogs, November 7, 2013, blogs.ifas.ufl.edu/ifascomm/2013/11/07/extension-can-do.

3. Ibid.

4. On the canned food industry, see Anne Zeide, *Canned: The Rise and Fall of Consumer Confidence in the American Food Industry* (University of California Press, 2018). For seminal works on California women in the canning industry, see Vicki L. Ruiz, *Cannery Women, Cannery Lives: Mexican Women, Unionization, and the California Food Processing Industry, 1930–1950* (University of New Mexico Press, 1987); Patricia Zavella, *Women's Work and Chicano Families: Cannery Workers of the Santa Clara Valley* (Cornell University Press, 1987). See also Lynne A. Rieff, "'Rousing the People of the Land': Home Demonstration Work in the Deep South, 1914–1950" (PhD diss., Auburn University, 1995), 80–81; Kelly Ann Minor, "Power in the Land: Home Demonstration in Florida, 1915–1960" (PhD diss., University of Florida, 2005), 111–166; "Early History of USDA Home Canning Recommendations," Critical Review of Home Preservation Literature and Current Research, https://nchfp.uga.edu/publications/usda/review/earlyhis.htm; Gregg Steven Pearson, "The Democratization of Food: Tin Cans and the Growth of the American Food Processing Industry, 1810–1940" (PhD diss., Lehigh University, 2016).

5. Agnes Ellen Harris, *Canning Clubs in Florida*, Bulletin 2, 3, University of Florida Institute for Food and Agricultural Sciences (IFAS) Extension Records, University Special Collections and Archives, George A. Smathers Library, University of Florida, Gainesville, Florida (hereafter cited as UF Archives). Home demonstration and Cooperative Extension Service records were merged and revised under the IFAS Extension Records, series 093, with four subseries of archival material, which includes the home demonstration records: https://findingaids.uflib.ufl.edu/repositories/2/resources/906.

6. Ibid., 5.

7. Ibid., 12–13.

8. Agnes Ellen Harris, *Home Demonstration Work in Florida*, Extension Bulletin no. 5 (T. J. Appleyard, State Printer, February 1916), 9–10, UF Archives.

9. *Canning Clubs in Florida*, 9.

10. "Annual Report for Home Demonstration Work, State of Florida for the Year July 1st, 1914 to July 1st, 1915," 7, information chart on unnumbered page, IFAS Extension Records, UF Archives. Lynne Rieff mentions, "Rural families raised a surplus of food and earned additional income selling their products. Marketing directly to the public was an

idea that interested rural people of both races and complemented the 'live-at-home' program. Rural women especially saw an opportunity to contribute to their families' income by selling extra canned goods, fresh fruits and vegetables, and other home-grown items." Lynne A. Rieff, "Improving Rural Life in Florida: Home Demonstration Work and Rural Reform, 1912–1940," in *Making Waves: Female Activists in Twentieth-Century Florida*, ed. Jack E. Davis and Kari Frederickson (University Press of Florida, 2003), 114.

11. Sarah Partridge, "Home Demonstration Annual Report, 1918, South and East Florida," 6–7, IFAS Extension Records, UF Archives.

12. *Canning Clubs in Florida*, 6–7. See also Minor, "Power in the Land," 111, 124–128; Ola Powell, *Successful Canning and Preservation: Practical Hand Book for Schools, Club, and Home Use* (Lippincott, 1917). One insightful work about the connection between women and markets is Nancy Grey Osterud, "Gender and the Transition to Capitalism in Rural America," *Agricultural History* 67, no. 2 (Spring 1993): 14–29.

13. Agnes Ellen Harris, *Home Demonstration Work in Florida*, 10.

14. Ibid.

15. "Annual Report for Home Demonstration Work, July 1st, 1914 to July 1st, 1915," 9.

16. Partridge, "Home Demonstration Annual Report, 1918," 8.

17. Agnes Ellen Harris, "Report of Assistant State Home Demonstration Agent, 1918," n.p., IFAS Extension Records, UF Archives. See also Minor, "Power in the Land," 11.

18. Agnes Ellen Harris, "Report of Assistant State Home Demonstration Agent, 1918," n.p.

19. "The War College," program, IFAS Extension Records, UF Archives.

20. See also Agnes Ellen Harris, "Report of the State Home Demonstration Agent, 1918," n.p., IFAS Extension Records, UF Archives; "Extension Home Economics—Meeting Everchanging Needs," in folder entitled "Bicentennial History: King & Hammer, 1976," 1–11, IFAS Extension Records, UF Archives. For more on Florida and World War I, see Gary R. Mormino, "All Disquiet on the Home Front: World War I and Florida, 1914–1920," *Florida Historical Quarterly* 97, no. 3 (Winter 2019): 249–299; Andy Huse, "War, Fear, and Bread in Tampa, 1917–1918," *Florida Historical Quarterly* 97, no. 3 (Winter 2019): 300–329; Tejal Rao, "Food Supply Anxiety Brings Back Victory Gardens," *New York Times*, March 26, 2020; Rose Hayden-Smith, *Sowing the Seeds of Victory: American Gardening Programs of World War* (McFarland & Company, 2014); Cecilia Gowdy-Wygant, *Cultivating Victory: The Women's Land Army and the Victory Garden Movement* (University of Pittsburgh Press, 2013); Elaine F. Weiss, *Fruits of Victory: The Woman's Land Army of America in the Great War* (Potomac Books, 2008).

21. Sarah Partridge, "Report of Progress of Home Demonstration Work for Quarter Ending September 30, 1922," 2, IFAS Extension Records, UF Archives.

22. Sarah Partridge, "Annual Report of Home Demonstration Work for Women and Girls, Calendar Year 1920, S. Florida," OEWS 753-p8, IFAS Extension Records, UF Archives; Sarah Partridge, "Brief Report of Home Demonstration Work in Poultry, 1921," 4, IFAS Extension Records, UF Archives; Sarah Partridge, "Report of the State Agent for Home Demonstration Work for the Calendar Year Ending December 31, 1920," 8, IFAS Extension Records, UF Archives.

23. Partridge, "Report of the State Agent for Home Demonstration Work for the Calendar Year Ending December 31, 1920," 12–14.

24. Isabelle S. Thursby, "Narrative Report of Isabelle S. Thursby, Foods and Marketing Agent, Florida, 1926," 20, IFAS Extension Records, UF Archives.

25. Flavia Gleason, "Excerpts from March 1926 Reports," May 8, 1926, 1, IFAS Extension Records, UF Archives. Cho-Cho was sponsored by and represented New York's Child Health Organization. The clown toured the country and appeared in advertisements to encourage children to adopt and maintain healthy practices. C. C. Carstens, "National Social Agencies Rendering Services to the Home and Family: (2) Child Welfare Organizations," *Annals of the American Academy of Political and Social Sciences* 105 (January 1923): 55–56; *Primary Education* 28, no. 1 (January 1920): 51; *Public Health Journal* 13, no. 3 (March 1922): 110; "Preaches Gospel of Health," *Tampa Tribune*, January 7, 1934, 7.

26. "Home Demonstration Work—A Pioneering Program," 1, in "Histories of Home Demonstration Work by A. Harris, M. Keown, Keown & Spencer, A. Warren, L. Kiser" folder, IFAS Extension Records, UF Archives.

27. "Cooperative Extension Work in Agriculture and Home Economics: Report of General Activities for 1917 with Financial Statement for the Fiscal Year Ending June 30, 1917," 72, IFAS Extension Records, UF Archives.

28. Ibid.

29. Partridge, "Home Demonstration Annual Report, 1918, South and East Florida," 8.

30. Partridge, "Annual Report of Home Demonstration Work for Women and Girls, Calendar Year 1920, S. Florida," OEWS 753-p7.

31. Frantz P. Lund to Wilmon Newell, December 14, 1922, IFAS Extension Records, UF Archives. See also Nicolaas Mink, "Selling the Storied Stone Crab: Eating, Ecology, and the Creation of South Florida Culture," *Gastronomica* 6, no. 4 (Fall 2006): 32–43; Nicolaas Mink, "Eating the Claws of Eden: Stone Crabs, Tourism, and the Taste of Conservation in Florida and Beyond," *Florida Historical Quarterly* 86, no. 4 (Spring 2008): 470–497; Jack E. Davis, *The Gulf: The Making of An American Sea* (Liveright Publishing, 2017).

32. Lucy Belle Settle, "South and East District—Annual Report—1923," 9, IFAS Extension Records, UF Archives.

33. Sarah Partridge, "Florida Home Demonstration Leader Annual Report, 1923," 5, IFAS Extension Records, UF Archives.

34. Flavia Gleason, "Excerpts from October 1926 Reports," November 29, 1926, 2, IFAS Extension Records, UF Archives.

35. Flavia Gleason, "Excerpts from October 1927 Reports," November 22, 1927, 4, IFAS Extension Records, UF Archives; Minor, "Power in the Land," 124–128.

36. Sarah Partridge, "Brief Report of Home Demonstration Work in Florida, 1920," 4, IFAS Extension Records, UF Archives.

37. Lonny I. Landrum, "Report of the District Agent of Home Demonstration Work in North and West Florida, for the Year, Ending December 31, 1921," 6, IFAS Extension Records, UF Archives.

38. Ibid.

39. "Home Demonstration Circular, 851," 1922, 9, IFAS Extension Records, UF Archives.

40. Flavia Gleason, "Annual Narrative of Home Demonstration Work in Florida, 1924," 10, IFAS Extension Records, UF Archives.

41. There was no official state agent for African American home demonstration work until 1929, when Julia Miller was "appointed the Local District Agent in charge of Negro Home Demonstration Agents." Before then, white HDAs and A. A. Turner supervised African American women. Barbara R. Cotton, *The Lamplighters: Black Farm and Home Demonstration Agents in Florida, 1915–1965* (U.S. Department of Agriculture and Florida A&M University, 1982), 44.

42. Agnes Ellen Harris, "Report of the State Home Demonstration Agent, 1918," 15–16.

43. Ibid., 16.

44. Partridge, "Report of the State Agent for Home Demonstration Work for the Calendar Year Ending December 31, 1920," 15–16.

45. Partridge, "Brief Report of Home Demonstration Work in Florida, 1920," 2.

46. Sarah Partridge, "Brief Report of Home Demonstration Work in Florida, June 1920," 1, IFAS Extension Records, UF Archives.

47. Partridge, "Report of the State Agent for Home Demonstration Work for the Calendar Year Ending December 31, 1920," 5. Tampa had the more "developed and diversified economy that included an industrial base built around cigar manufacturing. Its multicultural population consisted of whites and African Americans, as well as Spanish, Italians, and Cubans, both black and white." Eric Jarvis, "'Secrecy Has No Excuse': The Florida Land Boom, Tourism, and the 1926 Smallpox Epidemic in Tampa and Miami," *Florida Historical Quarterly* 89, no. 3 (Winter 2011): 321. According to the census table of "Country of Origin for Foreign White Stock," the Florida Cuban population was 6,613 in 1920 and 15,973 in 1930. *Fourteenth Census of the United States Taken in the Year 1920: Population Volume III, Showing the Composition and Characteristics of the Population for Counties, Cities, and Townships or Other Minor Civil Divisions* (Government Printing Office, 1932); *Fifteenth Census of the United States: 1930: Population Volume III, Part I Reports by States, Showing the Composition and Characteristics of the Population for Counties, Cities, and Townships or Other Minor Civil Divisions* (Government Printing Office, 1932)

48. "Tampa Truisms," 7, in Edith Young Barrus folder, IFAS Extension Records, UF Archives. She moved to the Palm Beach area in 1921 to serve as its HDA. "The women were always glad to see me," she later recalled, "for I was a shopping service, a nursing service, a news gatherer, a weather prophet, a welfare worker, a canner, a gardener, a sick children curer, and message carrier for the school board." Edith Young Barrus, "Report of Experience as Home Demonstration Agent in Florida, Prepared for Epsilon Sigma Phi," 3, IFAS Extension Records, UF Archives. A movie showing home demonstration work in 1919 used scenes from "the first 4-H club camp at Wimauma" that she helped lead. "Organizations and Associations Contributing to the Development of Home Economics in Florida," 3, in folder entitled "Bicentennial History: King & Hammer, 1976," IFAS Extension Records, UF Archives.

49. Farm and Home Maker's Short Course and Prize Contest handout, IFAS Extension Records, UF Archives.

50. Partridge, "Report of the State Agent for Home Demonstration Work for the Calendar Year Ending December 31, 1920," 16.

51. Ibid., 16–17.

52. Ibid., 17.

53. Ibid.

54. Unnamed report, likely from 1921, located in a folder entitled "Extension Work, 1921–1923," IFAS Extension Records, UF Archives.

55. "Activities Conducted under Project IV, Home Demonstration Work, September 1, 1920 to June 30, 1921," 4, IFAS Extension Records, UF Archives. See also A. A. Turner, *Farm and Home Makers' Clubs*, Bulletin 19 (March 1919), 1–8, IFAS Extension Records, UF Archives.

56. A. A. Turner, "Annual Report of Agricultural Extension Work among Negroes in Florida, from Jan. 1 to Dec. 31, 1921," 3, IFAS Extension Records, UF Archives.

57. Ibid.

58. Cotton, *Lamplighters*, 44.

59. A. A. Turner and S. W. Partridge, "Report of Home Makers' Clubs from Jan. 1 to Dec. 31, 1922," 1, IFAS Extension Records, UF Archives.

60. "Narrative Report of Negro Home Demonstration Work for Quarter Ending June 30, 1922," 1, IFAS Extension Records, UF Archives.

61. "Home Demonstration Work among Negroes: Narrative Report of Home Demonstration Work, in Florida, January first to March 31, 1922," 2, IFAS Extension Records, UF Archives.

62. Partridge, "Report of Progress of Home Demonstration Work for Quarter Ending September 30, 1922," 4. Also in Duval County, a discussion about white and African American federated club women included the comment, "An effort is being made to open in Jacksonville, with State Federation backing, a domestic science school for colored women." There was no indication if home demonstration would be involved, however. L. H. Hammond, *Southern Women and Racial Adjustment*, the Trustees of the John F. Slater Fund, Occasional Paper, no. 19, second edition 1920, 25, in Southern Education Foundation, folder 10, box 2, Archives Research Center, Robert W. Woodruff Library, Atlanta University Center.

63. A. A. Turner, "Annual Narrative Report of Farm and Home Makers Clubs in Florida from December 1st, 1923 to Nov. 30, 1924," 1, IFAS Extension Records, UF Archives.

64. "A Summary of Negro Home Demonstration Work in Florida 1915–1937 Inclusive," Beluah S. Shute, 2, IFAS Records, UF Archives.

65. A. A. Turner, "Annual Report of Agricultural Extension Work among Negroes in Florida, from Jan. 1 to Dec. 31, 1921," 1.

66. M. M. Lewey, "Recollections of Florida," *Modern Farmer*, March 1, 1929, 3.

67. "Annual Report of A.A. Turner, Local District Agent to A.P. Spencer, Vice Director: Cooperative Extension Work among Negroes in Florida, From Jan. 1st. to Dec. 31st. 1922," 1, IFAS Records, UF Archives.

68. For recent scholarship about the Florida land boom, see Christopher Knowlton, *Bubble in the Sun: The Florida Boom of the 1920s and How It Brought on the Great Depression* (Simon and Schuster, 2020); Gregg M. Turner, *The Florida Land Boom of the 1920s*

(McFarland & Company, 2015); Paul S. George, "Brokers, Binders, and Builders: Greater Miami's Boom of the Mid-1920s," *Florida Historical Quarterly* 65, no. 1 (June 1986): 27–51; Eric Jarvis, "'Secrecy Has No Excuse': The Florida Land Boom, Tourism, and the 1926 Smallpox Epidemic in Tampa and Miami," *Florida Historical Quarterly* 89, no. 3 (Winter 2011): 320–346; Andrew W. Kahrl, "The Sunbelt's Sandy Foundation," *Southern Cultures* 20, no. 3 (Fall 2014): 29–30; Andrew W. Kahrl, *The Land Was Ours: How Black Beaches Became White Wealth in the Coastal South* (University of North Carolina Press, 2016).

69. Mary Keown, "A Summarized History of Home Demonstration Work in Florida, 1912–1946," 5, IFAS Extension Records, UF Archives.

70. "Report of the Director of Extension, State of Florida, 1926," 9–10, IFAS Records, UF Archives.

71. Mary Keown, "Annual Narrative Report of Home Demonstration Work, East Florida, 1927," 1, IFAS Extension Records, UF Archives.

72. No author given, "Brief Report of Home Demonstration Work in Poultry, 1921," 3, IFAS Extension Records, UF Archives. Capons are castrated cockerel (roosters).

73. Sarah Partridge, "Annual Home Demonstration Summary, July 1st, 1918–July 1st, 1919," 3–4, IFAS Extension Records, UF Archives; "From Mrs. Partridge," April 29, 1922, 1, in Extension Work, 1921–1923 folder, IFAS Extension Records, UF Archives.

74. Flavia Gleason, "Brief Narrative Report of Negro Home Demonstration Work, Florida, 1925," 4, IFAS Extension Records, UF Archives.

75. "Lucy Belle Settle, District Home Demonstration Agent, South and East Florida, Annual Report, 1923," 4–5, IFAS Extension Records, UF Archives.

76. Ibid., 5.

77. *Rural Home Life in Florida* (Department of Agriculture, 1927), 90–91. Bertie Leah Edge information: *1920 U.S. Census*, Okaloosa County, Florida, population schedule, Garden, ED 125, p. 1A (penned), https://www.ancestry.com. Bertie Leah added to her income in the summer by picking blueberries at a local farm. *Rural Home Life in Florida*, 91.

78. "Cooperative Extension Work in Agriculture and Home Economics: Report of General Activities for 1917 with Financial Statement for the Fiscal Year Ending June 30, 1917," 73, IFAS Extension Records, UF Archives.

79. Gleason, "Annual Narrative Report of Home Demonstration Work in Florida, 1924," 10. The closest match I could find to this person in Manatee County is Marie M. Thompson, wife of Samuel K. Thompson. *1920 U.S. Census*, Manatee County, Florida, population schedule, Parrish, ED 114, p. 15B (penned), https://www.ancestry.com; *1930 U.S. Census*, Manatee County, Florida, population schedule, Precinct 11, ED 0024, p. 8B (penned), https://www.ancestry.com.

80. Gleason, "Annual Narrative Report of Home Demonstration Work in Florida, 1924," 10–11.

81. *New Smyrna Daily News*, November 18, 1925, 5.

82. Flavia Gleason, "Narrative Report of Home Demonstration Work Florida, 1925," 14, IFAS Extension Records, UF Archives.

83. Gleason, "Annual Narrative Report of Home Demonstration Work in Florida, 1924," 11.

84. Flavia Gleason, "Narrative Report of Home Demonstration Work Florida, 1926," 15, IFAS Records, UF Archives.

85. Flavia Gleason, "Annual Narrative Report of Home Demonstration Work in Florida, 1927," 12, IFAS Extension Records, UF Archives.

86. Ibid., 11.

87. Virginia P. Moore, "Narrative Report of Home Improvement and other Activities of Asst. State Home Demonstration Agent in Florida, 1926," 5, IFAS Extension Records, UF Archives.

88. Thursby, "Narrative Report of Isabelle S. Thursby, Foods and Marketing Agent, Florida, 1926," 1.

89. Ibid., 3.

90. Ibid., 2, 9. Margery/Marjorie Manitha Thomas Buchans information: *1920 U.S. Census*, DeSoto County, Florida, population schedule, Arcadia, ED 15, p. 9B (penned), https://www.ancestry.com; *1930 U.S. Census*, DeSoto County, Florida, population schedule, Precinct 8, ED 0011, p. 5A (penned), https://www.ancestry.com.

91. Flavia Gleason, "Excerpts from September 1926 Reports," October 9, 1926, 4, series 21, Agricultural Experiment Station, Campus and State Correspondence 1921–1947, UF Archives; Flavia Gleason, "Excerpts from October 1927 Reports," November 22, 1927, 1, IFAS Extension Records, UF Archives.

92. *Rural Home Life in Florida*, 150.

93. Ruby McDavid, "Annual Narrative Report of Home Demonstration Work, Northwest Florida, 1927," 4, IFAS Extension Records, UF Archives.

94. "All Year Garden Contest Story of Mrs. D. G. Hicks, Laurel Hill, Okaloosa County, Florida," October 1929, Home Demonstration Gardening and Food Conservation folder, 1929–1930, 1–2, UF Archives; Josie Lee Harrelson Hicks information: *1920 U.S. Census*, Okaloosa County, Florida, population schedule, Garden, ED 125, p. 4B (penned), https://www.ancestry.com; *1930 U.S. Census*, Okaloosa County, Florida, population schedule, Garden, ED 0014, p. 1A (penned) https://www.ancestry.com; "Josie Lee Harrelson Hicks," Find a Grave, accessed November 12, 2022, https://www.findagrave.com/memorial/21266789/josie-lee-hicks.

95. A. A. Turner, "Narrative Report of Farm and Home Makers Club in Florida from December 1st. 1924 to Nov. 30th. 1925," 1, IFAS Extension Records, UF Archives.

96. "Report of the Director of Extension, State of Florida 1926," 16, IFAS Extension Records, UF Archives.

97. Ibid., 18. See also "Report of the Director of Extension, State of Florida 1925," 16, IFAS Extension Records, UF Archives. A. A. Turner, "Narrative Report of Farm and Home Makers Club in Florida from December 1st. 1924 to Nov. 30th. 1925," 1.

98. "Report of the Director of Extension, State of Florida 1926," 18.

99. One HDA reported that women in central and southern Florida were showing more interest in ornamentals, with a growing bulb industry in some central Florida counties. "Report of the Director of Extension, State of Florida 1926," 19; "Report of the Director of Extension, State of Florida 1925," 17.

100. L. A. Hamilton, "Hillsboro County's Narrative Report," IFAS Extension Records, UF Archives.

101. Ibid.

102. "Leon County's Narrative, Report from Jan. 1st to July 1st, 1926," 1, IFAS Extension

Records, UF Archives. See also Lu Ann Jones, "Taking What She Had and Turning It into Money: The Female Farm Economy," in *Cornbread Nation 1: The Best of Southern Food Writing*, ed. John Edgerton (University of North Carolina Press, 2002), 229.

103. The capital city was singled out as an illustration of success: "The curb market in Tallahassee is an example of what this type of marketing means especially to the person who is farming on a small scale but who has a surplus of fresh vegetables." "1928 Program of Work for Negro Home Demonstration Agents," 2, IFAS Extension Records, UF Archives.

104. On February 15, 1935, in Pulaski County, Arkansas, Miller married Harvey Cincinnatus Ray, the first male African American employee hired by the Arkansas Agricultural Extension Service. Their daughter, Gloria Ray, became one of the "Little Rock Nine" in 1957. "Arkansas, Marriage Certificates, 1917–1972," https://www.ancestry.com; "Ray House," Preserve Arkansas, https://preservearkansas.org/ray-house; "Julia Miller Ray," Find a Grave, https://www.findagrave.com/memorial/31382505/julia-ray.

105. "Julia A. Miller, Negro Home Demonstration Agent, 1929 Narrative Report of Negro Home Demonstration Work in Florida," 1, IFAS Extension Records, UF Archives.

106. Ibid., 3.

107. Ibid., 8. See also Carmen V. Harris, "'Well I Just Generally Bes the President of Everything': Rural Black Women's Empowerment through South Carolina Home Demonstration Activities," *Black Women, Gender + Families* 3, no. 1 (Spring 2009): 91–112.

108. "Julia A. Miller, Negro Home Demonstration Agent," 7.

109. Ibid., 9–10.

110. The Okeechobee hurricane affected this area in September 1928. "Julia A. Miller, Negro Home Demonstration Agent, 1929 Narrative Report of Negro Home Demonstration Work in Florida," IFAS Extension Records, UF Archives. 10–12; "Business Satisfactory with Good Inquiries in Southeast," *Electrical World* 93, no. 3, January 19, 1929, 175; *The Story of the Southern Sugar Company* (January 1929), Florida Memory: State Library and Archives of Florida, https://www.floridamemory.com/items/show/333798?id=1. See also John A. Heitmann, "The Beginnings of Big Sugar, 1920–1945," *Florida Historical Quarterly* 77, no. 1 (Summer 1998): 39–61.

111. See also Minor, "Power in the Land," 168; Julia A. Miller, "Suggestive Outline for Plan of Work for Negro Home Dem. Clubs, 1929," 1–7, IFAS Extension Records, UF Archives.

112. See Kelly Anne Minor, "'Consumed with a Ghastly Wasting': Home Demonstration Confronts Disease in Rural Florida, 1920–1945," in *Entering the Fray: Gender, Politics, and Culture in the New South*, ed. Jonathan Daniel Wells and Sheila R. Phipps (University of Missouri Press, 2010), 68–95. Flavia Gleason stayed in Florida until the mid-1930s and then returned to her home state of Louisiana, where she was involved with Extension and Louisiana's Federation for Women's Clubs. "Flavia Gleason Mims," Find a Grave, https://www.findagrave.com/memorial/87233457/flavia-mims; "Miss Flavia Gleason Is New State Home Dem. Agt," *Kissimmee Valley Gazette*, July 27, 1923. Thank you to Philip Williams (M.A., MLIS) of the Wiregrass Regional Digital History Project for his help with this information.

113. *Rural Home Life in Florida*, 35.

114. Ibid.

115. Ibid., 92.

116. Ibid., 94–95.

117. Ruby McDavid, "Narrative Report of District Home Demonstration Agent for North and West Florida, 1925," 6, IFAS Extension Records, UF Archives.

118. Flavia Gleason, "Excerpts from March 1925 Reports," May 13, 1925, 10, IFAS Extension Records, UF Archives.

119. Mary Keown, "Report of Home Demonstration Agent in East Florida District, 1929," 37, IFAS Extension Records, UF Archives.

120. Gleason, "Narrative Report of Home Demonstration Work Florida, 1926," 18.

121. "Cooperative Extension Work in Agriculture and Home Economics: Report of General Activities for 1917," 73; "From Mrs. Partridge," 3, IFAS Extension Records, UF Archives.

122. *Rural Home Life in Florida*, 16. See also Flavia Gleason, "Narrative Report of Home Demonstration Work Florida, 1926," 18.

123. Gleason, "Narrative Report of Home Demonstration Work Florida, 1926," 18.

124. "Home Demonstration Circular, 851," 1922, 5, IFAS Extension Records, UF Archives.

125. Flavia Gleason, "Excerpts from December 1924 Reports," January 21, 1925, 13, IFAS Extension Records, UF Archives.

126. Flavia Gleason, "Excerpts from January 1925 Reports, February 26, 1925," 11, IFAS Extension Records, UF Archives.

127. Flavia Gleason, "1929 Annual Narrative Report of Home Demonstration Work in Florida," 19–20, IFAS Extension Records, UF Archives.

128. Flavia Gleason, "Excerpts from August 1925 Reports," September 15, 1925, 5. IFAS Extension Records, UF Archives.

129. Keown, "Report of Home Demonstration Agent in East Florida District, 1929," 37.

130. Flavia Gleason, "Excerpts from August 1925 Reports," September 15, 1925, 3.

131. Flavia Gleason, "Excerpts from August 1927 Reports," September 1927, 5, IFAS Extension Records, UF Archives; Hannah Palmquist King info: *1930 U.S. Census*, Osceola County, Florida, population schedule, Kissimmee, ED 0010, p. 1A (penned), https://www.ancestry.com.

132. Meade Love, "1928 Home Demonstration Work," 3–4, IFAS Extension Records, UF Archives.

133. See Jay Barnes, *Florida's Hurricane History* (University of North Carolina Press, 2012); "Great Miami Hurricane of 1926," National Weather Service, https://www.weather.gov/mfl/miami_hurricane; Jenny Staletovich, "Ninety Years Later, the Great Miami Hurricane a Scary, 'What If?,'" *Miami Herald*, June 3, 2016, https://www.miamiherald.com/news/weather/hurricane/article80378337.html.

134. Gleason, "Excerpts from October 1926 Reports," 7.

135. Keown, "Annual Narrative Report, 1927," 1–2.

136. Gleason, "Excerpts from October 1926 Reports," 7.

137. In Florida, it is ranked alongside 2018's Hurricane Michael and is probably comparable to 2022's Hurricane Ian. For more on the Okeechobee hurricane, see Christopher

M. Church, "The 1928 Hurricane in Florida and the Wider Caribbean," in *Environmental Disaster in the Gulf South: Two Centuries of Catastrophe, Risk, and Resilience*, ed. Cindy Ermus, 80–102 (Louisiana State University, 2018); Robert Mykle, *Killer 'Cane: The Deadly Hurricane of 1928* (Taylor Trade Publishing, 2006); "The Storm of '28," Historical Society of Palm Beach County, https://pbchistory.org/the-storm-of-28; "The Deadliest, Costliest and Most Intense United State Tropical Cyclones from 1851–2010 (and Other Frequently Requested Hurricane Facts)," *https://repository.library.noaa.gov/view/noaa/50155*; National Hurricane Center (NOAA Technical Memorandum NWS NHC-6), *https://www.nhc.noaa.gov/pdf/nws-nhc-6.pdf*;American Red Cross, *The West Indies Hurricane Disaster, September 1928: The Official Report of Relief Work in Porto Rico, the Virgin Islands and Florida* (American Red Cross, 1929), 73. The University of Florida also has 1928 hurricane information on its digital archival website: UF Digital Collections, *https://ufdc.ufl.edu*.

138. Barrus, "Report of Experience," 5.

139. Ibid.; "Resume of Extension Service E.Y. Barrus, 1918–1928," 4, IFAS Extension Records, UF Archives.

140. Barrus, "Report of Experience," 6.

141. Ibid., 14. See also "Story of Rebuilding Homes in Storm Zone Told Here," *Jacksonville Journal*, November 25, 1928.

142. Barrus, "Report of Experience," 14.

143. Flavia Gleason, "Programs and Plans for Development of Home Demonstration Work in Florida, 1929," 3, IFAS Extension Records, UF Archives.

144. Flavia Gleason, "Home Demonstration Division of Cooperative Extension Work in Agriculture and Home Economics, State of Florida," February 1929, 1, Gov. Doyle E. Carlton Records 1929–1932, Administrative Correspondence, box 41, series 204, State of Florida, Department of State Division of Archives.

145. "Report on Home Demonstration Florida Federation of Women's Clubs, 1929–1930, Mrs. Meade A. Love, Chairman," 3, IFAS Extension Records, UF Archives.

146. Gleason, "1929 Annual Narrative Report of Home Demonstration Work in Florida," 5.

CHAPTER FOUR. CURB MARKETS, FINDING CUSTOMERS, AND RIPENING BANK ACCOUNTS

1. "Price List Board—Decatur Curb Market—Morgan County," Alabama Cooperative Extension System Records, RG no. 71, Collections & Archives, Draughon Library, Auburn University, Alabama (hereafter cited as ACES Records); A. D. Livingston, *Cold-Smoking & Salt-Curing Meat, Fish, & Game* (Lyons Press, 2011), 41.

2. "Mrs. Mitchell Lives [Either 2 or 21 miles] from the Curb Market; In 22 Months She Sold $2000 Worth of Produce," ACES Records. The photo is with others from Decatur, Gadsden, and Tuscaloosa.

3. See Kathleen C. Hilton, "Both in the Field, Each with a Plow: Race and Gender in USDA Policy, 1907–1929," in *Hidden Histories of Women in the New South*, ed. Virginia Bernhard, Betty Brandon, Elizabeth Fox-Genovese, Theda Perdue, and Elizabeth Hayes Turner (University of Missouri Press, 1994), 126–127; Lynne A. Rieff, "Go Ahead and Do All You Can: Southern Progressives and Alabama Home Demonstration Clubs, 1914–

1940," in Bernhard et al., *Hidden Histories of Women*, 134–149; Melissa Walker, "Farm Wives and Commercial Farming: The Case of Loudon County, Tennessee," *Tennessee Historical Quarterly* 57, no. 1 (Spring/Summer 1998): 42–61.

4. See Mabel Feagin, "Outline of Work 1923–1924, Bullock County," 1–2, in Girls' Club, 1923, folder, ACES Records; Gladys McCain, "Annual Report of County Extension Workers, Coosa County, Alabama, 1924," 15, ACES Records. For more on the Farm Bureau, see Nancy K. Berlage, *Farmers Helping Farmers: The Rise of the Farm and Home Bureaus, 1914–1935* (Louisiana State University Press, 2016).

5. "Annual Report—1927, Home Demonstration Work, State Home Demonstration Agent," 67, ACES Records; "Tuscaloosans Pay Visit to Rome to See Curb Market," *Tuscaloosa News & Times Gazette*, October 16, 1923, 2.

6. In a 1927 report, a list of curb markets indicates Gadsden's market opened in November 1923, Tuscaloosa's in May 1924, Selma's in April 1925, and Anniston's in May 1926. However, other records indicate Anniston's opened before Selma's. "Annual Report—1927, Home Demonstration Work, State Home Demonstration Agent," 68.

7. "Formal Opening of Curb Market Was Big Success," *Gadsden Daily Times*, November 17, 1923, 1.

8. Lynne A. Rieff, "'Rousing the People of the Land': Home Demonstration Work in the Deep South, 1914–1950" (PhD diss., Auburn University, 1995), 134; clipping from unknown newspaper, possibly from April or May 1927, in Mamie C. Thorington, "Annual Report of Extension Work in Montgomery County, Alabama, 1927," 14(?), ACES Records.

9. Minnie Slone, "Annual Report of Extension Work in Calhoun County, Alabama, for 1927," 7, ACES Records.

10. Isadora Williams, "Annual Report of County Extension Agents, Tuscaloosa County, Alabama, 1924," 8, ACES Records.

11. Ibid., 9.

12. Ibid., 9–10, 16.

13. "Jena Preparing for Curb Market," *Tuscaloosa News & Times Gazette*, March 28, 1924, 7. The small article notes the Tuscaloosa curb market was first scheduled to open on April 15, 1924, rather than the May 1 date that appears in other sources.

14. Isadora Williams, "Annual Report of County Extension Agents, Tuscaloosa County, Alabama, 1924," 9–10; "Pike Road Club Shows Interest in Move to Locate Curb Market in Montgomery," *Montgomery Advertiser*, month not given, 1927, in Thorington, "Annual Report of Extension Work, 1927," 13(?); Isadora Williams, "Annual Report of Extension Work in Tuscaloosa, Alabama for 1926," 17, ACES Records. See also Rebecca Sharpless, *Grain and Fire: A History of Baking in the American South* (University of North Carolina Press, 2022).

15. Isadora Williams, "Annual Report of County Extension Agents, Tuscaloosa County, Alabama, 1924," 9–10.

16. Ella Hamilton, "Annual Report of County Extension Agents, Conecuh County, Alabama, June 9, 1924 to December 1, 1924," 6, ACES Records.

17. Elizabeth Striplin, "Annual Report of County Extension Agents, Cullman County, Alabama, 1924," 2, 11, ACES Records.

18. Elizabeth Striplin, "Annual Report of County Extension Workers, 1925, Cullman County, Alabama," 6, ACES Records.

19. Ibid.

20. Ibid.

21. Stella Harms, "Annual Report of County Extension Workers, Calhoun County, Alabama, 1923," 11, ACES Records.

22. Ila Dean Griffin and Blanche Heard, "Annual Report of Extension Workers, Limestone County, Alabama, 1924," 6, ACES Records.

23. Zelma Gaines Jackson, "Annual Report of County Extension Workers, 1926, Chambers County, Alabama," 4, ACES Records.

24. Carrie Torbert, "Annual Report of Extension Workers, Elmore County, Alabama, 1924," 8, ACES Records.

25. The counties listed are indicated by the district notations in Agnes Ellen Harris, "Annual Report of Extension Work in Alabama for 1926," 175, ACES Records.

26. Counties in district 1 include Blount, Colbert, Cullman, Fayette, Franklin, Jackson, Jefferson, Lauderdale, Lamar, Lawrence, Limestone, Madison, Marion, Morgan, Walker, and Winston, according to the map in Harris, "Annual Report of Extension Work in Alabama for 1926," 175; Cecile Hester, "Narrative Report for Lauderdale County, Alabama, November 10, 1928," 8–9, ACES Records; "Caroline 'Carrie' Powell Delano," Find a Grave, https://www.findagrave.com/memorial/76381164/caroline-delano.

27. Cecile Hester, "Narrative Report for Lauderdale County, Alabama, November 10, 1928," 8–9.

28. Annie J. Smith, "Annual Report of County Extension Workers for Colbert County, Alabama, 1927," 5, ACES Records.

29. Elizabeth DeLoney, "Annual Report of Extension Work in Franklin County, Alabama, 1927," 16, ACES Records.

30. Blanche Heard, "Annual Report of Extension Work for 1927 in Limestone County, Alabama," n.p., ACES Records; Blanche Heard and Ila Dean Griffin, "Annual Report of Extension Workers, 1924 in Limestone County, Alabama," 6, ACES Records.

31. Sallye Hamilton, "Annual Report of County Extension Workers for 1927, Morgan County Alabama," 31–32, 28, ACES Records.

32. Sallye Hamilton, "Annual Report of County Extension Workers, Morgan County, Alabama, 1927," 29, ACES Records.

33. Sallye Hamilton, "Annual Report of County Extension Workers for 1927, Morgan County Alabama," 26.

34. Ibid., 32.

35. Ibid.

36. District 2 counties include Bibb, Calhoun, Chambers, Cherokee, Chilton, Clay, Cleburne, Coosa, DeKalb, Etowah, Marshall, Randolph, Shelby, St. Clair, Talladega, Tallapoosa, and Tuscaloosa, according to the map in Harris, "Annual Report of Extension Work in Alabama for 1926," 175.

37. Isadora Williams, "Annual Report of County Extension Agents, Tuscaloosa County, Alabama, 1924," 9. Ada Marlow Pate is listed as "Mrs. J. T. Pate," but records indicate her husband was Thomas Jackson Pate. *1920 U.S. Census*, Tuscaloosa County, Alabama, census

place, Buhl, Enumeration District (ED) 136, p. 7A (penned), https://www.ancestry.com; *1930 U.S. Census*, Tuscaloosa County, Alabama, census place, Buhl, ED 0051, p. 2A (penned), https://www.ancestry.com; "Ada Jane Pate," Find a Grave, accessed October 26, 2022, https://www.findagrave.com/memorial/62878604/ada-jane-pate.

38. One unnamed Tuscaloosa County woman bought a "large refrigerator" with the profits from selling angel food cakes on the curb market. Sarah Reid, "Annual Report of County Extension Agents, Tuscaloosa County Alabama, 1925," II, IV, ACES Records.

39. Isadora Williams, "Annual Report of County Extension Agents, Tuscaloosa County, Alabama, 1925," 4a, ACES Records; Mada Rebecca Windham West information: *1920 U.S. Census*, Tuscaloosa County, Alabama, census place, Taylorville, (ED) 135, p. 2A (penned), https://www.ancestry.com; *1930 U.S. Census*, Tuscaloosa County, Alabama, census place, Taylorville, (ED) 0049, p. 4B (penned), https://www.ancestry.com; "Mada Rebecca Windham West," Find a Grave, accessed March 14, 2020, https://www.findagrave.com/memorial/155806663/mada-rebecca-west.

40. Isadora Williams, "Annual Report of Extension Work in Tuscaloosa, Alabama for 1926," 19. The report also identified West as a former schoolteacher.

41. Ibid.

42. Ibid., 19–20.

43. Agnes Ellen Harris, "Annual Report of Extension Work in Alabama for 1926," 29.

44. Isadora Williams, "Annual Report of Extension Work in Tuscaloosa, Alabama for 1926," 16; Elizabeth Collings, "Annual Report of County Extension Workers, Tuscaloosa County, Alabama, 1928," 10, ACES Records.

45. Isadora Williams, "Annual Report of Extension Work in Tuscaloosa, Alabama for 1926," 17.

46. Ibid.

47. Ibid.

48. Agnes Ellen Harris, "Annual Report of Extension Work in Alabama for 1926," 30.

49. "Much Interest in Curb Market" (1927 newspaper clipping, possibly from the *Montgomery Advertiser),* in Thorington, "Annual Report of Extension Work in Montgomery County, Alabama, 1927," 14(?); Mary Emma Maddox Hewitt Robertson information: *1920 U.S. Census*, Tuscaloosa County, Alabama, census place, Dunns, ED 101, p. 3B (penned), accessed May 15, 2020, https://www.ancestry.com; *1930 U.S. Census*, Tuscaloosa County, Alabama, census place, Dunns, ED 0001, p. 8A (penned), accessed May 15, 2020, https://www.ancestry.com.

50. Some records spell Neighbors as "Nabors." *Mrs. J. E. Spiller and Her Daughter Selling Flowers from Her Car at the Tuscaloosa Curb Market* (photo), April 13, 1928, ACES Photographs Collection, https://content.lib.auburn.edu/digital/collection/autest/id/336/rec/408; Isadora Williams, "Annual Report of County Extension Workers, Tuscaloosa County, Alabama, November 1, 1925 to November 1, 1926," 17, ACES Records; Kate Neighbors Spiller information: *1920 U.S. Census*, Tuscaloosa County, Alabama, census place, Taylorville, ED 135, p. 7A (penned), https://www.ancestry.com; *1920 U.S. Census*, Tuscaloosa County, Alabama, census place, Taylorville, ED 135, p. 7A (penned), https://www.ancestry.com; *1930 U.S. Census*, Tuscaloosa County, Alabama, census place, Taylorville, ED 63–49, p. 91 (penned), https://www.ancestry.com; "Kate Neighbors Spiller," Find

a Grave, https://www.findagrave.com/memorial/12683808/kate-spiller. Advertisement about figs seen in the *Tuscaloosa News*, July 19, 1926, 7.

51. Helen Johnston, "Annual Report Home Demonstration Work—Alabama 1929," 70–71, ACES Records; Lulu Elizabeth "Bessie" Stephens Smith information: *1920 U.S. Census*, Tuscaloosa County, Alabama, census place, Taylorville, ED 135, p. 10A (penned), https://www.ancestry.com; *1930 U.S. Census*, Tuscaloosa County, Alabama, census place, Tuscaloosa, ED 0026, p. 3B (penned), https://www.ancestry.com; "Bessie Stephen Smith," Find a Grave, https://www.findagrave.com/memorial/51966085.

52. Johnston, "Annual Report Home Demonstration Work—Alabama 1929."

53. Ibid.

54. Mrs. D. B. (Diana B.) Williams, "Annual Report of Extension Work in Etowah County, Alabama, 1927," 22, 12–13, ACES Records; Lula Bankson (Swann) information: *1920 U.S. Census*, Etowah County, Alabama, census place, Coats Bend, ED 101, p. 9A (penned), https://www.ancestry.com; Dora Jane Callan Aldridge information: *1930 U.S. Census*, Etowah County, Alabama, census place, Short Creek, ED 0039, p. 2B (penned), https://www.ancestry.com; "Dora Jane Callan Aldridge," Find a Grave, https://www.findagrave.com/memorial/150205065; Minnie May Millican/Milligan Anderson information: *1920 U.S. Census*, Etowah County, Alabama, census place, Coats Bend, ED 101, p. 9A (penned), https://www.ancestry.com; *1930 U.S. Census*, Etowah County, Alabama, census place, Coats Bend, [ED] 0052, p. 1A (penned), https://www.ancestry.com; "Minnie Mae Anderson," Find a Grave, accessed February 25, 2020, https://www.findagrave.com/memorial/54045018.

55. "Turkey Trot at Curb Market for Thursday," *Gadsden Times*, January 2, 1924, 1.

56. Mrs. D. B. (Diana B.) Williams, "Annual Report of Extension Work in Etowah County, Alabama, 1927," 13.

57. Mrs. D. B. (Diana B.) Williams, "Annual Report of County Extension Workers, Etowah County, Alabama, November 1, 1927, to November 1, 1928," 7, ACES Records.

58. Ibid.

59. Mrs. D. B. (Diana B.) Williams, "Annual Report of County Extension Workers, Etowah County, Alabama, 1928," 8–9, ACES Records; Irene Griffin Freeman information: *1930 U.S. Census*, Etowah County, Alabama, census place, Altoona, ED 0054, p. 3B (penned), https://www.ancestry.com; "Irene Griffin Freeman," Find a Grave, https://www.findagrave.com/memorial/85056542.

60. Mrs. D. B. (Diana B.) Williams, "Annual Report of Extension Work in Etowah County, Alabama for 1929," 11, ACES Records.

61. "The Curb Market" (undated clipping from unknown newspaper), in D. B. (Diana B.) Williams, "Annual Report of Extension Work in Etowah County, Alabama, 1927," 28.

62. Mrs. D. B. (Diana B.) Williams, "Annual Report of Extension Work in Etowah County, Alabama for 1929," 20–21; Mary Catherine Dempsey Satterfield information: *1930 U.S. Census*, Etowah County, Alabama, census place, Hokes Bluff, ED 0016, p. 1B (penned), https://www.ancestry.com; "Mary Catherine Dempsey Satterfield," Find a Grave, https://www.findagrave.com/memorial/191517632.

63. Mrs. D. B. (Diana B.) Williams, "Annual Report of Extension Work in Etowah County, Alabama for 1929," 20.

64. Mrs. D. B. (Diana B.) Williams, "Annual Report of County Extension Workers, Etowah County, Alabama, 1928," 8.

65. Harriet Plowder, "Annual Report of County Extension Workers, Talladega County, Alabama, 1928," 5, ACES Records.

66. Ibid., 11.

67. Ibid., 14.

68. Ibid.; Sue/Susan Wallis Carpenter information: *1920 U.S. Census*, Talladega County, Alabama, census place, Talladega, ED 133, p. 1A (penned), https://www.ancestry.com; *1930 U.S. Census*, Talladega County, Alabama, census place, Talladega, ED 0014, p. 15B (penned), https://www.ancestry.com; "Susan Carpenter," accessed May 5, 2020, Find a Grave, https://www.findagrave.com/memorial/7709335.

69. Harriet Plowder, "Annual Report of County Extension Workers, 1927, Talladega County, Alabama," 9, ACES Records; Daisy Jane Brown information: *1920 U.S. Census*, Talladega County, Alabama, census place, Talladega, ED 133, p. 10A (penned), https://www.ancestry.com; "Daisy Jane Brown London," *Alabama, Death and Burials Index, 1881–1974*, accessed June 2, 2020, https://www.ancestry.com.

70. District 3 counties include Autauga, Barbour, Bullock, Dallas, Elmore, Greene, Hale, Lee, Lowndes, Macon, Marengo, Montgomery, Perry, Pickens, Russell, Sumter, and Wilcox according to the map in Harris, "Annual Report of Extension Work in Alabama for 1926," 175; Thorington, "Annual Report of Extension Work in Montgomery County, Alabama, 1927," 10–11, ACES Records.

71. Thorington, "Annual Report of Extension Work in Montgomery County, Alabama, 1927," 10–11; undated clipping from unknown newspaper in Thorington, "Annual Report of Extension Work in Montgomery County, Alabama, 1927," 13(?).

72. Clare Livingston, "Annual Report of Extension Work, Elmore County, Alabama, 1927," 21, ACES Records; Ruth Dobyne, "Annual Report of County Extension Workers, Autauga County, Alabama, 1929," 11, ACES Records.

73. Dobyne, "Annual Report of County Extension Workers, Autauga County, Alabama, 1929," 11.

74. Ibid., 10. Local peaches from Autauga and Montgomery Counties were also sold when available. "First Peaches of Season Reach Local Curb Market," *Montgomery Advertiser*, May 27, 1928, 1.

75. *Montgomery Advertiser*, May 11, 1928, 15. C. E. Douglass might be Clyde Edgar Douglass, whom the census identifies as an inspector with the state capitol and a farmer. *1920 U.S. Census*, Montgomery County, Alabama, census place, Montgomery Ward 1, ED 94, p. 4B (penned), https://www.ancestry.com; *1930 U.S. Census*, Montgomery County, Alabama, census place, Killough, ED 0041, p. 15B (penned), https://www.ancestry.com.

76. "State Home Demonstration Agent, Annual Report—1927, Home Demonstration Work," 69–70; Julia Augusta See Clare information: *1930 U.S. Census*, Montgomery County, Alabama, census place, Snowdoun, ED 0063, p. 8A (penned), https://www.ancestry.com; "Julia Clare," Find a Grave, accessed June 2, 2020, https://www.findagrave.com/memorial/142629985.

77. Helen Johnston, "Annual Report Home Demonstration Work—Alabama 1929," 63–64.

78. Dobyne, "Annual Report of County Extension Workers, Autauga County, Alabama, 1929," 12.

79. "Bess Fleming, Annual Report of Extension Work in Girls' Club Work, 1929," 39–40, ACES Records.

80. "Annual Narrative Report of L. C. Hanna State Agent for Negro Women, State of Alabama, for the Year Ending December 31, 1928," 3, ACES Records.

81. Ibid., 21 or 27; "Society News and Activities of Selma, Alabama," *Birmingham Reporter*, August 25, 1928, 6; "Annual Report by L. N. Duncan, Director, Alabama Extension Service, December 31, 1929," 76–77, ACES Records; *1920 U.S. Census*, Spalding County, Georgia, census place, Orrs, ED 172, p. 22B (penned), https://www.ancestry.com; *1940 U.S. Census*, census place, Montgomery, ED 51–51, p. 12A (penned);obituary in the *Montgomery Advertiser*, January 30, 1983, 57; Margalit Fox, "Amelia Boynton Robinson Dies at 104," reprinted in the *Anniston Star*, August 27, 2015, 6A; "Amelia Boynton Robinson," National Park Service, https://www.nps.gov/people/amelia-boynton-robinson.htm; "Negro Home Agent Starts Work Here," *Selma Times-Journal*, April 9, 1929, 10. She married Samuel W. Boynton, the Dallas County farm agent, in 1936. Her HDA reports are located in the African American Extension Records, 1930–1932, at Ralph Draughon Library, Auburn University. By the time of the 1940 census, she was no longer an HDA and was instead listed as a "housewife." *1940 U.S. Census*, census place, Selma, Dallas, Alabama, ED 24–37, p. 6B (penned).

82. Rosa B. Jones, "Supplement to the Annual Report of the Agricultural Extension Work among Negroes (in Alabama), for the Year Ending December 31, 1926," 4–5, ACES Records.

83. Ibid., 5.

84. "Annual Narrative Report of L. C. Hanna State Agent for Negro Women, State of Alabama, for the Year Ending December 31, 1928," 10.

85. Ibid., 11 or 22.

86. Ibid., 3. Emma Jackson Taylor information: *1920 U.S. Census*, Montgomery County, Alabama, census place, Robertson Cross Roads, ED 117, p. 13A (penned), https://www.ancestry.com; *1930 U.S. Census*, Montgomery County, Alabama, census place, Robertson Crossroads, ED 0042, p. 15B (penned), https://www.ancestry.com. Sadie Jordan appears to be Sadie Davis Jordan, wife of Noble Jordan. *1920 U.S. Census*, Montgomery County, Alabama, census place, Mount Meigs, ED 136, p. 8A (penned), https://www.ancestry.com; *1930 U.S. Census*, Montgomery County, Alabama, census place, Mount Meigs, ED 0062, p. 8B (penned), https://www.ancestry.com; obituary in the *Montgomery Advertiser*, March 5, 1968, 5.

87. "Annual Narrative Report of L. C. Hanna State Agent for Negro Women, State of Alabama, for the Year Ending December 31, 1928,", 22–23. Eva Jones—maiden name possibly Goldsmith—information: *1930 U.S. Census*, Autauga County, Alabama, census place, Beat 1, ED 0002, p. 35A(?) (penned), https://www.ancestry.com; "Eva Jones," Find a Grave, accessed February 21, 2020, https://www.findagrave.com/memorial/13236852.

88. Annette S. Tyndall, "Annual Report of Extension Work, Dallas County, Alabama, 1925," 7, ACES Records.

89. Ibid.

90. Ibid., 8.
91. Ibid., 7; untitled article, *Selma Times-Journal*, April 9, 1925, 12.
92. Untitled article, *Selma Times-Journal*, April 9, 1925, 12.
93. "Kiwanis Told about Plan of Curb Market," *Selma Times-Journal*, January 21, 1925, 8.
94. "Residents of Nearby Counties May Sell on the Curb Market, It Is Announced by Manager; Places for Negro Truck Raisers," *Selma Times-Journal*, April 9, 1925, 12.
95. Tyndall, "Annual Report of Extension Work, Dallas County, Alabama, 1925," 7; "Curb Market Enjoys Play by the Children," *Selma Times-Journal*, May 10, 1925, 10.
96. "Curb Market Enjoys Play by the Children," *Selma Times-Journal*, May 10, 1925, 10.
97. Ibid.
98. "Residents of Nearby Counties," 12. The same article notes that when the curb market is open, "no hucksters will be allowed to sell door to door. . . . When the market closes at 10 a.m. the sales of vegetables may be made by hucksters who may visit their regular customers if they so desire." Pearl Stanfill Hain information: *1920 U.S. Census*, Dallas County, Alabama, census place, Kings, ED 92, p. 2B (penned), https://www.ancestry.com; *1930 U.S. Census*, Dallas County, Alabama, census place, River, ED 0011, p. 9A (penned), https://www.ancestry.com; "Pearl Stanfill Hain," Find a Grave, https://www.findagrave.com/memorial/18545165.
99. Annette Breeden, "Annual Report of Extension Work in Dallas County, Alabama, 1927," 8, ACES Records.
100. Annette Breeden, Annual Report of Extension Work, Dallas County, Alabama, 1928, page numbers not given, ACES Records.
101. Annette Breeden, "Annual Report of Extension Work, Dallas County, Alabama, 1929," 25, ACES Records; Emma Price Thornton information: *1930 U.S. Census*, Dallas County, Alabama, census place, Selma, ED 0031, p. 3A (penned), https://www.ancestry.com; "Emma M. Price Thornton," Find a Grave, accessed April 2, 2020, https://www.findagrave.com/memorial/159067246.
102. Mabel Feagin, "Annual Report of Extension Work in Bullock County, Alabama, 1927, 5, ACES Records.
103. "Curb Market to Begin Saturday," *Montgomery Advertiser*, February 5, 1927, 5.
104. Lida Jones, "Annual Report of County Extension Workers, Macon County, Alabama, 1928," 5, ACES Records.
105. Dobyne, "Annual Report of County Extension Workers, Autauga County, Alabama, 1929," 9; Emmie Adams DeRamus information: *1930 U.S. Census*, Autauga County, Alabama, census place, Beat 1, ED 0002, p. 20B (penned), https://www.ancestry.com; "Emmie A. DeRamus," Find a Grave, https://www.findagrave.com/memorial/172980291.
106. She was listed in home demonstration reports as Mrs. A. J. Smilie. Mamie Thorington, "Annual Report of County Extension Workers, Montgomery County, Alabama, 1928," 9, ACES Records: Daisy Wright Smilie information: *1930 U.S. Census*, Montgomery County, Alabama, census place, Pine Level, ED 0044, p. 7A (penned), https://www.ancestry.com; "Daisie Wright Smilie," Find a Grave, accessed May 4, 2020, https://www.findagrave.com/memorial/54480486.
107. Mary Bailey, "Annual Report of Extension Work in Lee County, Alabama, 1927,"

6, ACES Records; Ermine Ruby Watson Orr information: *1930 U.S. Census*, Lee County, Alabama, census place, Opelika, ED 0006, p. 15B (penned), https://www.ancestry.com; "Ermine Ruby Orr," Find a Grave, accessed June 2, 2020, https://www.findagrave.com /memorial/126171818.

108. Bailey, "Annual Report of Extension Work in Lee County, Alabama, 1927,", 7. This is same Florence Ellington Robertson mentioned in the introduction.

109. Ibid., 9.

110. Ibid., 8. According to census records, this might be Margaret Elizabeth Flanagan Newton, but it cannot be confirmed.

111. "Curb Market Sale of Produce Heavy," *Montgomery Advertiser*, March 27, 1927, 17.

112. Mary Bailey, "County Home Demonstration Agent [for Lee County, Alabama], Nov 1, 1927–Nov 2, 1928," 2, ACES Records. She mentioned that two curb markets had been established in the county but did not specify where the second market was located.

113. District 4 counties include Baldwin, Butler, Choctaw, Clarke, Coffee, Conecuh, Covington, Crenshaw, Dale, Escambia, Geneva, Henry, Houston, Mobile, Monroe, Pike, and Washington according to the map in Harris, "Annual Report of Extension Work in Alabama for 1926," 175. Louise Riley, "Annual Report of County Extension Work, 1927, Mobile County, Alabama," 15–16, ACES Records.

114. Riley, "Annual Report of County Extension Work, 1927, Mobile County, Alabama," 15–16.

115. Ibid., 12.

116. Clippings from unknown newspapers, likely from 1927, in Riley, "Annual Report of County Extension Work, 1927, Mobile County, Alabama," n.p.

117. Riley, "Annual Report of County Extension Work, 1927, Mobile County, Alabama," 15. These sales figures are assumed to represent the period from May to October 1927.

118. Ibid., 16, 20.

119. Clippings from unknown newspapers, likely from 1927, in Riley, "Annual Report of County Extension Work, 1927, Mobile County, Alabama," n.p.

120. Clippings from unknown newspapers, likely from 1928, in Louise Riley, "Annual Report of County Extension Workers, Mobile County, Alabama, 1928," n.p., ACES Records.

121. Ibid.

122. Letter to Louise M. Riley from Mrs. F. A. Tucker, state home demonstration agent, in "Annual Report—1927, Home Demonstration Work," 91, ACES Records; Lucy Elizabeth Brawner/Browner Tucker information: *1930 U.S. Census*, Mobile County, Alabama, census place, Crawfords, ED 0036, p. 8A (penned), https://www.ancestry.com.

123. Louise Riley, "Annual Report of County Extension Work, November 1, 1928 to November 30, 1929, Mobile County, Alabama," 22, ACES Records.

124. W. G. (Wyche G.) Pruett, "Annual Report of County Extension Workers, Houston County, Alabama, November 1, 1926 to November 1, 1927," 24, ACES Records.

125. W. G. (Wyche G.) Pruett, "Annual Report of County Extension Workers, Houston County, Alabama, 1929," 19, ACES Records; Milbra Kelley Halstead information: *1930 U.S. Census*, Houston County, Alabama, census place, Center Schoolhouse–Keytons Siding,

ED 0017, p. 10A (penned), https://www.ancestry.com; "Milbra E. Halstead," Find a Grave, accessed April 2, 2020, https://www.findagrave.com/memorial/57592645.

126. Pruett, "Annual Report of County Extension Workers, Houston County, Alabama, 1929,", 20; Effie Waddell Holland information: *1930 U.S. Census*, Houston County, Alabama, census place, Brannan Stand and Hawthorns Store, ED 0002, p. 2A (penned), https://www.ancestry.com; "Effie Waddell Holland," Find a Grave, accessed April 2, 2020, https://www.findagrave.com/memorial/73423701.

127. Eula Hester, "Annual Narrative Report of Eula Hester, County Home Demonstration Agent, Pike County, Alabama, Year 1928," 8, ACES Records (there is a second report of this 1928 record, with the same name, which indicates the amount was $10,116.01 [p. 11]); "Kiwanis Endorses Troy Curb Market," *Montgomery Advertiser*, April 24, 1927, 21.

128. Hester, "Annual Narrative Report of Eula Hester, County Home Demonstration Agent, Pike County, Alabama, Year 1928" [second report], 21; Shirley Vernetta Wilson Smart Wilkins information: *1930 U.S. Census*, Pike County, Alabama, census place, Darbys, ED 0019, p. 10A (penned), https://www.ancestry.com; "Shirley Vernetta Wilson Wilkins," Find a Grave, accessed January 11, 2020, https://www.findagrave.com/memorial/74102032.

129. Mary Segers, "Annual Report of County Extension Workers for 1927, Escambia County Alabama," 9, ACES Records.

130. Thelma Tisdale, "Annual Report of Extension Work in Butler County, Alabama, for 1927," 15, ACES Records.

131. Harris, "Annual Report of Extension Work in Alabama for 1926," 30.

132. Ibid., 31–33.

133. Clipping from unknown newspaper, likely from 1927, in Riley, "Annual Report of County Extension Work, 1927, Mobile County, Alabama," n.p.

134. "State Home Demonstration Agent, Annual Report—1927, Home Demonstration Work," 68.

135. *Digest* 6, no. 7 (April 1929): 12–13; *Digest* 7, no. 7 (April 1930): 24; L. N. Duncan, "Annual Report of Extension Work in Alabama, for 1929," 41, ACES Records.

136. Mrs. D. B. (Diana B.) Williams, "Annual Report of Extension Work in Etowah County, Alabama for 1929," 12.

137. Duncan also included the number of girls' clubs (516) and the number of girls enrolled (12,032). "Annual Report by L. N. Duncan, Director, Alabama Extension Service, December 31, 1929," 32–33, ACES Records.

138. "Annual Report by L. N. Duncan, Director, Alabama Extension Service, December 31, 1929," 40–41.

139. Ibid., 77.

140. Ibid., 76.

141. Ibid., 77.

142. Dobyne, "Annual Report of County Extension Workers, Autauga County, Alabama, 1929," 12.

143. Ibid., 13–14.

144. Sarah Partridge, "Annual Home Demonstration Summary, July 1st, 1918–July 1st, 1919," 14, University of Florida Institute for Food and Agricultural Sciences (IFAS) Exten-

sion Records, University Special Collections and Archives, George A. Smathers Library, University of Florida, Gainesville, Florida (hereafter cited as UF Archives); "Emergency Law To Control New Market Passed," *Miami Daily Metropolis*, August 2, 1918, 8. Home demonstration and Cooperative Extension Service records were merged and revised under the IFAS Extension Records, series 093, with four subseries of archival material, which includes the home demonstration records: https://findingaids.uflib.ufl.edu/repositories/2/resources/906

145. "Orlando to Have a 'Liberty Kitchen,' and Curb Market," *Orlando Sentinel*, April 10, 1918, 5; "Curb Market Will Be Opened in Orlando at Early Date," *Orlando Evening Star*, April 10, 1918, 4.

146. "The Voice of the People," *Orlando Sentinel*, April 25, 1918, 2. According to census records, George Harris was a "peddler" and then a truck farmer: *1920 U.S. Census*, Orange County, Florida, population schedule, Orlando, Enumeration District [ED] 117, p. 5B (penned), https://www.ancestry.com; *1930 U.S. Census*, Orange County, Florida, population schedule, Orlando, Enumeration District [ED] 0016, p. 22A (penned), https://www.ancestry.com.

147. *Miami Metropolis*, May 3, 1918, 4; "Growers Deny Any Profiteering on the Curb Market," *Miami Daily Metropolis*, September 24, 1919.

148. "Curb Market Again Tomorrow," *Miami Herald*, May 17, 1918, 3.

149. "Flowers to Be Sold," *Miami News*, May 20, 1918, 9.

150. "New Crop Grapefruit at the City Market," *Miami News*, September 4, 1918, 2.

151. "From Mrs. Partridge," 2–3, IFAS Extension Records, UF Archives. In 1918, it was already considered "a valuable Miami institution." "Miami's Curb Market a Success," *Tampa Times*, May 24, 1918, 4; "Two Extreme Types Presented by State Social Workers," *Miami Metropolis*, April 8, 1922, 8; "Housewives Are Urged to Come Out to Market," *Miami Metropolis*, July 18, 1918, 3.

152. "Police Commissioner after Curb Market," *Miami Metropolis*, February 4, 1921, 2. See also "Growers Deny Any Profiteering on the Curb Market," *Miami Daily Metropolis*, September 24, 1919; "Council to Pass Law to Protect the Curb Market," *Miami Metropolis*, July 20, 1918, 2.

153. "100 Stalls Added to Miami Curb Market," *Tampa Sunday Tribune*, September 17, 1922, 14-C.

154. "Miami's Curb Market," *Miami Daily Metropolis*, March 8, 1922, 6.

155. "Easter Eggs a Feature of Curb Market Today," *Miami Daily Metropolis*, April 19, 1919, 1.

156. "Chinese Cabbage Grows Popular as Vegetable," *Miami Daily Metropolis*, December 15, 1921, 5. The paper noted that Lowe and her parents had moved to the Miami area from Indiana and her father was president of a music publishing company in Miami.

157. "Frost Effects Noticed at Curb Market Today," *Miami Metropolis*, January 7, 1920, 2.

158. "Children at the Curb Market," *Miami Metropolis*, February 4, 1921, 5.

159. "Many Redlands People Support Curb Market," *Miami Daily Metropolis*, December 19, 1921, 3; "Chinese Cabbage Grows Popular as Vegetable." *Miami Daily Metropolis*, December 15, 1921, 5.

160. "Biscayne Park Club Market Now Open," *Miami Daily Metropolis*, January 14, 1922, 11.

161. "Florida Grower Does Not Know about Successful Curb Market Conducted Under City Auspices in This City," *Miami Daily Metropolis*, April 13, 1923, 3.

162. "Districts Are Well Represented in Big Creditable Displays," *Miami Daily Metropolis*, February 23, 1922, 3. Bertha Benson Kjorsvik was a Minnesota native and was married to Hilmer/Helmar Kjorsvik, a factory fruit grower. *1920 U.S. Census*, St. Lucie County, Florida, population schedule, Indrio, ED 172, p. 4B (penned), https://www.ancestry.com.

163. "Miami Bananas Are on Market," *Miami Daily News and Metropolis*, April 26, 1924, 19. Pawpaws are also known as custard apples or Quaker delight, among other nicknames. Andrew Moore, *PawPaw: In Search of America's Forgotten Fruit* (Chelsea Green Publishing, 2015).

164. "Clever Dolls Made from Coconut Palms," *Miami Daily Metropolis*, December 19, 1921, 3.

165. Ibid.

166. "Indian at the Fair Attract Attention," *Miami Daily Metropolis*, February 27, 1922, 12. For more on the "marketing" of Seminole Tribe members, see Andrew K. Frank, "Authenticity for Sale: The Everglades, Seminole Indians, and the Construction of a Pay-Per-View Culture," in *Destination Dixie: Tourism and Southern History*, ed. Karen L. Cox (University Press of Florida, 2014), 285–308; Mikaëla M. Adams, "Savage Foes, Noble Warriors, and Frail Remnants: Florida Seminoles in the White Imagination, 1865–1934," *Florida Historical Quarterly* 87, no. 3 (Winter 2009): 404–435; Henry Knight, "'Savages of Southern Sunshine': Racial Realignment of the Seminoles in the Selling of Jim Crow Florida," *Journal of American Studies* 48, no. 1 (February 2014): 251–273.

167. "Curb Market a War Measure," *Daily Democrat*, July 26, 1918, 2; *Daily Democrat*, July 22, 1918, 2.

168. *Daily Democrat*, August 6, 1921, 7.

169. "Curb Market Opened Well," *Daily Democrat*, April 8, 1922, 1. "Rascal Square" on South Adams Street was likely the market's location as late as 1926. It later moved to Boulevard Street. "Rascal Square Has Moved to Another Place," *Tallahassee Daily Democrat*, August 6, 1926, 4.

170. "Narrative Report of Home Demonstration Work for Quarter Ending June 30, 1922," 2, IFAS Extension Records, UF Archives.

171. Ibid.

172. Ibid.

173. "Notice Farmers Curb Market," *Daily Democrat*, April 13, 1922, 6. One particular letter to the editor piques the interest, from a George Benton who penned an apology to curb market patrons: "The city had moved me from my location . . . and won't allow me to sell fish there," Benton wrote, "but if I locate anywhere else in town I will let you know my whereabouts. . . . I will keep you posted." *Daily Democrat*, April 29, 1922, 4.

174. "Putting State Road Fort Myers Through," *Tampa Morning Tribune*, October 5, 1921, 4; "From Mrs. Partridge," April 29, 1922, 2, IFAS Extension Records, UF Archives; *Rural Home Life in Florida* (Department of Agriculture, 1927), 196–198.

175. *Rural Home Life in Florida*, 196–198.
176. *Cooperative Extension Work in Agricultural and Home Economics, State of Florida*, Circular 838 (March 2, 1922), 1, IFAS Extension Records, UF Archives.
177. "Home Demonstration Circular, 851," 1922, 11, IFAS Extension Records, UF Archives; *Rural Home Life in Florida*, 196–198.
178. "New Vegetable Market Here Is a Big Success," *Fort Myers Press*, January 14, 1922, 1.
179. "The Curb Market," *Palm Beach Post, May 8, 1918, 2;* "Woman's Club Endorses Curb Market," *Palm Beach Post*, May 7, 1918, 3; "Special Meeting Will Be Held to Talk at Curb Market," *Palm Beach Post*, September 18, 1918.
180. "Curb Market Started," *Miami Metropolis*, June 3, 1918, 7; "Hundreds Patronize Curb Market First Day," *Palm Beach Post*, June 2, 1918, 3; "Curb Market Will Open with Plenty of Produce Offered by Farmers," *Palm Beach Post*, May 31, 1918, 1.
181. Fruit Sold at Curb Market for Red Cross," *Palm Beach Post*, June 23, 1918, 3.
182. Edith Young Barrus, "Report of Experience as Home Demonstration Agent in Florida, Prepared for Epsilon Sigma Phi," 14, IFAS Extension Records, UF Archives.
183. Lucy Belle Settle, "Annual Narrative Report of Home Demonstration Work, Central and South Florida [1927]," 5, IFAS Extension Records, UF Archives.
184. Flavia Gleason, "Excerpts from August 1927 Reports," September 1927, 1, IFAS Extension Records, UF Archives.
185. Flavia Gleason, "Excerpts from April 1927 Reports," May 19, 1927, 14 (the document has two pages numbered 13), IFAS Extension Records, UF Archives.
186. Mary Keown, "Annual Narrative Report of Home Demonstration Work, East Florida, 1927," 5, IFAS Extension Records, UF Archives.
187. *Punta Gorda Herald*, May 16, 1918, 6; "Is City Market Desired by the People?," *Tampa Times*, June 1, 1918, 4.
188. Ruby McDavid, "Report of Home Demonstration Work of Northwest Florida, 1929," 19, IFAS Extension Records, UF Archives.
189. Flavia Gleason, "Excerpts from March 1925 Reports," May 13, 1925, 13, IFAS Extension Records, UF Archives.
190. Ruby McDavid, "Narrative Report of Home Demonstration Work in Northwest Florida, 1926," 2, IFAS Extension Records, UF Archives.
191. Ruby McDavid, "1929 Annual Narrative Report of Ruby McDavid, District Home Demonstration Agent, Florida," 19, IFAS Extension Records, UF Archives.
192. Flavia Gleason, "Excerpts from July 1927 Reports," August 11, 1927, 2, IFAS Extension Records, UF Archives.
193. "Must Patronize at the Curb Market," *Ocala Evening Star*, June 29, 1922, 1.

CHAPTER FIVE. HARVESTING TROPICAL FRUITS AND MILK AND USING FLORIDA GROWN

1. W. A. McRae, "Florida Tourist," *Florida Quarterly Bulletin of the Department of Agriculture* 31, no. 4 (October 1, 1921). Tracy J. Revels writes that the "tin can" tourist helped in making Florida "no longer just the southernmost state, but a region of increasing attraction and accessibility." Tracy J. Revels, *Sunshine Paradise: A History of Florida Tourism* (University

Press of Florida, 2011), 71. See also Karen L. Cox, *Dreaming of Dixie: How the South Was Created in American Popular Culture* (University of North Carolina Press, 2011), 112.

2. For more on the marketing and tourism of Florida, see David J. Nelson, *How the New Deal Built Florida Tourism: The Civilian Conservation Corps and State Parks* (University Press of Florida, 2019); Jerry T. Watkins III, *Queering the Redneck Riviera: Sexuality and the Rise of Florida Tourism* (University Press of Florida, 2018); Lu Vickers and Cynthia Wilson-Graham, *Remembering Paradise Park: Tourism and Segregation at Silver Springs* (University Press of Florida, 2015); Harvey H. Jackson, *The Rise and Decline of the Redneck Riviera: An Insider's History of the Florida-Alabama Coast* (University of Georgia Press, 2013); Gary R. Mormino, *Land of Sunshine, State of Dreams: A Social History of Modern Florida* (University Press of Florida, 2008); Kevin Kokomoor, "'In The Land of the Tarpon': The Silver King, Sport, and the Development of Southwest Florida, 1885–1915," *Journal of the Gilded Age and Progressive Era* 11, no. 2 (April 2012): 191–224; Nicole C. Cox, "Selling Seduction: Women and Feminine Nature in 1920s Florida Advertising," *Florida Historical Quarterly* 89, no. 2 (Fall 2010): 186–209; William C. Barnett, "Inventing the Conch Republic: The Creation of Key West as an Escape from Modern America," *Florida Historical Quarterly* 88, no. 2 (Fall 2009): 139–172; Larry R. Youngs, "The Sporting Set Winters in Florida: Fertile Ground for the Leisure Revolution, 1870–1930," *Florida Historical Quarterly* 84, no. 1 (Summer 2005): 57–78.

3. Nicolaas Mink, "Eating the Claws of Eden: Stone Crabs, Tourism, and the Taste of Conservation in Florida and Beyond," *Florida Historical Quarterly* 86, no. 4 (Spring 2008): 475.

4. Mary A. Stennis, "Annual Report of Food Nutrition and Health, 1929," 7, University of Florida Institute for Food and Agricultural Sciences (IFAS) Extension Records, University Special Collections and Archives, George A. Smathers Library, University of Florida, Gainesville, Florida (hereafter cited as UF Archives). Home demonstration and Cooperative Extension Service records were merged and revised under the IFAS Extension Records, series 093, with four subseries of archival material, which includes the home demonstration records: https://findingaids.uflib.ufl.edu/repositories/2/resources/906.

5. Flavia Gleason, "Report of the Home Demonstration Agent, July 15 to Nov. 30, 1923," 6, IFAS Extension records, UF Archives; Mary A. Stennis, "Annual Report of Nutrition 1927," 4, IFAS Extension records, UF Archives. See also Angela Jill Cooley, *To Live and Dine in Dixie: The Evolution of Urban Food Culture in the Jim Crow South* (University of Georgia Press, 2015); Laura Shapiro, *Perfection Salad: Women and Cooking at the Turn of the Century* (University of California Press, 2009).

6. Agnes Ellen Harris, *Home Demonstration Work in Florida*, Extension Bulletin no. 5 (T. J. Appleyard, State Printer, February 1916), 22, IFAS Extension Records, UF Archives.

7. *Rural Home Life in Florida* (Department of Agriculture, 1927), 170, IFAS Extension Records, UF Archives. See also Kelly Ann Minor, "Power in the Land: Home Demonstration in Florida, 1915–1960" (PhD diss., University of Florida, 2005), 124; Isabelle Thursby, *Save the Surplus*, Bulletin 50 (Cooperative Extension Work in Agricultural and Home Economics, State of Florida, November 1928), https://ufdc.ufl.edu/UF00026354/00001/2j.

8. Harris, *Home Demonstration Work in Florida*, 14.

9. Sarah W. Partridge, "Annual Home Demonstration Summary, July 1st, 1918–July 1st, 1919," 19, IFAS Extension Records, UF Archives.

10. *Rural Home Life in Florida*, 174, 176.

11. *Cooperative Extension Work in Agricultural and Home Economics, State of Florida*, Circular 838, 7, IFAS Extension Records, UF Archives.

12. Flavia Gleason, "Narrative Report of Home Demonstration Work Florida, 1925," 15, IFAS Extension Records, UF Archives.

13. Flavia Gleason, "1926 Home Demonstration Program of Work for Florida," 6, IFAS Extension Records, UF Archives.

14. Mary Keown, "Annual Narrative Report of Home Demonstration Work, East Florida, 1927," 6, IFAS Extension Records, UF Archives.

15. Flavia Gleason, "Narrative Report of Home Demonstration Work Florida, 1926," 15, IFAS Extension Records, UF Archives.

16. Flavia Gleason, "Excerpts from March 1926 Reports," May 8, 1926, 5, IFAS Extension Records, UF Archives.

17. "Florida Products Made into Holiday Sweets for Feasts," *Miami News*, January 4, 1924, 15.

18. *Rural Home Life in Florida*, 170–174. Ruby Geddie Richardson was a clerk and stenographer for the "state college" in 1920 and a bookkeeper in 1930. *1920 U.S. Census*, Leon County Florida, population schedule, Tallahassee, Enumeration District (ED) 108, p. 19B, https://www.ancestry.com; *1930 U.S. Census*, Leon County, Florida, population schedule, Tallahassee, ED 0015, p. 10B (penned), https://www.ancestry.com.

19. Joy Sheffield Harris, *A Culinary History of Florida: Prickly Pears, Datil Peppers & Key Limes* (History Press, 2014), 103–104.

20. Harriet B. Layton, "Report of the Assistant State Home Demonstration Agent, Ending December 31, 1920," 7, IFAS Extension Records, UF Archives.

21. These demonstrations reflected an earlier plan to "develop vineyards and create a market in the State and elsewhere for the delicious muscadine grape juice and other products." By late 1920, however, the reality was obvious: "At present, however, due to the high price of the Thomas grapes on the local market . . . it seems inadvisable to urge making juice for commercial purposes." Ibid., 3–4; Harriet B. Layton, "Report of Work of Assistant State Home Demonstration Agent, 1919–1920," 1.

22. Estelle Bozeman, "Report of Conservation Specialist in Home Demonstration Work, 1921," 3, IFAS Extension Records, UF Archives.

23. "Lucy Belle Settle, District Home Demonstration Agent, South and East Florida, Annual Report, 1923," 9–10, IFAS Extension Records, UF Archives. See also Mink, "Eating the Claws of Eden," 470–497.

24. Bozeman, "Report of Conservation Specialist in Home Demonstration Work, 1921," 3.

25. Manatee and Lee Counties sent exhibits to the Madison Square Garden event. "Report of Isabelle S. Thursby, Foods and Marketing Agent," in *Cooperative Extension Work in Agriculture and Home Economics Report of General Activities for 1924 with Financial Statement for the Fiscal Year Ending June 30, 1924* (Agricultural Extension Service, University of Florida, 1943), 89–90.

26. "Dainty Things to Be Taken to Chicago," *Bradenton Herald*, October 24, 1925, 9. *Rural Home Life in Florida* later described Felts's garden as being "in a lovely subtropical setting" (65).

27. Flavia Gleason, "Excerpts from January 1925 Reports," February 26, 1925, 12, IFAS Extension Records, UF Archives.

28. "Everybody Drinks," *Official Record of the United States Department of Agriculture* 4, no. 47 (November 25, 1925), 6.

29. Ibid.; *Rural Home Life in Florida*, 177–179; Flavia Gleason, "Excerpts from August 1925 Reports," September 15, 1925, 6, IFAS Extension Records, UF Archives.

30. Lucy Belle Settle, "Narrative Report of District Home Demonstration Agent of South and East Florida, 1925," 15IFAS Extension Records, UF Archives. Jennie (Boyd, Gardner, or Boyd Gardner) Cady, a Scottish native, and her husband moved from Massachusetts to Florida between 1920 and 1930. *1930 U.S. Census*, Volusia County, Florida, population schedule, DeLand, ED 0015, p. 5A (penned), https://www.ancestry.com; obituary in the *Orlando Sentinel*, February 14, 1957, 14; "Jennie B. Cady," Find a Grave, https://www.findagrave.com/memorial/97350551/jennie-b-cady.

31. Flavia Gleason, "Excerpts from May and June 1927 Reports," July 25, 1927, 3, IFAS Extension Records, UF Archives; Keown, "Annual Narrative Report of Home Demonstration Work, East Florida, 1927," 4; Adah Odum Cubbedge Stanley Rowe information: *1930 U.S. Census*, Volusia County, Florida, population schedule, Oak Hill, ED 0047, p. 5A (penned), https://www.ancestry.com; "Adah A. Odum Cubbedge Stanley Rowe," Find a Grave, https://www.findagrave.com/memorial/64699893/adah-a_cubbedge_stanley-rowe.

32. Keown, "Annual Narrative Report of Home Demonstration Work, East Florida, 1927," 5.

33. Mary Keown, "Report of Home Demonstration Agent in East Florida District, 1929," 37, IFAS Extension Records, UF Archives; Lena May Ritter Link information: *1930 U.S. Census*, Dade County, Florida, population schedule, Precinct 71, ED 0115, p. 3A (penned), https://www.ancestry.com; "Lena May 'Aunt Lena' Ritter Link," Find a Grave, https://wwww.findagrave.com/memorial/206691923/lena-may-link; Maria Florence Gazzam Kosel information: *1920 U.S. Census*, Dade County, Florida, population schedule, Redland, ED 39, p. 2B (penned), https://www.ancestry.com; *1930 U.S. Census*, Dade County, Florida, population schedule, Precinct 71, ED 0115, p. 4B (penned), https://www.ancestry.com. According to her obituary, she was the first woman to have her own Redland homestead. "Maria Florence Gazzam Kosel," Find a Grave, https://www.findagrave.com/memorial/209068358/maria-florence-kosel; "Kosel Homestead," Historical Marker Database, https://www.hmdb.org/m.asp?m=146232.

34. Flavia Gleason, "Excerpts from December 1924 Reports," January 21, 1925, 12, IFAS Records, UF Archives.

35. Flavia Gleason, "Home Demonstration Work, 1928," 5, IFAS Extension Records, UF Archives.

36. "Women's, Girls Clubs Use County Products for Holiday Sweets," *Palm Beach Post*, December 18, 1929, 9.

37. *Rural Home Life in Florida*, 176, 65.

38. Ibid., 190. In 1930 she listed her occupation as fruit farmer. Edna M. Kirkpatrick

information: *1930 U.S. Census*, Pinellas County, Florida, population schedule, Belleair, ED 0053, p. 1A (penned), https://www.ancestry.com; "Edna McMullen Kirkpatrick," Find a Grave, https://www.findagrave.com/memorial/12673771/edna-kirkpatrick.

39. Gleason, "Excerpts from December 1924 Reports," 12; Keown, "Annual Narrative Report of Home Demonstration Work, East Florida, 1927," 5.

40. *Rural Home Life in Florida*, 193; Isabelle S. Thursby, "Narrative Report of Isabelle S. Thursby, 1926," 17 IFAS Extension Records, UF Archives; Gleason, "Excerpts from December 1924 Reports," 12; Jessie McEwen Shaw information: *1930 U.S. Census*, Pinellas County, Florida, population schedule, Clearwater, ED 0046, p. 2A (penned), https://www.ancestry.com.

41. Thursby, "Narrative Report of Isabelle S. Thursby, Foods and Marketing Agent, Florida, 1926," 18.

42. *Rural Home Life in Florida*, 195; Thursby, "Narrative Report of Isabelle S. Thursby, Foods and Marketing Agent, Florida, 1926," 18–19; Isabelle Thursby, "Helping Florida Feed Herself," Garden Series No. 15, April 8, 1929, 3–4, IFAS Extension Records, UF Archives; Cina/Cena Stromstadt Stewart information: *1930 U.S. Census*, Dade County, Florida, population schedule, Precinct 71, ED 0115, p. 3B (penned), https://www.ancestry.com.

43. Thursby, "Narrative Report of Isabelle S. Thursby, Foods and Marketing Agent, Florida, 1926," 9. Rebecca Sharpless says of rural women and the relationship between producers and consumers: "[They] added value to their raw food products and reaped the profits of their time as some urban women decided that paying a country woman for her labor was a better use of their resources than processing the food for themselves." "'She Ought to Have Taken Those Cakes': Southern Women and Rural Food Supplies," *Southern Cultures* 18, no. 2 (Summer 2012): 53.

44. "Home Demonstration Circular, 851," 1922, 12; Thursby, "Narrative Report of Isabelle S. Thursby, Foods and Marketing Agent, Florida, 1926," 7–8; Etta Spear Huff Weed information: *1920 U.S. Census*, Putnam County, Florida, population schedule, Palatka, ED 150, p. 5A (penned), https://www.ancestry.com; *1930 U.S. Census*, Putnam County, Florida, population schedule, Palatka, ED 0007, p. 4A (penned), https://www.ancestry.com; "Etta Weed," Find a Grave, accessed October 31, 2022, https://www.findagrave/com/memorial/101941976/etta-weed.

45. "Home Demonstration Circular, 851," 1922, 12.

46. *Rural Home Life in Florida*, 93–94.

47. Sarah Partridge, "Narrative Report Home Demonstration Work, Florida, 1921," 12, IFAS Extension Records, UF Archives. The 1920 census lists a Vera Alderman in the same presumed age range living in DeSoto County. *1920 U.S. Census*, DeSoto County, Florida, population schedule, Bowling Green, ED 24, p. 11A (penned), https://www.ancestry.com.

48. Robert Hochmuth, UF/IFAS, email message to the author, October 28, 2019; Lawrence Richard O'Connor, UF/IFAS, email message to the author, October 29, 2019; Eugene McAvoy, UF/IFAS, email message to the author, October 28, 2019; David Wright, University of Florida, email message to the author, October 28, 2019; Bridget C. Stice, UF/IFAS, email message to the author, October 31, 2019; Libbie Johnson, UF/IFAS, email message to the author, October 28, 2019; "USDA/NASS 2018 State Agriculture Overview for Florida," National Agricultural Statistics Service, U.S. Department of Agriculture,

https://www.nass.usda.gov/Quick_Stats/Ag_Overview/stateOverview.php?state
=FLORIDA; "USDA—National Agricultural Statistics Service—Florida," https://www
.nass.usda.gov/Statistics_by_State/Florida/index.php; "The Watermelon Special," Florida
Memory: State Library and Archives of Florida, July 7, 2019, https://www.floridamemory
.com/items/show/342061; "2019 Plant Breeding and Variety Development Overview,"
University of Florida Institute of Food and Agricultural Sciences, https://ifas.ufl.edu
/media/researchifasufledu/docs/pdf/2019-Plant-Breeding-Packet_FOR-WEB.pdf.

49. "Annual Report for Home Demonstration Work, State of Florida for the Year July 1st, 1914 to July 1st, 1915," 5–6, IFAS Extension Records, UF Archives.

50. Virginia Moore, "Narrative Report of Home Improvement and Other Activities of Asst. State Home Demonstration Agent in Florida, 1926," 1–2, IFAS Extension Records, UF Archives.

51. Anna Hamilton, "Bottling Hell: Marketing St. Augustine, Florida's Datil Pepper," *Southern Cultures* 21, no. 1 (Spring 2019): 59–72. See also Joy Harris, *Culinary History of Florida*, 111–122.

52. *Rural Home Life in Florida*, 29.

53. Moore, "Narrative Report of Home Improvement and Other Activities of Asst. State Home Demonstration Agent in Florida, 1926," 3.

54. *Rural Home Life in Florida*, 148–149.

55. "Lonny I. Landrum, District Home Demonstration Agent—Florida, 1921," 5, IFAS Extension Records, UF Archives; Isabelle Thursby, "Helping Florida Feed Herself," Garden Series No. 14, February 4, 1929, 2, UF Archives.

56. Flavia Gleason, "Annual Narrative Report of Home Demonstration Work in Florida, 1924," 9, IFAS Extension Records, UF Archives. "Venezuela nuts" might be referring to cashews.

57. Flavia Gleason, "Excerpts from August 1927 Reports," September 1927, 1, IFAS Extension Records, UF Archives.

58. *Rural Home Life in Florida*, 163; Isabelle Thursby, "Narrative Report of Isabelle S. Thursby, Foods and Marketing Agent, Florida, 1926," 13. Roselle was the subject of experimental work to see what products could be made from it in the research laboratory, along with the sweet potato. Sarah Partridge, "Brief Report of Home Demonstration Work in Florida, June 1920," 8, IFAS Extension Records, UF Archives.

59. *Rural Home Life in Florida*, 150.

60. Ruby McDavid, "Report of Home Demonstration Work of Northwest Florida, 1929," 10–11, IFAS Extension Records, UF Archives.

61. Flavia Gleason, "Excerpts from March 1925 Reports," May 13, 1925, 2, IFAS Extension Records, UF Archives.

62. *Rural Home Life in Florida*, 191.

63. Flavia Gleason, "Excerpts from September 1926 Reports," October 9, 1926, 2, IFAS Extension Records, UF Archives.

64. Gleason, "Excerpts from August 1927 Reports," 1; Lucy C. Cushman and Lonny I. Landrum, "Report of the District Agent of Home Demonstration Work in North and West Florida, December 1920," 3, IFAS Extension Records, UF Archives.

65. *Rural Home Life in Florida*, 191.

66. "Home Demonstration Work, South, 1922, State of Florida," 2A-12, IFAS Records, UF Archives.

67. Ruby McDavid, "Narrative Report of Home Demonstration Work in Northwest Florida, 1926," 7, IFAS Extension Records, UF Archives; Teresa Madden Sperring: *1930 U.S. Census*, Suwannee County, Florida, population schedule, Padlock, ED 0018, p. 2A (penned), https://www.ancestry.com; Stella Williams: *1930 U.S. Census*, Suwannee County, Florida, population schedule, Suwannee, ED 0009, p. 4B (penned), https://www.ancestry.com; Henrietta Hatcher Weaver/Ettie Weaver: *1930 U.S. Census*, Suwannee County, Florida, population schedule, Nebo, ED 0015, p. 3A (penned); Susie Lee Henry Childress: *1930 U.S. Census*, Suwannee County, Florida, population schedule, Live Oak, ED 0002, p. 4B (penned), https://www.ancestry.com.

68. Ruby McDavid, "Narrative Report of District Home Demonstration Agent for North and West Florida," 1925, 7, IFAS Extension Records, UF Archives. (This report has "1926?" written on the front, but it appears to be a 1925 report, because of the folder in which it is located.)

69. Flavia Gleason, "Excerpts from October 1926 Reports," November 29, 1926, 2, IFAS Records, UF Archives; Landrum, "District Home Demonstration Agent—Florida, 1921," 12–13. Mrs. J. D. Johnson may be Miriam Victoria Johnson, wife of James D. Johnson, who lived in Spring Warrior. *1920 U.S. Census*, Taylor County, Florida, population schedule, Spring Warrior, ED 164, p. 1B (penned), https://www.ancestry.com.

70. Flavia Gleason, "Excerpts from July 1927 Reports," August 11, 1927, 1, IFAS Records, UF Archives.

71. Chayotes are still grown in south Florida but on less acreage than before. Jeff Wasielewski, commercial tropical fruit Extension agent, UF/IFAS, Miami–Dade County, email message to the author, February 11, 2020.

72. *Rural Home Life in Florida*, 150–152.

73. Isabelle Thursby, "1927 Plan of Work," n.p., IFAS Extension Records, UF Archives.

74. *Rural Home Life in Florida*, 152; McDavid, "Report of Home Demonstration Work of Northwest Florida, 1929," 6.

75. McDavid, "Report of Home Demonstration Work of Northwest Florida, 1929," 6.

76. One county agent report noted this area was the "horticultural portion of the state where citrus fruits and winter vegetables are the main income crops." "Report of the Director of Extension, State of Florida 1926," 9, IFAS Records, UF Archives. Interestingly, key limes are not specifically referenced in the HDA or the women's report. According to Joy Sheffield Harris, Florida's official state pie has a varied history, possibly dating back to 1931 or even earlier, as human and environmental interference had "wiped out" the key lime crops in the 1920s. Joy Sheffield Harris, *Florida Sweets: Key Lime Pie, Kumquat Cake & Citrus Candy* (Arcadia Publishing, 2017), 52–58; Stella Parks, *BraveTart: Iconic American Desserts* (Norton, 2017), 252–254; Steve Garbarino, "Real-Deal Key Lime Pie," *Wall Street Journal*, May 14, 2011; Melissa Locker, "The Mysterious Origin of Key Lime Pie," *Southern Living*, August 6, 2018, https://www.southernliving.com/news/key-lime-pie-history; Gwen Filosa, "We All Know Key Lime Pie Was Invented in the Keys, Right? Seems Not Everyone Agrees," *Miami Herald*, July 31, 2018, https://www.miamiherald.com/living/food-drink/article215758680.html.

77. Thursby, "Narrative Report of Isabelle S. Thursby, Foods and Marketing Agent, Florida, 1926," 12–14.

78. *Rural Life in Florida*, 142.

79. Ibid., 148, 145; Jonathan H. Crane and Jeff Wasielewski, "Tropical Fruit Acreage in Florida," IFAS Extension, accessed March 14, 2020, https://sfyl.ifas.ufl.edu/media/sfylifasufledu/miami-dade/documents/tropical-fruit/Tropical-Fruit-Acreage.pdf. Sapodillas, sugar apples, and carambola are still grown in and around the Miami-Dade area. Other tropical fruit grown in south Florida includes lychee, passion fruit, jackfruit, pitaya, and mamey sapote, which is popular in Latin America, the Caribbean, and Cuba in milkshakes and ice creams. In some reports, "coco plum" is written as "cocoa plum." "Cocoplum," University of Florida/IFAS Extension Gardening Solutions, https://gardeningsolutions.ifas.ufl.edu/plants/trees-and-shrubs/shrubs/cocoplum.html.

80. "Advertisement for Orange County, 1924," Florida Memory: State Library and Archives of Florida, https://floridamemory.com/items/show/318842.

81. Isabelle S. Thursby, Circulars 22, 23, 24, and 25, IFAS Records, UF Archives.

82. Bozeman, "Report of Conservation Specialist in Home Demonstration Work, 1921, 1–3; Minor, "Power in the Land," 124–125. An early promoter of south Florida foods was the Aid Society of the First Presbyterian Church of Miami, publisher of the 1912 *Florida Tropical Cook Book* (https://babel.hathitrust.org/cgi/pt?id=hvd.rsmakr&view=1up&seq=13). The society created the cookbook "to answer the first question asked by new residents on seeing a new fruit or vegetable, 'Now tell me how to prepare it for the table.'"

83. Gleason, "Excerpts from December 1924 Reports," 11.

84. Flavia Gleason, "Excerpts from August 1926 Reports," September 28, 1926, 2, IFAS Records, UF Archives.

85. Mary Keown, "Report of Home Demonstration Agent in East Florida District, 1929," 41.

86. *Rural Home Life in Florida*, 156; Crane and Wasielewski, "Tropical Fruit Acreage in Florida, 2018." Guava cultivation is mainly confined to home gardens and to commercial acreage in Miami–Dade County and other Florida counties. "Guavas Are Good for You," accessed February 25, 2020, https://wwww.floridamemory.com/items/show/297380.

87. Gleason, "Annual Narrative Report of Home Demonstration Work in Florida, 1924," 15; *Rural Home Life in Florida*, 158.

88. Other food-themed events included Alachua County's Cabbage Week, when cash prizes were given for the best recipes and uses of cabbage. *Rural Home Life in Florida*, 158–159; Gleason, "Excerpts from August 1925 Reports," 7–8; Joy Harris, *Culinary History of Florida*, 116; Keown, "Report of Home Demonstration Agent in East Florida District, 1929," 47.

89. Gleason, "Excerpts from September 1926 Reports," 2.

90. Gleason, "Annual Narrative Report of Home Demonstration Work in Florida, 1924," 16.

91. "Home Demonstration Circular, 851," 1922, 12. Cora Hooten Spears information: *1930 U.S. Census*, Orange County, Florida, population schedule, Orlando, ED 0016, p. 42A (penned), https://www.ancestry.com.

92. Gleason, "Narrative Report of Home Demonstration Work Florida, 1926," 15.

Unsurprisingly, guavas were sold at curb markets. "Guavas in Quantities Find Ready Sale on City's Curb Market," *Miami Metropolis*, August 6, 1919, 8.

93. Kristin L. Hoganson, *Consumers' Imperium: The Global Production of American Domesticity, 1865–1920* (University of North Carolina Press, 2007), 110.

94. *Rural Home Life in Florida*, 154.

95. Ibid., 154–156.

96. Ibid., 154.

97. Gleason, "Excerpts from May and June 1927 Reports," 1.

98. "Mangoes Go Fast at Curb Market," *Fort Myers Press*, May 25, 1929, 1, 3.

99. *Rural Home Life in Florida*, 159, 163–165.

100. "Eighteen Wagons at Curb Market; Move Next Week," *Miami News*, May 11, 1918, 1.

101. "Pageant Bugle Blast to Sound Papaya Merit Round the World," *Miami Daily News*, January 13, 1929, 2nd news section, 7.

102. Bridget C. Stice, Extension agent 3–livestock, UF/IFAS Extension Polk County, email message to the author, October 31, 2019. Okeechobee, Highlands, and Osceola were top-ranking counties for cattle. "Florida Agriculture Overview and Statistics," Florida Department of Agriculture and Consumer Services, https://www.fdacs.gov/Agriculture-Industry/Florida-Agriculture-Overview-and-Statistics; "2018 State Agriculture Overview: Florida," https://www.nass.usda.gov/Quick_Stats/Ag_Overview/stateOverview.php?state=FLORIDA; "Southern Region News Release Milk Production," National Agricultural Statistics Service, U.S. Department of Agriculture, https://www.nass.usda.gov/Statistics_by_State/Florida/Publications/Livestock_Releases/Milk_Production/2019/index.php.

103. "Narrative Report of Projects for Year Ending November 30, 1922, State of Florida," 6, IFAS Extension Records, UF Archives.

104. "Home Demonstration Dairy Projects for Women and Girls, July 20, 1922," IFAS Extension Records, UF Archives; "Dairy Products Club, 36 Suggestions to Read Frequently and Followed, Circular No. 823," IFAS Extension Records, UF Archives; May Morse, "Summary of Home Demonstration Dairy Work, 1920–1921," 1–3, IFAS Extension Records, UF Archives; Stennis, "Annual Report of Food Nutrition and Health, 1929," 20; Joy Harris, *Culinary History of Florida*, 104–105; "Quart of Milk to Every Child Plan Formed by Florida Women," U.S. Department of Agriculture *Weekly News Letter* 6, no. 30 (February 1919), 11.

105. Oral interview by the author with Lynnell Reynolds Fulmer, granddaughter of Annie McDonald Reynolds McCormick, February 4, 2020.

106. E. R. Culley, "Narrative Report of Home Dairy and Nutrition Work 1925," 8, IFAS Extension Records, UF Archives.

107. McDavid, "Report of Home Demonstration Work of Northwest Florida, 1929," 8.

108. Mary Keown, "Report of Home Demonstration Work in East Florida District, 1929," 46, IFAS Extension Records, UF Archives.

109. *Rural Home Life in Florida*, 123. Tillie Snyder was Matilda Catherine Smith Snyder. *1920 U.S. Census*, Hillsborough County, Florida, population schedule, Sydney, ED 85, p. 5A (penned), https://www.ancestry.com.

110. Flavia Gleason, "Narrative Report of Home Demonstration Program of Work, Florida, 1926," 11, IFAS Extension Records, UF Archives.

111. Sarah Partridge, "Narrative Report of Home Demonstration Program of Work, Florida, 1921," 18, IFAS Extension Records, UF Archives.

112. *Rural Home Life in Florida*, 123.

113. See Alan Marcus, *Land of Milk and Honey: The Creation of the Southern Dairy Industry* (Louisiana State University Press, 2021); Mark Kurlansky, *Milk! A 10,000-Year Food Fracas* (Bloomsbury Publishing, 2018); Kendra Smith-Howard, *Pure and Modern Milk: An Environmental History since 1900* (Oxford University Press, 2017); Anne Mendelson, *Milk: The Surprising Story of Milk through the Ages* (Knopf, 2008); E. Melanie Dupuis, *Nature's Perfect Food: How Milk Became America's Drink* (New York University Press, 2002).

114. See Gary R. Mormino, *Land of Sunshine, State of Dreams: A Social History of Modern Florida* (University Press of Florida, 2008), 185–228.

CONCLUSION. REAPING THE PROFITS FROM GARDENS TO GRAPEFRUIT

1. Harriet Leonard, "My Curb Market Experience," located in folder labeled "Home Demonstration Work, Alabama, 1930," 73, ACES Records; Harriet Leonard Beyer information: *1930 U.S. Census*, Limestone County, Alabama, census place, Athens, ED 0006, p. 12A (penned), https://www.ancestry.com; "Harriet Leonard Beyer," Find a Grave, https://www.findagrave.com/memorial/98405117/harriet-beyer. In the letter, Harriet's name is spelled "Harriett."

2. Mrs. Franklin D. Roosevelt (Eleanor Roosevelt), *It's Up to the Women* (Frederick A. Stokes Company, 1933), 15. See also Lizabeth Cohen, *Making a New Deal: Industrial Workers in Chicago, 1919–1939* (Cambridge University Press, 1991); Jane Ziegelman and Andrew Coe, *A Square Meal: A Culinary History of the Great Depression* (HarperCollins, 2016).

3. Lu Ann Jones, *Mama Learned Us to Work: Farm Women in the New South* (University of North Carolina Press, 2002), 79.

4. Rebecca Sharpless, "'She Ought to Have Taken Those Cakes': Southern Women and Rural Food Supplies," *Southern Cultures* 18, no. 2 (Summer 2012): 47; Lu Ann Jones, "Taking What She Had and Turning It into Money: The Female Farm Economy," in *Cornbread Nation 1: The Best of Southern Food Writing*, ed. John Edgerton (University of North Carolina Press, 2002), 224–226. See also Marcie Cohen Ferris, *The Edible South: The Power of Food and the Making of an American Region* (University of North Carolina Press, 2014), 154–156.

5. Elizabeth S. D. Engelhardt, *A Mess of Greens* (University of Georgia Press, 2011), 184.

6. Sweet Grown Alabama, www.sweetgrownalabama.org. One newer venture is Flavors of the Black Belt, https://www.alabamablackbeltadventures.org/flavors/, which is associated with Alabama's Black Belt Adventures tourism venture.

7. "Fresh from Florida," https://followfreshfromflorida.com. Two magazines also tout the variety in Florida: *Edible South Florida*, https://ediblesouthflorida.ediblecommunities.com/, and *Edible Northeast Florida*, https://ediblenortheastflorida.ediblecommunities.com/.

8. The Citrus Tower in Clermont, built in 1956, is a tourist attraction that visitors can

climb to view the numerous citrus groves in the surrounding areas. "The Citrus Tower," Atlas Obscura, accessed March 14, 2020, https://www.atlasobscura.com/places/citrus-tower; Citrus Tower, accessed March 14, 2020, https://www.citrustower.com.

9. "Florida Spring Training History," Florida Grapefruit League," www.floridagrapefruitleague.com/home/history; Michael Clair, "Grapefruit League Earned Its Name from a Prank," MLB.com, March 13, 2020, https://www.mlb.com/news/wilbert-robinson-caught-grapefruit-from-a-plane. The Grapefruit League is composed of fifteen teams, including the Atlanta Braves, the St. Louis Cardinals, the Boston Red Sox, the Baltimore Orioles, the Pittsburgh Pirates, the Tampa Bay Rays, the Miami Marlins, the New York Yankees, and the New York Mets.

10. "History: Orange Bowl," NCAA.com, December 21, 2023, https://www.ncaa.com/news/football/article/2013-12-13/history-orange-bowl; Cheez-It Citrus Bowl History," Cheez-It Citrus Bowl, *https://cheezitcitrusbowl.com/history/*; "Orange Blossom Classic Returning to South Florida with Community Events Leading Up to Big Game," CBS News, September 1, 2021, http://miami.cbslocal.com/2021/09/01/orange-blossom-classic-game-community-events; Mark Stallworth, "Orange Blossom Classic Returns to Miami," *Miami Times*, September 4, 2021, https://www.miamitimesonline.com/sports/orange-blossom-classic-returns-to-miami/article_fb862bba-0a72-11ec-9f24-bb6b4d7d5eff.html.

11. Jim Korkis, "WDW Chronicles: The Florida Orange Bird's Colorful History," *AllEars*, no. 963 (March 6, 2018), https://allears.net/wdw-chronicles-the-florida-orange-birds-colorful-history/; Nicole Cantore, "Disney Eats: Foodie Guide to Flavors of Florida Presented by CORKCICLE 2023," Disney Parks blog, June 20, 2023, https://disneyparks.disney.go.com/blog/2023/06/disney-eats-foodie-guide-to-flavors-of-florida-presented-by-corkcicle-2023/.

12. Melissa Walker, "Home Extension Work among African American Farm Women in East Tennessee, 1920–1939," *Agricultural History* 70, no. 3 (Summer 1996): 495.

13. Grace Elizabeth Frysinger, *Home Demonstration Agent* (Washington, D.C., U.S. Department of Agriculture Miscellaneous Publication No. 178, December 1933), 3.

INDEX TO RECIPES

angel food cake, 115
avocado: punch, 121; sandwich, 122; and scrambled eggs, 117
avocado and scrambled eggs, 117
avocado punch, 122
avocado sandwich, 121

baked eggplant, 117
baked goods, 111–115
barbeque sauce no. 1, 120
biscuits, 111

cabbage: 4-H garden club sandwich, 120–121; 4-H health sandwich, 121
cake: angel food, 115; lemon cheese/layer, 112; orange dessert, 114
candies and jellies, 123–125
canned pork salad, 117
carrot: 4-H health sandwich, 121; goulash, 119; Pine Bark stew, 118
casserole rabbit, 117
chayote, 4-H health sandwich, 121
cheese cake, 112; lemon, 112
chile sauce, 120
cocoanut, 124
cocoanut candy, 124
corn bread, 111; spider, 112
crystalized whole grapefruit, 123
cucumbers: 4-H health sandwich, 121; olive oil pickles, 119; stuffed tomato salad, 115–116
custard, frozen honey, 122

eggplant: baked, 117; creole, 116
eggplant creole, 116
eggs, hard-cooked/hard boiled: canned pork salad, 117; 4-H garden club sandwich, 120–121

figs: Florida sandwich, 121; sweet fig paste, 123–124
fish, 118
Florida fruit cup, 118
Florida sandwich, 121

4-H garden club sandwich, 120–121
4-H health sandwich, 121
frozen desserts: frozen honey custard, 122; grape sherbert no. 1, 122; guava ice cream, 122
frozen honey custard, 122
frozen treats and juices, 122–123
fruit butter, Florida sandwich, 121

gingerbread, guava, 113
goulash, 119
grape, 122
grapefruit: crystalized whole, 123; Florida fruit cup, 118
grape sherbert no. 1, 122
greens (leafy), Mustard or turnip greens or rutabaga tops, 116–117
greens cooked "Spanish," 116–117
green tomatoes, 116
guava: duff, 112–113; Florida fruit cup, 118; gingerbread, 113; gumdrops, 125; Hollywood highball, 122–123; ice cream, 122
guava duff, 112–113
guava gingerbread, 113
guava gumdrops, 125
guava ice cream, 122

hard-cooked/hard boiled eggs: canned pork salad, 117; 4-H garden club sandwich, 120–121
Hollywood highball, 122–123
honey: frozen honey custard, 122; guava gingerbread, 113; Hollywood highball, 122–123; topping, 114
honey topping, 114

ice cream, guava, 122

jelly, mint, 124
juices: avocado punch, 122; Hollywood highball, 122–123

layer cake, 112
lemon: avocado sandwich, 121; cheese

lemon (*continued*)
cake, 112; Florida fruit cup, 118; grape sherbert no. 1, 122; guava gingerbread, 113; guava gumdrops, 125; guava ice cream, 122; papaya whip, 113; roselle gelatine salad, 124; sauce, 113–114
lemon cheese cake, 112
lemon sauce, 113
lime: avocado punch, 122; avocado sandwich, 121; Florida fruit cup, 118; Hollywood highball, 122–123

Marglobe special, 121
meat: canned pork salad, 117; casserole rabbit, 117–118; goulash, 119; stuffed tomato salad fillings, 115–116
mint jelly, 124

nut molasses candy, 124
nuts: Florida sandwich, 121; 4-H health sandwich, 121; guava gumdrops, 125; nut molasses candy, 124; roselle gelatine salad, 124; stuffed tomato salad fillings, 116

olive oil pickles, 119
onion: avocado sandwich, 121; barbeque sauce no. 1, 120; canned pork salad, 117; casserole rabbit, 117–118; chile sauce, 120; eggplant creole, 116; 4-H garden club sandwich, 120–121; goulash, 119; greens cooked "Spanish," 116–117; olive oil pickles, 119; Pine Bark stew, 118; tomato soup, 115
orange: Florida sandwich, 121; Hollywood highball, 122–123; mint jelly, 124; orange dessert cake, 114
orange dessert cake, 114

Palm Beach sandwich, 121
papaya whip, 113
peach, 119–120
peanut butter, 121
peanuts: 4-H health sandwich, 121; Marglobe special, 121; nut molasses candy, 124
peppers: chile sauce, 120; eggplant creole, 116; 4-H garden club sandwich, 120–121; goulash, 119; greens cooked "Spanish," 116–117; Pine Bark stew, 118
pickles: olive oil, 119; sweet peach, 119–120
pickles and sauces, 119–120
pie, strawberry, 114–115
pineapple: Florida fruit cup, 118; Hollywood highball, 122–123; Palm Beach sandwich, 121; roselle gelatine salad, 124; stuffed tomato salad fillings, 116–117
Pine Bark stew, 118
pork, canned, 117
pork salad, canned, 117

rabbit, casserole, 117–118
rolls, 111
rose-apple, 118
roselle gelatine salad, 124

salad: canned pork, 117; roselle gelatine salad, 128; stuffed tomato, 115–116
sandwiches, 120–121; avocado, 121; Florida, 121; 4-H garden club, 120–121; 4-H health, 121; Marglobe special, 121; Palm Beach, 121
sauce: barbeque sauce no. 1, 120; chile, 120; lemon, 113–114
sherbert no. 1, grape, 122
sides and entrées, 115–119
soups and stews: goulash, 119; Pine Bark, 118; tomato, 115
spiced green tomatoes, 116
spider corn bread, 112
strawberry pie, 114–115
stuffed tomato salad, 115–116; fillings for, 116
sweet fig paste, 123–124
sweet peach pickle, 119–120

tamarind juice, 123
tomato: chile sauce, 120; 4-H garden club sandwich, 120–121; goulash, 119; Marglobe special, 121; Pine Bark stew, 118; soup, 115; spiced green, 116; stuffed salad, 115–116
tomato soup, 115
topping, honey, 114

INDEX

Adams, Lewis, 22
Adams, Mildred, 50
African American Extension Service work, 20, 23, 25, 30, 53–57, 60–63
Alabama Agricultural and Mechanical University (Alabama A&M University), 20, 21–22
Alabama Cooperative Extension System (ACES), 22
Alabama's "Black Belt," 29–30
Alderman, India, 50
Alderman, Vera, 96–97
Aldridge, Dora Callan, 74
Allen, Mrs. J. D., 79–80
All-Florida Soda Fountain (Farmer's Week, 1925), 93–94
American Country Girl, The (Crow), 16–17
American Country Life Association, 18
Anderson, Minnie Millican, 74
Anna T. Jeanes Foundation, 36
Arnold, Stella, 42–43
Association for the Advancement of Negro Country Life, 18
Association of American Agricultural Colleges and Experiment Stations, 15
Auburn University, 20, 21, 22, 24, 37

Bailey, Liberty Hyde, 14–16, 19; *The Country Life Movement in the United States*, 16; Rural Science Series, 16
Bailey, Mary, 3, 80
Baldwin County, Ala. (Mobile), curb market, 80–81
Bankson, Lula, 74
Barrett, Charles S., 15
Barrus, Edith Young, 54–55, 66; work with Cuban and Latin women and girls, 54–55
basketry and baskets, 34, 40, 42–43, 46, 48, 53, 60, 61, 63, 64–65, 91–94, 99, 109; in Clay County, 43–45; at curb markets, 73, 75, 81, 82, 85
Beard, William A., 15

Bedsole, Mary Lessie Beaty, 43
bees, 35, 40–41, 51–52
Bellenger, Fannie, 74–75
boll weevil, 28–29
Boswell, Mrs. T. J., 65
Bow, Clara, 45
Boynton, Annie Mae, 77
Bozeman, Estelle, 96, 101–102
Brown, Floy, 50–51
Bryce, Ellie Ruth, 63
Buchanan, James, 12
Buchans, Margery Thomas, 60
Buckman Act, 24
Bullock County, Ala. (Union Springs), curb market, 79
Burleigh, Mrs., 52
Butler County, Ala. (Greenville), curb market, 82
Butterfield, Kenyon L., 15
Buttrick, Wallace, 19

Cady, Jennie B., 94
cakes, 42, 59, 60, 102, 106; at curb markets, 69, 71, 73, 74, 75, 79, 81, 85, 87, 88
Calhoun County, Ala. (Anniston), curb market, 69, 70
Calkins, Mrs., 96
Callier, Gertrude, 78
Calloway, Josephine Schooler, 31
Camp, Mrs. H. C., 95–96
Campbell, Thomas Monroe (T. M.), 23, 25, 33, 35
canning, 25, 26, 35, 36, 42, 53–54, 56, 63, 82, 90, 100; fish and seafood, 52–53; fruits and vegetables, 40, 41–42, 49–51, 60, 63, 64, 76, 85, 96, 99, 101, 102; meat, 40, 41, 53, 79, 87, 99, 100; soups, 41, 42, 53
canning clubs, 21, 26, 29, 39–40, 49–51; tomato, 7–8, 26, 49–51, 64
Cannon, Winifred, 96
Capper-Ketcham Act of 1928, 21
Carney, Mabel, 36

Carpenter, Sue Wallis, 75
cars, 10, 28, 45, 48, 56, 59, 70, 74, 75, 76, 79, 80, 109
Childress, Susie Lee Henry, 99
Cho-Cho the Health Clown, 52
Citrus Bowl, 108
Claire, Julia See, 76
Clay County Basket Association (Ala.), 43–45
Colbert County, Ala. (Sheffield), curb market, 71
Coleman, Nannie Juanita, 33–34
Connecticut Experiment Station, 13–14
Coolidge, Grace Goodhue, 47
Cooperative Extension Service, 7, 8, 9, 11, 19–25, 30–31, 35, 54, 56–57, 60–61
Cornell University, 12, 14–15, 37
Cotton, Barbara, 9, 25, 26, 56
Councill, William Hooper, 22
Council of Home Demonstration Women, Escambia County, Fla., 88
Country Life and the Country School (Carney), 36
Country Life Commission, 14–16, 19
Country Life Movement, 11, 14–19, 63
Country Life Movement in the United States, The (L. H. Bailey), 16
Country Life Reader (Stevenson), 16
Crisis, The, 20, 32
Crow, Martha Foote, 16–17
crystallized fruits, 59, 93, 94, 95–96, 101–102, 109
curb markets: development of, 8–9, 68–69, 71, 84, 86–87; products sold, 68, 69, 76, 85–86, 88; support and promotion of, 69, 71, 72, 73, 78, 80–81, 84–85, 86–87, 88. *See also* discrimination and segregation

Dade County, Fla. (Miami), curb market, 84–86, 88, 94
dairies and milk, Florida, 24, 53, 89, 90, 94, 104–105
Dallas County, Ala. (Selma), curb market, 68, 77–79, 82
Daly, Laura, 34
Davis, Posey Oliver (P. O.), 43
Davis, Rosebud Baker, 41–42

Delano, Caroline Powell, 70–71
DeLoney, Elizabeth, 39
Department of Home Economics (Florida State College for Women), 26, 37, 49
DeRamus, Emmie Adams, 38, 79, 83
DeShong, Pettie, 50
discrimination and segregation, 3, 8, 9, 10, 14, 20, 29–32, 47–48, 53, 63, 108–109; in curb markets, 76–78, 83, 84, 87; Jim Crow, 9, 32, 56–57; *Knight v. Alabama*, 22; *Plessy v. Ferguson* (1896), 13; "Project VI," 25; racial violence, 4, 31–32; in Smith-Lever Act, 20; *U.S. v. Cruikshank* (1876), 12–13. *See also* Great Migration
Dorsett, Alice, 51
Duncan, Luther N. (L. N.), 77, 83

Eddy, Josephine, 46–48
Edge, Bertie Leah, 59
Edge, Fannie Lee Kaley, 59
Ellis, Lois, 60
Engelhardt, Elizabeth S. D., 7, 107
Escambia County, Ala. (Brewton), curb market, 82
Etowah County, Ala. (Gadsden), curb market, 68–69, 74–75, 82–83

fairs: Alabama, 35, 42, 43, 46, 47; Florida, 53, 57, 86, 92, 93, 99, 103
fans, 46–47
Farely, Mrs. M. M., 87
Farm and Homemaker's clubs, 25, 36, 55, 56
"Farm and Home Maker's Short Course and Prize Contest," 55
Farm Boys and Girls (McKeever), 16
farmer's institutes, 14, 23, 25, 36
Federal Farm Loan Act of 1916, 21
Felts, Beulah, 93
Fennell, Whitlock, 65
Fink, J. K., 85
Fischer, Mrs. Samuel (Ida Stewart Fischer), 32
Fletcher, Hattie, 100
Florida Agricultural & Mechanical University (Florida A&M University), 24–26, 54, 108
Florida Agricultural College, 24. *See also* University of Florida

Florida Agricultural Experiment Station, 24
Florida Gift Packages and gift boxes, 90–93, 105
Florida State University (Florida State College for Women), 24, 26, 37, 49, 51, 54, 99; Department of Home Economics, 26, 37, 49
flowers, 65, 69, 72–74, 79, 81, 84, 85, 88, 99
Foster, W. F., 22
4-H, 35, 43, 99
4-H Basket shop (Clay County, Ala.), 43
Freeman, Irene Griffin, 74–75
Fruit Festival, Homestead, 96

Gadsden County, Fla. (Quincy), curb market, 88
General Education Board, 19
George, James Z., 14
George Peabody College for Teachers, 18–19, 37
Givens, Gladys, 50
Gleason, Flavia, 58, 59, 60, 63, 64–65, 66, 91, 100
Gravitt, Walter, 22
Great Migration, 4, 29–31, 57, 61
Green, Emma Mitchell, 45
Greene, Mary, 77
Guava Week and Guava Day, 102

Hain, Pearl Stanfill, 78
Halstead, Milbra Kelley, 81–82
Hamilton, L. A., 61
handicrafts, 33, 35, 45–48, 60, 61, 64–65, 75, 99
Hanna, Luella, 22, 34, 36, 76–77
Harris, Agnes Ellen, 26, 38, 49, 54
Harris, Mrs. D. C., 45
Harris, George, 84
Hatch, William, 14
Hatch Act of 1887, 11, 14
Haupt, Martha, 37
Haynes, Claudia, 64
Heard, Blanche, 46
Hester, Uva, 23
Hicks, Josie Lee Harrelson, 60
Holland, Effie Waddell, 82

Holloway, Ethyl, 63–64
home demonstration: agents, 7, 19–21, 25–26, 29, 37–39, 51, 53–55, 62–63, 109; education, 37; gender, 6–7, 9, 16–17, 20–21, 26, 37–39, 107. *See also* discrimination and segregation
home demonstration shops and exchanges, 43–45, 59, 64–65, 66, 94–95
Hoover, Herbert, 73
Hoover, Lou Henry, 73
Houston County, Ala. (Dothan), curb market, 81–82
Hubert, Benjamin F., 17–18
Hudson, Mertie, 42
Hull, Bertha Cox, 46
Humphries, Frederick S., 12–13
Hurricanes, Great Miami and Okeechobee, 58, 65–66, 87

Institute of Food and Agricultural Sciences (IFAS), University of Florida, 24

Jeanes Supervising Industrial Teachers, 35–37
Jesup, Morris K., 23
Jim Crow. *See* discrimination and segregation
Johnson, Mrs. J. D., 100
Johnson, Samuel William, 13–14
Jones, Bessie Dean, 45
Jones, Eva, 77
Jones, Lu Ann, 7, 9, 10, 107
Jones, Rosa B., 34–35, 47–48, 77
Jordan, Sadie, 77

Keller, Lula Brown, 48
Kelley, Mrs. J. B. (Anna Lee Goza Kelley), 43
Keown, Mary, 52, 57–58, 91, 102
King, Allie, 46
King, Hannah Palmquist, 65
Kirkpatrick, Edna McMullen, 95
Kjorsvik, Bertha Benson, 86
Knapp, Seaman A., 18–19
Knapp School of Country Life, 18–19
Kosel, Florence Gazzam, 94
Kraemer, Delaware Short, 96

land-grant (Morrill Acts), 11–14, 20–21, 22, 24
Lauderdale County, Ala. (Florence), curb market, 70–71
Lawrence, Juanita, 58–59
leatherworks, 45–46, 65
Lee County, Ala. (Opelika), curb market, 3, 79–80, 82
Lee County, Fla. (Fort Myers), curb market, 87, 88
Leonard, Harriet, 106
Leon County, Fla. (Tallahassee), curb market, 84, 86–87, 88
Lightfoot, Martha Visscher, 46–47
Limestone County, Ala. (Athens), curb market, 70, 71, 106
Lincoln, Abraham, 12
Lingo, Victoria, 39, 42
Link, Lena Ritter, 94
London, Daisy Jane Brown, 75
Loveman, Joseph, and Loeb Department Store (Birmingham, Ala.), 43, 48, 75
Lowe, Ellythe, 85
Lund, Frantz, P., 52

Macon County, Ala. (Tuskegee), curb market, 79
Mahan, Nellie, 85
Mahue, Ella, 62
Malloy, Flossie Bonner, 40
Manuel, R., 87
Marion County, Fla. (Ocala), curb market, 88
Martin, Mrs. John, 95
Mason, Annelu Hairston, 43
Mauldin, Elizabeth, 68
Mayo, Nora, 45
McCleary, Ann E., 8, 38
McCormick, Annie McDonald Reynolds, 104
McEwen, Jessie Lorenia, 95
McGlathery, Audrey, 71–72
McKeever, William A., 16
McKeown, Ruth, 63
McKown, Mrs. J. W., 64
Michigan State University (Agricultural College of the State of Michigan), 11
Miles, B., 87

Miller, Julia, 25, 62–63
millinery and hats, 34, 47–48, 56, 61, 64, 82
Mobile County, Ala. (Mobile), curb market, 80–81
Montgomery County, Ala. (Montgomery), curb market, 69, 75–77, 78, 79, 83
Moore, Virginia, 60, 97–98
Morall, Arimentha, 62
Morgan, Anne, 18
Morgan County, Ala. (Decatur), curb market, 68, 71–72
Morrill, Justin Smith, 11–13
Morrill Act of 1862 (Morrill Land-Grant Act), 11–13, 21; list of Morrill Act of 1862 universities and colleges, 12, 21, 24
Movable School (Tuskegee University), 23, 33–34

Nassau County, Fla. (Fernandina Beach), curb market, 88, 94
National Association for the Advancement of Colored People (NAACP), 20, 32
National Civic Federation, Woman's Department, 18; Ellen Wilson Chair of Rural Nursing, 18
National Federation of Colored Farmers, 4
Newell, Wilmon, 52
New South, 3–4
Newton, Mrs., 80
Nicholson, Margaret, 98–99
Nordman, Mrs. Herman, 59
Norton, John Pitkin, 13–14

Orange Blossom Classic, 108
Orange Bowl, 107–108
Orange County, Fla. (Orlando), curb market, 84
oranges and citrus fruits, 41, 52, 61, 84–85, 90, 91, 92–96, 101, 102, 107
Orr, Ermine Watson, 79
Owen, Marie Bankhead, 18

Page, Walter H., 15
Parrish, Amanda, 56
Partridge, Sarah, 52, 54, 55, 56, 90
Pasco County, Fla. (Dade City), curb market, 87

Pate, Ada Marlow, 72
Pickett, Laurie, 48
Pike County, Ala. (Troy), curb market, 82
Pilkenton, Fannie, 99
Pinchot, Gifford, 15
Pinellas County, Fla. (Clearwater), curb market, 87–88
Plunkett, Horace, 15
Preston, Miss, 54

rabbits, 41, 51, 74, 76, 81, 99
Ray, Tisby Luella, 34
Report of the Commission on Country Life (1909 and 1911), 14–15, 17
Richardson, Ruby Geddie, 91–92
Robertson, Florence Ellington, 3, 79
Robertson, Mary Maddox, 73
Rogers, Catherine, 35
Rolfs, Peter Henry (P. H.), 25
Roosevelt, Eleanor, 106–107
Roosevelt, Theodore, 14–15
Rudd, Mrs. J. E. (Janie Elizabeth Simmons Rudd), 43–45
Rural Home Life in Florida, 63–64, 90, 97–98, 105
Rural Science Series (L. H. Bailey), 16
Russellville Furniture Company, 48

Satterfield, Catherine Dempsey, 75
Seckinger, Yvonne, 50
Second Morrill Act of 1890 (Agricultural College Act of 1890), 11, 12–13, 22; list of Second Morrill Act of 1890 universities and colleges, 13, 22, 24–25
Semi-Centennial Celebration of the Founding of Agricultural Colleges, 15
Seminole County, Fla. (Sanford), curb market, 88
Settle, Lucy Belle, 87, 93
Sharpless, Rebecca, 8, 107
Smart, Shirley Wilson, 82
Smilie, Daisie Wright, 79
Smilie, Louise, 76
Smith, Bessie Stephens, 73–74
Smith, Estrella, 99
Smith, Ida, 95
Smith-Hughes Act of 1917, 21, 36

Smith-Lever Act of 1914, 8, 11, 19–21, 26, 28, 49
Snyder, Tillie Smith, 104
Southern Sugar Company (Sugar Mill Negro Quarters / Southern Sugar Mill Quarters), 62–63
Southern Workman, 18–19
Spears, Cora Hooten, 103
Speed, Mary, 62
Spencer, A. P., 57
Sperning, Bessie, 99
Sperring, Teresa Madden, 99
Spiller, Kate Neighbors, 73
Stanley, Adah, 94
Stevenson, O. J., 16
Stewart, Cena Stromstadt, 95–96
Stewart, Inez McGraw, 46
Strudwick, Mary, 37
Summers, Joe, 87
Suwannee County, Fla. (Live Oak), curb market, 88
Sykes, Anna, 50

Talladega County, Ala. (Talladega), curb market, 75
Taylor, Mrs. T. H. (Emma Jackson Taylor), 77
Thomas, Essie, 45
Thompson, Mrs. H. K., 59
Thompson, Mrs. T. C., 76
Thornton, Emma Price, 78–79
Thursby, Isabelle, 60, 93, 100–101
Tipping, Hazel, 96
Tompkins, Eva Ingram, 47
tourism and tourists, 59, 85, 89, 96, 102, 104
Townsend, Clara, 64
Trantham, Eula, 50
True, Alfred Charles, 20–21
Trumbull, Lyman, 11–12
Tucker, Lucy Brawner, 81
Turner, Arthur Anderson (A. A.), 25, 54, 56, 57, 60–61
Turner, Jonathan Baldwin, 11–12
Turner, Mrs., 77
Tuscaloosa County, Ala. (Tuscaloosa), curb market, 68, 69, 72–74, 80
Tuskegee University, 17, 20, 21–23, 25, 31, 33, 47

Tuskegee University Cooperative Extension Program (TUCEP), 22–23
Tyner, Pearl, 99

University of Florida, 24, 26, 93

Volusia County, Fla. (Deland), curb market, 94

Walker, Melissa, 8, 108
Walker, Ruth, 64
Wallace, Henry, 15
Walt Disney World, 89; Florida Citrus Commission and Florida Orange Bird, 108
Walton County, Fla. (DeFuniak Springs), curb market, 88
Washington, Booker T., 22, 23, 33
Washington, Margaret Murray, 33
Washington, Minnie E. J., 56–57

Washington County, Fla. (Chipley), curb market, 88
Watkins, Hampton, 87
Weaver, Ettie Hatcher, 99
Weed, Etta Spear Huff, 96
West, Mada Windham, 72
Wetmore, Maude A. K., 18
Williams, Diana, 74
Williams, Isadora, 70, 73, 80
Williams, Mabel, 65
Williams, Stella, 99
World War I, 25–26, 29, 51, 54, 84, 85, 87; Food and Fuel Control Acts, 29; Food Production Act, 29; Home Demonstration Kitchens, 29, 95; "War College for Women," 51

Yale University, Connecticut Experiment Station, 12–14
Young, Mrs. Frank, 86

www.ingramcontent.com/pod-product-compliance
Lightning Source LLC
Chambersburg PA
CBHW030705200226
39916CB00044B/330